Prevention

THE DIABETES DTOUR DIET

COOKBOOK

200 UNDENIABLY DELICIOUS RECIPES TO BALANCE YOUR BLOOD SUGAR AND MELT AWAY POUNDS

RODALE

Barbara Quinn, MS, RD, CDE, and the Editors of *Prevention*

Prevention® is a registered trademark of Rodale Inc.
Diabetes DTOUR Diet™ is a trademark of Rodale Inc.

Printed in the United States of America
Rodale Inc. makes every effort to use acid-free ♾, recycled paper ♻.

Photographs by Kana Okada
Food stylist: Stephana Bottom
Prop stylist: Deborah Williams

Library of Congress Cataloging-in-Publication Data

Quinn, Barbara.
    The diabetes DTOUR diet cookbook : 200 undeniably delicious recipes to balance your blood sugar and melt away pounds / Barbara Quinn and the editors of Prevention.
        p.   cm.
    Includes index.
    ISBN-13: 978–1–60529–566–4   hardcover
    ISBN-10: 1–60529–566–3   hardcover
    1.Diabetes—Diet therapy—Recipes.   2. Reducing diets—Recipes.   I. Prevention (Emmaus, Pa.)
    II. Title.
    RC662.Q56   2009
    641.5'6314—dc22   2009039054

     4   6   8   10   9   7   5   hardcover

We inspire and enable people to improve their lives and the world around them

For more of our products visit **rodalestore.com** or call 800-848-4735

To all those who believe
that good health begins
with good food

CONTENTS

INTRODUCTION

When we set out to develop the Diabetes DTOUR Diet, our purpose was clear: We wanted to show readers how they could use food to rein in their blood sugar and lose weight, too. Our plan had to be sensible and scientifically sound—no extreme eating or dietary deprivation. And of course, the food couldn't be anything less than fabulous!

DTOUR delivers on this promise, and then some. Beginning with our eight original test panelists, who lost as much as 25 pounds in 6 weeks while stabilizing or lowering their blood sugar, the stories of DTOUR success have been truly amazing. They affirm the effectiveness of DTOUR's core principles: meals and snacks in reasonable portions at regular intervals throughout the day, with essential nutritional support from the Fat-Fighting 4.

We did notice one rather consistent request from our DTOUR-ists: They wanted more—more recipes, more variety, more choices. This book delivers, with 200 brand-new recipes for eating DTOUR-style. Glance through the pages ahead, and you'll see dishes that you probably wouldn't expect to find in a healthy eating plan, much less one that can melt away pounds and help control blood sugar. But every one has been prepared and evaluated in our very own test kitchen, so we know that they meet DTOUR's nutritional standards. Bonus: They taste awesome!

If you're new to DTOUR, we encourage you to read through the first three chapters, which lay out the basics of the plan and offer helpful pointers for choosing your calorie level and designing your own daily menus. You'll also get acquainted with the Fat-Fighting 4, the quartet of nutrients—fiber, calcium, vitamin D, and omega-3s—that play no small part in DTOUR's effectiveness for weight loss and blood sugar control.

What if you're already following DTOUR? First, we say kudos to you for your continued commitment to taking care of yourself and your health! The information in the early chapters may be familiar to you, but it's a good refresher nonetheless. You'll find new stuff, too—like our DTOUR Dozen, the 12 superfoods that deliver exceptional amounts of one or more of the Fat-Fighting 4. You'll see these foods as key ingredients in many of the DTOUR recipes; they also are excellent add-ons for meals.

As you browse through the recipes, you'll discover several special features that we hope will make your meal planning and preparation as quick and convenient as possible. Let's say you're pressed for time (and really, who isn't these days?). Watch for recipes with the Make It Fast icon; it means those particular dishes go from kitchen to dining table in 30 minutes or less. Be sure to check out the Make It Ahead tips, too. They provide instructions for prepping certain ingredients—and sometimes entire recipes—and then storing them for later use.

For the budget-conscious, there's Make It Again, which shows how to transform one meal's leftovers into a tasty new dish. And speaking of meals, Make It a Meal suggests food pairings to guide you as you build your own daily menus. (Or choose from the 14 days of menus that begin on page 304.)

We've included all of these bells and whistles so that you can focus on the best part: eating! Really, we want you to love this food and this plan. And the better DTOUR fits into your lifestyle, the more likely you are to stay with it. That's the secret to lifelong weight maintenance and blood sugar control.

—The editors of *Prevention*

Note: If you have diabetes, please be sure to consult your doctor or nutritionist before making any changes to your diet. Once you start losing weight, you may need to adjust your medication. But please, never change your dosage or stop taking a medicine without your doctor's knowledge and consent.

PART 1

FOOD IS THE SOLUTION

Lose Weight and Balance
Your Blood Sugar
While Eating
What You
Love

CHAPTER 1

EAT THE DTOUR WAY

etour (verb). *To avoid by going around; to bypass.*

There are lots of things in life that you'd probably detour, if given the choice. Like long lines. Or taxes. Or visits with the in-laws.

We can't do much about those things, sorry to say. But we can show you a way to detour diabetes—by getting rid of those extra pounds and reining in your blood sugar. If you already have diabetes, we can help you dodge complications and perhaps medications (or at least reduce your dosage).

That's why we call our plan the Diabetes DTOUR Diet—although we'll venture to say that it's completely unlike any diet you may have tried in the past: DTOUR emphasizes what you *can* eat, not what you can't. Studies have shown quite convincingly that certain foods—or, more precisely, certain nutrients in foods—enhance weight loss, balance blood sugar, and improve insulin resistance. And that, in turn, can reduce your risk for diabetes or give you better control of the disease.

When we talk about foods, we don't mean your typical diet food. Far from it! When was the last time you ate French toast on a diet? Or shepherd's pie? Or cheesecake? On DTOUR, you can enjoy all these classics—though we're confident that you'll discover a lot of new favorites, too. We want you to enjoy eating, to look forward to your meals (and snacks!), to have fun with food. We promise you that you will never feel like you're "on a diet"—even though the bathroom scale (and your jeans) may say otherwise!

That's not to say you won't need to make some adjustments to your current eating habits. Then again, eating more often throughout the day doesn't seem so bad, does it? DTOUR recommends three meals plus two snacks daily, spread out at roughly 3-hour intervals. It's the secret to keeping your blood sugar on an even keel. As a bonus, it prevents the between-meal hunger pangs and cravings that can make sticking with any eating plan that much harder.

Whether you're new to DTOUR or you're back for more delicious recipes and menus, you're in for a treat! In Part 2 of this book, you'll find 200 brand-new recipes guaranteed to delight your taste buds and satisfy your appetite. Every one meets the DTOUR guidelines for calories, carbohydrates, and fat and contributes to your daily intake of the Fat-Fighting 4—the quartet of supernutrients that boosts weight loss and blood sugar control.

Now that we've tempted you, you're probably eager to get cooking! But before you do, let's take a few minutes to explore how weight gain and high blood sugar feed into each other—and why the DTOUR principles can solve both problems deliciously!

DTOUR WINNER

"Our family has completely revamped how we shop, how we eat, how we look at food. That's unprecedented in our house, and we're really proud about it."

–KRIS SUMEY
Lost 24 points and 10 inches on DTOUR

BLOOD SUGAR, BEHAVING BADLY

For both diabetes and prediabetes, the distinguishing characteristic is higher-than-normal blood sugar. And high blood sugar is an indicator that your body's ability to process blood sugar is compromised.

When you eat carbohydrates—which come from all kinds of foods, from fresh fruits and vegetables to packaged baked goods and sweets—your body breaks them down into glucose. As your blood levels of glucose—that is, your blood sugar—start to rise, your pancreas releases the hormone insulin. The job of insulin is to escort blood sugar out of your bloodstream and into cells, which then convert it to fuel.

As long as insulin is able to do its job properly, your blood sugar stays within a healthy range. Sometimes, though, your cells don't pay attention to insulin as well as they should. If blood sugar can't gain entry to cells, it just builds up in the bloodstream instead. That's when your blood sugar level starts to climb.

In the meantime, because the fuel supply to your cells has been cut off, they can't produce the energy that they need to function. Your pancreas responds by cranking out even more insulin, but it can't keep up the pace. Eventually, insulin production falters, leaving the hormone in short supply.

Normal fasting blood sugar should be below 100 mg/dL. If yours is 126 mg/dL or higher, it means that you have diabetes. (For our purposes here, *diabetes* refers to type 2. Type 1 is an autoimmune disease in which the pancreas can't produce insulin at all.) The range in between is considered prediabetes.

Many experts describe diabetes and prediabetes as lifestyle diseases, meaning that lifestyle factors—especially diet—are the primary causes. In a way, that's a good thing, because lifestyle factors are within your control. You can eat better; you can exercise more; you can get rid of any extra weight, especially around your midsection. All of these things will help bring your blood sugar to a healthy level and keep it there.

FIGHT FAT WITH FOOD

Perhaps you're reading this book because you (or your doctor) have decided that you should lose a few pounds. It's a smart move on your part, because slimming down can do wonders for your blood sugar. DTOUR can do more than just whittle away any jiggle around your middle. It helps to target the deeper layer of fat—what's known as visceral fat—that has the most serious health effects.

Because of its location, visceral fat can mess with your internal organs, including the insulin-producing pancreas. It also contributes to chronic inflammation, which in itself is a risk factor for diabetes, among other conditions. As if that weren't enough, visceral fat can elevate LDL cholesterol, the unhealthy kind that can set the stage for heart disease.

When the eight members of our DTOUR test panel took the plan for a test run, they lost between 3 and 10 inches from their waistlines in just 6 weeks. Their results are even more impressive when you consider that they didn't make any changes to their activity levels. Eating DTOUR-style did the trick!

If you're just starting out on DTOUR, we suggest taking a measure of your waistline, just above your midsection. Then check again about every 2 to 4 weeks. You should notice that as your waistline shrinks, your blood sugar becomes more stable.

Keep in mind, too, that a steady blood sugar reading can help with weight loss and maintenance. That's because you're less likely to experience the cravings and hunger pangs that can happen as your blood sugar spikes and dips.

3 MEALS + 2 SNACKS = 1 GREAT PLAN

DTOUR is all about the right foods, in the right amounts, at the right times of day. That last part is important. Studies confirm that eating smaller meals (and snacks!) at regular intervals is good for your blood sugar as well as your waistline. We suspect you'll feel a whole lot better, too, because you'll have more energy throughout the day.

Now, don't let the phrase "smaller meals" fool you. While our DTOUR recipes follow very specific guidelines for calories (as well as carbohydrates, proteins, and fats), they definitely don't skimp on flavor or satisfaction. In fact, several of our DTOUR test panelists were pleasantly surprised by how full they felt, even though they were eating less than they had been accustomed to. That's because we make ample use of calorie-dense ingredients that pack a heaping helping of nutrition into few calories per serving.

On DTOUR, you'll be eating three meals plus two snacks a day. All of our "meal" recipes provide between 350 and 400 calories per serving, while the "snack" recipes deliver 150 to 200 calories. The similar calorie values mean that you can mix and match to create a new menu virtually every day. We haven't done the math, but we're pretty sure that the potential combinations are almost endless!

You will need to set a daily calorie budget for yourself; Chapter 3 explains how. Basically, the DTOUR recipes support both a 1,400- and a 1,600-calorie-a-day plan. We don't recommend going below this range, but you may be able to go a bit higher, depending on your starting and goal weights, activity level, and gender.

And let's not forget portion sizes! It's essential to pay attention to these. If you eat more than a serving of any particular food, you need to account for the extra calories accordingly. Using measuring cups and spoons, as well as a scale, can keep you on track until you're able to eyeball servings accurately.

MEET THE FAT-FIGHTING 4

Just by diversifying your mealtimes and practicing portion control, you'll notice a difference on the scale and in your blood sugar levels. But DTOUR gives you a little something extra as insurance for achieving optimal results. We call them the Fat-Fighting 4: fiber, calcium, vitamin D, and omega-3s. Each of them has physiological effects that make slimming down and stabilizing your blood sugar a little bit easier. So imagine what they can do together!

Because the Fat-Fighting 4 are so important to the success of DTOUR, we'll spend some time here exploring what they do and how much of each you need. They're built right into the DTOUR recipes, so you're sure to get enough.

FIBER

If the word *fiber* conjures a mental image of the powdery supplement on display in the digestive health section of your drugstore, what you're about to read may change your mind. As you'll see, dietary fiber is outstanding as a natural weight loss and blood sugar aid.

Fiber's benefits come from its ability to pass through your digestive system more or less intact. As it does, it reduces the amount of carbohydrate that your body absorbs from the foods you eat. As a result, your postmeal blood sugar level doesn't rise and fall as much.

When you follow a fiber-rich eating plan like DTOUR, you'll notice how you feel fuller even though you're eating less. That's fiber at work. It gives "bulk" to food, which slows transit time through your digestive tract. This buys time for your stomach to alert your brain that it's at capacity. Your brain responds by turning off your hunger switch—and you realize that you've had enough.

Fiber also forces you to put more effort into chewing your food. It may not seem like a big deal, but consider this: When you chew slowly and thoroughly, you're more mindful of what and how much you're eating.

The evidence in favor of a fiber-rich eating plan such as DTOUR for weight loss and blood sugar control continues to mount. Here's just a sampling of what studies have found so far.

◆ Over a 10-year span, people who ate more fiber from cereal grains were much less likely to develop diabetes, compared with those who ate less.

◆ Getting just 5 grams of fiber a day from vegetables can reduce diabetes risk.

◆ In general, people who follow high-fiber diets tend to have less body fat than those who don't get much fiber from dietary sources.

On DTOUR, your fiber goal is 25 grams per day. That's quite a bit more than the 16 grams per day in the typical American diet. It's surprising that most people get so little, really, because fiber is so plentiful in plant foods. Just take a stroll through the produce aisle of your supermarket and feast your eyes on the fresh, juicy berries, the crisp greens, the bright orange yams. All are excellent fiber sources, as are the kidney beans that you toss into a pot of chili and the whole grains that you serve as a side dish. Not surprisingly, all of these are feature ingredients in our DTOUR recipes.

When you eat these foods, you're getting not just your fiber but a whole host of natural disease-fighters called phytochemicals. Scientists continue to learn more about these substances, but the résumé so far is impressive: Phytochemicals offer protection against heart disease and other diabetes-related complications, as well as certain cancers. And like fiber, they're found only in plants.

Fiber has a whole lot of good going for it, but it does come with one caveat: If you're not accustomed to eating fiber-rich foods, increase your intake gradually, over the course of a few weeks. Your digestive system needs a little time to adjust to the change. Otherwise, it could respond with unpleasant symptoms like gas and bloating.

CALCIUM AND VITAMIN D

Calcium is best known for building bones, but it does so much more in your body. Your heart depends on calcium to keep beating, while your nerves use the mineral to help send signals to one another. And if that weren't enough, this essential mineral may help you to lose weight.

For proof, consider the findings of a 2004 study in which volunteers—all obese—followed a reduced-calorie diet. One group of volunteers ate a minimum of dairy foods, providing a total of 400 to 500 milligrams of calcium, while another augmented their diet with an 800-milligram calcium supplement. A third group increased their calcium intake by eating at least three servings of low-fat dairy daily, supplying 1,200 milligrams of calcium total.

Over the course of 6 weeks, all of the groups lost weight.

DTOUR WINNER

"When my doctor told me that I'd have to take medications [for my diabetes], I told him I didn't want to. He replied that I didn't have a choice. But he also said that if my blood sugar stabilized, I might be able to get off medication. That was motivation for me to give DTOUR a shot."

—RANDY SUMEY
Lost 23 pounds and lowered blood sugar by 182 points on DTOUR

But the group getting the highest daily dose of calcium from foods lost the most—11 percent of body weight, compared with 8.6 percent for those taking the 800-milligram supplement and 6 percent for those getting 400 to 500 milligrams from foods. Even better, the people with the highest calcium intakes lost more body fat, and more of that fat came from around their midsections. Other studies have shown similar results with calcium and dairy foods.

But calcium can't work its magic without the help of vitamin D. Your body needs vitamin D to absorb calcium from foods. That's why these two nutrients appear in tandem in our Fat-Fighting 4.

Let's not relegate vitamin D to supporting-role status, however. If the latest research is any indication, this powerhouse nutrient is emerging as a key player with significant health benefits in its own right. For example, researchers have linked low blood levels of vitamin D to an increased risk of insulin resistance and diabetes. And a 2006 study found that over a 20-year period, women who got plenty of vitamin D and calcium in their diets were one-third less likely to develop diabetes.

As with fiber, most Americans come up short on calcium and vitamin D. The best food sources of both nutrients come from the dairy case of your supermarket—milk, yogurt, and cheese. We make ample use of all of these ingredients, plus other respectable food sources, in our DTOUR recipes. In fact, you'll see an occasional suggestion to serve a dish with a glass of fat-free milk for a substantial boost to your daily calcium and vitamin D tallies.

On DTOUR, you should be getting about 1,200 milligrams of calcium and 155 IU of vitamin D per day. That's less than the current government guidelines of 200 to 600 IU for vitamin D (depending on age), but the idea is that you'll be making up the difference with sun exposure and—if necessary—supplements. We'll say more on this subject in Chapter 3.

DTOUR WINNER

"I used to eat whatever I wanted to whenever I wanted to, and that had to change. Once I started DTOUR, my blood sugar came down after about the third day."

–THOMAS COLBAUGH
Lost 21 pounds and lowered blood sugar by 78 points on DTOUR

OMEGA-3S

Even if the omega-3s didn't promote weight loss, we'd make a place for them in our DTOUR recipes. They deliver a boatload of benefits—and not just for your heart, though that's reason enough to increase your intake. (Bear in mind that heart disease is a common complication of diabetes, so the heart-protective effects of the omega-3s are an important perk.)

These beneficial fats are more precisely known as omega-3 fatty acids. Unlike saturated fats, which can clog your arteries and elevate your cholesterol, the omega-3s are unsaturated—a minor distinction in chemistry, perhaps, but it's what gives the omega-3s an edge over other fats. Studies have found the omega-3s to be effective for boosting HDL cholesterol (the good kind) and improving arterial function. They also reduce chronic inflammation, which we mentioned earlier as a risk factor for diabetes and other conditions.

Researchers investigating the role of the omega-3s in weight loss have identified another interesting effect of these beneficial fats: Much like fiber, they appear to dampen hunger by promoting fullness and satisfaction. This was demonstrated in a 2008 study in which people who were overweight or obese followed an eating plan either high or low in omega-3s. The participants kept track of how hungry they felt just after dinner and again 2 hours later. Those who were getting the most omega-3s reported fewer hunger pangs at both times.

As if that weren't enough reason to appoint the omega-3s to our Fat-Fighting 4, another 2008 study found a correlation between omega-3 intake and insulin resistance. For this study, the research team recruited volunteers—all overweight or obese—from several European countries. All of the participants followed a low-calorie diet, but one version featured a lot of fatty fish while the other did not. A third group didn't eat seafood but took fish oil capsules instead. Those getting their omega-3s from foods showed improvement in insulin resistance, a marker for prediabetes and diabetes.

Fatty fish such as salmon, tuna, and sardines are the best sources of omega-3s, though you can get a particular kind of omega-3 called alpha-linolenic acid (ALA) from certain plant foods. In this case, your body must convert ALA to EPA and DHA, which are more usable forms.

We realize that many people don't like fish all that much. But we've found ways to integrate it into recipes so that you're getting your omega-3s without the "fishy" taste. The general recommendation is 1,100 milligrams (1.1 grams) for women and 1,600 milligrams (1.6 grams) for men every day. But we think the health benefits of the omega-3s are so important that we've upped the ante for DTOUR. With our recipes, you'll be getting between 2,500 milligrams and 2,700 milligrams per day.

Now that you're acquainted (or reacquainted) with DTOUR's core philosophy and principles, let's get to the real reason you've come to this book: the food! Chapter 2 introduces you to the DTOUR Dozen, 12 foods that provide exceptional amounts of the Fat-Fighting 4. They're staples on this plan, so you'll want to know how to use them for maximum nutritional benefit. Then, in Chapter 3, you'll learn how to customize daily menus from the DTOUR recipes.

So let's get cooking!

GET TO KNOW THE DTOUR DOZEN

As you browse through and sample the recipes that we've created especially for the Diabetes **DTOUR Diet,** you'll notice certain main ingredients making repeat appearances. They're our DTOUR Dozen, the 12 "super-foods" that are central to eating DTOUR-style.

With all of the food choices out there, what makes these 12 so special that they've earned a mention here?

◆ They're superior sources of at least one of the Fat-Fighting 4 nutrients—and in many cases more than one. So they can help melt away pounds while balancing your blood sugar.

◆ They're exceptionally versatile. You can use them in recipes, as add-ons to meals, or as stand-alone snacks. Do you have a favorite dish that you're reluctant to give up even though it may not meet the DTOUR nutritional guidelines? No worries! Serve up one of the DTOUR Dozen as a side or dessert for a low-calorie dose of one (or more) of the Fat-Fighting 4—and enjoy your meal guilt free!

◆ They taste great. Let's face it: No matter how healthy and appealing a food is, you're not likely to eat it if you don't like it. That's why the DTOUR recipes and menus build on ingredients that hit the spot for flavor and satisfaction. That these same ingredients also help with weight loss and blood sugar control is just gravy.

Because the DTOUR Dozen do come up in the ingredient lists fairly often, they help save money on meal preparation, especially if you're able to buy in bulk. So be sure to reserve a place for these foods in your pantry, refrigerator, and freezer. You'll discover so many different and delicious ways of preparing them that you'll never grow tired of them—promise!

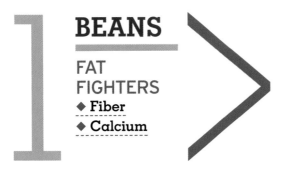

1 BEANS

FAT FIGHTERS
◆ **Fiber**
◆ **Calcium**

The U.S. Department of Agriculture maintains lists of foods that are the best sources of various nutrients. If you were to glance at the roster of high-fiber foods, you'd quickly draw a couple of conclusions about beans. Number one, they tend to be excellent sources of fiber. Number two, they come in all shapes and sizes: There are navy beans, pinto beans, black beans, and white beans. Kidney beans and lima beans. Garbanzo beans—the beans so nice they're named twice (you might know them as chickpeas). Beans that are baked and beans that are refried. And all of them are fiber powerhouses.

As you'll remember from Chapter 1, fiber earned its place among the Fat-Fighting 4 because of its exemplary ability to enhance satiety—meaning you feel full on less food, so you take in fewer calories—and to prevent postmeal spikes in blood sugar. And beans are a convenient, tasty way to bump up your fiber intake. Just ½ cup of black beans delivers more than 7 grams of fiber, which is about one-quarter of the 25 to 30 grams that we recommend on DTOUR. Other kinds of beans provide even more fiber per serving.

Beyond fiber, beans pack a decent amount of calcium, another of the Fat-Fighting 4. In ½ cup of white beans, you'll get almost 100 milligrams of calcium, while ½ cup of cooked soybeans—also called edamame—supplies 130 milligrams. So one serving of either bean would satisfy about 10 percent of DTOUR's daily requirement for calcium, which is 1,200 milligrams.

Beans are an excellent source of protein, which your body uses for all kinds of things. Unlike other proteins common in the American diet, such as red meat, beans are very low in saturated fat—the kind of fat that can contribute to clogged arteries and heart disease. Consider that ½ cup of soybeans provides 11 grams of protein and about 0.5 gram of saturated fat, compared with 1 cup of canned beef stew that contains the same amount of protein but more than 5 grams of saturated fat (not to mention an entire day's worth of sodium).

Perhaps not surprisingly, research has shown that eating beans every day for just a few weeks may help lower your cholesterol. And since they break down relatively slowly, they're great for keeping your blood sugar on an even keel.

As impressed as we are with their nutritional profile, what we really love about beans is how adaptable they are. You can toss them into hot soups or cold salads. You can mash them into refried beans (which are surprisingly low in saturated fat, despite their name) or hummus. You can buy

DTOUR WINNER

"I'm a very busy person, so it's very easy to fall into the habit of grabbing whatever is quick to eat. Now we're sitting down at the table and eating and talking with each other. My daughter was home for the weekend, and she had dinner with us. She said 'This is good—it isn't a diet!'"

–JEAN NICK
Lost 20 pounds and 6½ inches on DTOUR

them precooked for convenience or dry for cost savings. And they come in such a wide variety that you could conceivably eat beans every day for a week (or more) and not have the same kind twice.

Serving size: ½ cup cooked

For best use: If you can't spare the time for the lengthy soaking and cooking that dry beans require, then stick with canned. The only caveat is that the liquid in which the beans are packed is high in sodium, so be sure to rinse and drain them before using them.

If you're not accustomed to eating beans, then introduce them to your diet gradually. Taking in all that extra fiber at once could trigger gas and bloating. Give your digestive system a chance to adjust, and it should handle the beans just fine.

2 DAIRY FOODS

FAT FIGHTERS
- ◆ Calcium
- ◆ Vitamin D

If we had a national animal, it might very well be the cow, because we sure love our dairy foods. In 2007, the average American ate nearly 33 pounds of cheese and bought 21 gallons of milk. Food manufacturers, meanwhile, fed our desire for dairy by churning out 1.6 billion gallons of ice cream and related frozen desserts.

From a DTOUR perspective, you aren't going to find a better source of calcium and vitamin D than dairy. You can get these nutrients from other foods (like the beans mentioned above), but the amount per serving is relatively modest. This is especially true for vitamin D; other than milk, which has been fortified since the 1930s, very few foods contain the vitamin.

As you'll see, we make abundant use of dairy in our DTOUR recipes, even recommending a glass of fat-free milk as an accompaniment on occasion. So you'll want to get acquainted with the dairy section of your supermarket, if you aren't already. Our most important piece of advice to guide your shopping is to stick with fat-free or low-fat versions of your favorite dairy foods. "Regular" dairy has a lot of saturated fat, which you should limit as much as possible.

Serving size: cheese, reduced-fat or fat-free—1 ounce; cottage cheese, low-fat—½ cup; milk, fat-free—8 ounces; soy or rice milk, low-fat, fortified with calcium and vitamin D—8 ounces; yogurt, fat-free, plain—8 ounces (1 cup); yogurt, fat-free or low-fat, flavored—6 ounces (⅔ cup)

For best use: If you have lactose intolerance—and as many as 50 million Americans do—your body doesn't produce enough of the enzyme that helps break down lactose, the primary protein in dairy. Because this food group is such an important source of calcium and vitamin D, scientists are working hard to find ways to help people better tolerate dairy. You probably are familiar with Lactaid, a dietary supplement that replaces the missing enzyme. Your supermarket also may carry lactose-free versions of certain dairy products.

Even if you're lactose intolerant, you may be able to handle up to 8 ounces of milk at a time without discomfort. Pairing your glass of milk with food can help prevent symptoms, too. By consuming a little bit of dairy on a regular basis, you can "train" the beneficial bacteria that reside in your small intestine—where most digestion and absorption takes place—to break down the lactose that comes their way.

3+4 SALMON AND TUNA

FAT FIGHTERS
◆ Omega-3s
◆ Calcium
◆ Vitamin D

Of the Fat-Fighting 4, the omega-3s are the new kids on the nutritional block. From what scientists have learned so far, the protective effects of these healthy fats extend well beyond the heart, though that research is impressive in its own right. And since diabetes and heart disease often go hand in hand, you have even more reason to increase your omega-3 intake.

Fatty fish such as salmon and tuna are rich in omega-3s, which is why the American Heart Association advises those without heart disease to eat a serving of fish at least twice a week. For those with heart disease, the guideline is more specific: 1 gram (or 1,000 milligrams) of EPA and DHA—both specific kinds of omega-3s—per day. DTOUR aims even higher, with a goal of 2,500 to 2,700 milligrams daily. For comparison, a 3-ounce serving of farm-raised Atlantic salmon provides as much as 1,800 milligrams of omega-3s; in a similar-size serving of fresh tuna, you'll get 1,300 milligrams of these beneficial fats.

DTOUR WINNER

"I have two boys, 5 and 3 years old. They say to me, 'Your belly is getting smaller' and 'Dad, are you supposed to eat that?' They keep me honest."

–SCOTT NEWHARD
Lost 16 pounds and 5½ inches on DTOUR

Aside from the omega-3s, salmon and tuna provide respectable amounts of calcium and vitamin D. You'll get 181 milligrams of calcium from a 3-ounce serving of canned salmon with bones. Three ounces of tuna canned in oil delivers 200 IU of vitamin D, making it one of the few significant sources of the vitamin this side of fortified milk.

Serving size: 3 ounces cooked

For best use: You can get your omega-3s from fish oil supplements, but we really encourage you to try the fish dishes that we've created especially for DTOUR. Even if you're not a big fish-eater, you'll get hooked on these recipes . . . pardon the pun! They'll show you lots of inspired ways to prepare salmon, tuna, and other fish to pique your interest and your appetite.

Short on time for cooking? You can get your omega-3s to go. Stock up on canned tuna and pouches of salmon, which you can turn into a quick sandwich or snack (served with whole wheat crackers). You should be able to find the pouched salmon near the canned tuna in your supermarket.

5 BARLEY

FAT FIGHTERS
- ◆ **Fiber**
- ◆ **Calcium**

Although barley is a common crop in the United States, most of it is used as feed for livestock or as an ingredient in beer. A relatively small amount makes it to the supermarket for us to eat. But that may soon change, experts say, as the grain's health benefits propel it into the spotlight.

Barley is rich in a specific kind of soluble fiber called beta-glucan. Extensive research has shown that beta-glucan can lower total and LDL cholesterol by trapping it in your small intestine, so it can't be absorbed. According to a 2008 review of barley's health benefits in the *Journal of Nutrition*, getting just 3 grams of beta-glucan daily could lower your total cholesterol by as much as 8 percent. You get about 2.5 grams from a single serving of barley.

Thanks to its fiber content, barley also can help steady your blood sugar while creating a sense of fullness that discourages overeating—a bonus for your weight loss efforts. The grain even provides a modest amount of calcium.

Serving size: $\frac{1}{2}$ cup cooked

For best use: Look for hulled barley, which isn't as refined as the pearl barley that supermarkets usually carry. You may need to visit a health food store to find it. Be sure to soak it overnight before cooking; then add it to soups, stews, or rice pilaf. You can also buy barley flakes and barley flour, which work well in baked goods.

OATS

FAT FIGHTERS
◆ Fiber

Like barley and beans, oats earn a spot in the DTOUR Dozen because of their outstanding fiber content. A ½ cup serving of 1-minute "quick oats" supplies 4 grams of fiber, half of which is soluble.

Also like barley, oats contain beta-glucan, the special kind of soluble fiber that helps to rein in cholesterol. In a 2009 review of the effects of whole grains on heart disease, researchers combined the results of 10 studies, eight of which involved oats. The studies lasted from 4 to 8 weeks and tracked adults with heart disease or risk factors for it, such as being overweight or having high cholesterol. Based on the study findings, the researchers were able to link the consumption of oat-containing foods to a drop in both total and LDL cholesterol.

But the health benefits of oats don't end there. In other research, people who were overweight or obese were able to improve their insulin sensitivity by eating whole grains such as oats. All that soluble fiber slows the rate at which your body breaks down and absorbs carbohydrates, which means your blood sugar stays more stable.

Serving size: ½ cup cooked oatmeal

For best use: Perhaps the most convenient way to get your oats is straight from your cereal bowl. Just stroll the cereal aisle of your supermarket to find a wide range of plain and flavored oatmeal—some that cook quickly, others that take more time. If you prefer the flavored instant oatmeal, be sure to choose a kind that says "lower sugar" on the label. Otherwise, you may be defeating the purpose of eating oatmeal in the first place.

Another, sneakier option is to add oats to all kinds of recipes, from pancakes to meat loaf to desserts. Even breakfast oats needn't be ordinary; for a change of pace, you might try our Breakfast Oats with Pears (page 83) or the Oat Griddle Cakes with Melted Cheddar (page 87).

7 BERRIES

FAT FIGHTERS
♦ Fiber

Berries are nature's candy. Their taste is sweet to the tongue, and their bright colors are appealing to the eye. But unlike the sugary treats at the candy counter, berries are loaded with nutrients that are good for your health, particularly if you are overweight or have high blood sugar.

At the top of the list is fiber, which—as we've already seen—is an excellent weight loss aid and blood sugar regulator. A cup of blackberries supplies 7.6 grams of fiber, and a cup of blueberries has 3.5 grams.

Berries also are rich in polyphenols, naturally occurring plant chemicals with cardiovascular benefits. For a study published in the *American Journal of Clinical Nutrition* in 2008, people with heart disease risk factors ate either berries and berry-containing foods or non-berry foods for 8 weeks. Those in the berry group experienced reductions in blood pressure and increases in HDL cholesterol (the good kind). The researchers concluded that eating berries regularly could help prevent cardiovascular disease.

Serving size: ½ cup

For best use: Berries are wonderful by themselves or sprinkled onto oatmeal, ice cream, even salads. Fresh berries are very perishable, but they freeze well. So if you aren't going to eat them right away, store them in your freezer; that way you'll always have some on hand.

8 DATES

FAT FIGHTERS
◆ Fiber

Dates don't offer much in the looks department. They're plain and brown, a little sticky, and unassuming in general. But pop one in your mouth and you'll be rewarded with a sweet taste and a delightfully chewy texture.

Because of their palate-pleasing qualities, as well as their generous fiber supply, dates are a perfect DTOUR snack. Just seven Deglet Noor dates deliver 4 grams of fiber.

Dates are also an excellent source of antioxidants. In a 2004 study comparing the antioxidant capacity of various plant foods on a per-serving basis, dates came out ahead of antioxidant powerhouses such as grapes, oranges, broccoli, and peppers.

Serving size: 7 dates

For best use: Stuff dates with pecan or walnut halves for a chewy, nutty snack, or use them as an ingredient in pies, cookies, breads, and cakes. (We suggest our Gooey Date Bars on page 275!)

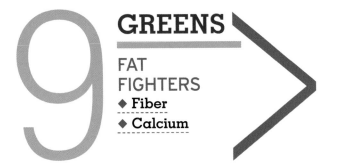

9 GREENS

FAT FIGHTERS
◆ Fiber
◆ Calcium

Mention "greens," and most people think "lettuce." In fact, this category of vegetable—a staple of Southern cooking—is incredibly diverse, with choices such as turnip greens, mustard greens, beet greens, and chard. All are outstanding sources of two of our Fat-Fighting 4. Just 1 cup of any of the aforementioned greens, cooked, supplies between 2.8 and 5.6 grams of fiber, plus 102 to 249 milligrams of calcium. If you're not a fan of dairy, greens might be a good alternative.

Greens also may be good for your heart, thanks to the folate they contain. This B vitamin appears to lower homocysteine, an amino acid that in too-high amounts may be a risk factor for heart disease. Since diabetes and heart disease often occur together, getting enough folate may help protect you against a serious diabetes complication.

Research has shown that getting 400 micrograms of folate a day can lower homocysteine by about 25 percent. A cup of cooked turnip greens provides 170 micrograms. It's important to note that the studies so far focus on elevated homocysteine levels. Whether folate's heart-protective effects extend to people with normal levels remains unclear.

Serving size: 1 cup raw or ½ cup cooked

For best use: Unless you've grown up with greens, you might consider them an acquired taste. But prepared just right, they're delicious—really! We've used them in entrées, salads, and sandwiches. For an even simpler dish, try tossing mustard, collard, or beet greens with artichoke hearts and then sautéing in olive oil.

Greens have a tendency to catch dirt and grit during harvesting, which you'll definitely taste if you don't clean them thoroughly. Trim off the stems and wash the greens in a bowl of cold water before cooking. Boil them for just a few minutes, then sauté if you wish.

DTOUR WINNER

"For me, the most fun part of DTOUR was that I could mix and match the meals that I like and create menus for a whole week at a time. Then I'd make my grocery list, go shopping, and prepare as much food as I could ahead of time."

–JOSI FERREIRA-GARCIA
Lost 7 pounds and 3 inches on DTOUR

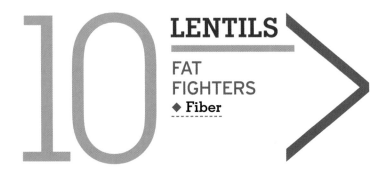

10 LENTILS

FAT FIGHTERS
◆ Fiber

Beans, peas, and lentils fall into the general category of legumes. Like beans, lentils are very high in fiber, with 1 cup cooked providing a substantial 16 grams. That same cup also delivers close to 360 micrograms of folate, just shy of the 400 micrograms that adults need each day. As we discussed previously, folate may help lower homocysteine to a heart-healthy level.

For those who eat little or no meat, lentils are a good alternative source of protein. They contain a variety of minerals, too.

Serving size: $\frac{1}{2}$ cup cooked

For best use: Add lentils to soups and pastas for extra texture, or enjoy them as a side dish instead of beans. Feeling more adventurous? Try any of the spicy Indian dishes that use lentils as a staple ingredient, such as *tadka dal,* made with green chiles and garlic.

11 FLAXSEED

FAT FIGHTERS
◆ Omega-3s
◆ Fiber

They may be little, but the seeds of the flax plant pack a big nutritional punch. Flaxseed is best known as a source of fiber and alpha-linolenic acid (ALA), which your body converts to EPA and DHA, both omega-3s. In several large studies, researchers have established an association between an increased intake of ALA and a reduced risk of coronary artery disease, heart attack, and other heart-related health problems.

Flaxseed has also shown promise for lowering both cholesterol and blood sugar. Whether the seeds help promote weight loss isn't clear, though their high fiber content points to a possible benefit.

Serving size: 1 tablespoon

For best use: Between flaxseed and flaxseed oil, definitely go for the seeds. That's where you'll get your fiber, along with the ALA. But flaxseed isn't all that digestible, so if you buy the whole seeds, use a coffee grinder to grind them. You can add ground

THE DTOUR SUPPORTING PLAYERS

You might not expect to find the following foods in an eating plan to lose weight and balance your blood sugar—but then again, DTOUR isn't just any plan! Our philosophy is that every food can have its place in DTOUR, as long as portions are sensible. And in the case of these foods, they actually may help you to meet your weight loss and blood sugar goals.

Rice and pasta: These can contribute to your daily fiber intake, as long as you choose brown rice and whole wheat or whole grain pasta over the refined varieties. In fact, the "diabetes pyramid" developed by the American Diabetes Association suggests getting at least 6 servings of grains and starches per day.

Peanut butter: Believe it or not, some studies have linked peanut butter consump-tion to reduced diabetes risk. The fiber content may have something to do with it! And since this classic comfort food contains mostly monounsaturated fat, it's considered heart-healthy. The calories are on the high side, however, so pay close attention to serving size.

Dark chocolate. Rich in antioxidant flavanols, this deceptively decadent sweet may help improve your good and bad cholesterol and reduce your blood pressure. One ounce contains 136 calories and 8.5 grams of fat, so nibble just a little rather than treating dark chocolate as its own food group.

Trail mix. Can you think of a better on-the-go snack? One ounce of trail mix—made with nuts, seeds, and chocolate chips—has just 137 calories. Even better, most of the fat is the unsaturated kind.

flaxseed to all kinds of foods, such as oatmeal, low-fat cottage cheese, and fruit smoothies. Store any extra flaxseed in the refrigerator or freezer.

Another option is flax meal, made from preground flaxseed. Look for it in your supermarket or your local health food store.

12 WALNUTS

FAT FIGHTERS
- ◆ **Fiber**
- ◆ **Omega-3s**

Just 1 ounce of English walnuts—about 14 halves—delivers almost 2 grams of fiber plus 2.6 grams of ALA, the precursor to EPA and DHA. You also get about 185 calories in that ounce, so eat walnuts sparingly.

Serving size: 1 ounce

For best use: Count out a set number of shelled walnuts for a snack rather than eating them by the handful. That way you're less likely to overdo it. Or choose the whole nuts, so you have to work a bit to get the meat out of them—another deterrent to overindulging. Chopped walnuts make a great topping for salads and add a bit of crunch to cookies and brownies (like our Double-Chocolate Walnut Brownies on page 276).

CHAPTER 3

BUILD YOUR OWN DTOUR MENUS

There's an adage attributed to Socrates that, loosely translated, means "Eat to live, not live to eat." With all due respect to the ancient Greek philosopher, we must disagree. We believe that eating for health and eating for pleasure can—and should—coexist. We've designed the Diabetes DTOUR Diet to embrace both.

The recipes in the pages that follow adhere to the science-supported nutritional guidelines that are the foundation of DTOUR. Each dish delivers a good dose of at least one—and often more—of our Fat-Fighting 4, along with just the right mix of carbohydrate, protein, and fat.

But a stellar nutritional profile in and of itself isn't enough for a recipe to make the DTOUR cut. Flavor and satisfaction are just as important. We won't eat something that we don't like, and we don't expect you to, either. That's why we taste-tested just about every recipe in this book. No matter what your food preferences, we promise that you'll find new favorites here!

Before you get cooking, let's review the basic principles of eating DTOUR-style. No worries—we've made it easy for you. All you need to do is set your calorie intake, then start building menus around three meals and two snacks a day. That's all there is to it!

EATING AS EASY AS 1-2-3

One of the things we learned from our DTOUR test panel is that people who follow eating plans tend to fall into one of two groups. Some like a lot of structure—"Just tell me what to eat!" they would say—while others prefer flexibility. We've designed DTOUR to accommodate both. The basic framework provides for a certain number of calories and a certain number of meals and snacks per day. Then you get to make up your own menus. With 200 recipes to choose from, the hardest part may be deciding what to try first!

To make the most of your DTOUR experience, you do need to follow a few simple steps, which we've outlined here. They're essential to the success of this plan—and to getting your weight and blood sugar to where you want them to be.

1. PICK YOUR CALORIE LEVEL

The "secret" to weight loss is not so much a secret as basic math: calories in < calories out = pounds gone. Because all of the DTOUR recipes adhere to strict calorie guidelines, you'll naturally lower your calorie intake without having to count. If you're thinking that fewer calories means less food, you may be pleasantly surprised to find that you're eating more than usual. That's because we use ingredients that deliver a lot of nutritional value—and satisfaction—for relatively few calories.

On DTOUR, you can choose from two different calorie levels: 1,400 and 1,600. We recommend 1,400 calories a day if you're a woman who's short in stature and relatively sedentary. If you're a woman who's taller or more active, or if you're a man, then aim for 1,600 calories a day.

These are very general guidelines, of course; you may want to talk with your doctor or a nutritionist to help choose the best level for you. The beauty of DTOUR is that you can adjust the calories to your needs, especially as you lose weight. All you need to remember is to eat three meals and two snacks per day and to choose recipes that fit your calorie budget. We'll explain how to do that next.

2. CHOOSE YOUR MEALS AND SNACKS

Most of us grew up eating the standard three square meals a day. As the science now shows, this may not be the healthiest menu for losing weight or controlling blood sugar. We're more likely to overindulge after a long period of not eating, which means taking in more calories than we should. And all that food going into our bodies at once can cause blood sugar to spike and dip—not what you want if high blood sugar is an issue for you.

With the three meals and two snacks on DTOUR, you'll be eating more often throughout the day, which has a couple of benefits. One, you're less likely to eat too much in one sitting because you won't be starving yourself between meals. And two, your blood sugar will stay on a more even keel.

Eating five times a day might seem like a lot—perhaps too much to lose weight. But the science is so strong that no less prestigious an organization than the American Dietetic Association has embraced this eating style. The ADA's 2009 position paper on weight management states that "total caloric intake should be distributed

PORTION SIZES AT A GLANCE

Scales and measuring cups are the best tools for keeping tabs on portion sizes. But it's not always convenient to use them. In those situations, some simple visual cues can help ensure that you're putting the right amount of food on your plate. Here's a handy guide.
◆ 3 ounces of cooked meat = a deck of cards
◆ 3 ounces of grilled fish = a checkbook

◆ 1 cup of potatoes, rice, pasta, and other starches = your fist
◆ 1 ounce of cheese = a Ping-Pong ball
◆ 1 teaspoon of mayonnaise or margarine = the tip of your thumb
◆ 1 medium orange or apple = a baseball
◆ 1 pancake or tortilla = a CD

throughout the day, with the consumption of four to five meals/snacks per day including breakfast."

The point about "total calorie intake" is critical. Even though you're eating five times a day, you need to stick with your calorie budget. This means watching your portions. All of our DTOUR recipes include information on serving size, so you don't have to guess at what looks about right. And they're more generous than you might expect, thanks to those calorie-dense ingredients that we mentioned earlier.

Fiber, one of our Fat-Fighting 4, does an excellent job of filling you up without filling you out. It's unique to plant foods—the fresh fruits and vegetables, beans, and whole grains that figure so prominently in the DTOUR recipes. In a recent University of Minnesota study, people who ate fruits, vegetables, and other fiber-rich foods lost an average of 2 to 3 pounds more than those on a low-fiber diet. And in a Finnish study of more than 4,000 people, those who ate the most fiber were 61 percent less likely to develop diabetes than those who ate the least.

You'll get a healthy dose of fiber, along with the rest of the Fat-Fighting 4, by following our three-meals-plus-two-snacks rule. As you set about creating your daily menus, it might help to think of the DTOUR recipes as building blocks, with each meal providing between 300 and 400 calories and each snack providing between 150 and 200 calories. So you'd want to aim toward the lower end of each range to get 1,400 calories per day or toward the upper end to get 1,600 calories per day.

We've designed the DTOUR recipes so that each breakfast, soup, sandwich, salad, and entrée counts as a "meal," and each appetizer, side, dessert, and beverage counts as a "snack." Feel free to mix and match as you wish; for instance, you could combine two appetizers for lunch or

DTOUR WINNER

"When I was pregnant with my youngest daughter, I developed gestational diabetes. That means I'm more likely to get full-blown diabetes. When DTOUR came along, I said to myself, *Now is the time to change my eating habits so I can beat the odds.*"

–COURTNEY MATTHEWS
Lost 8 pounds and 3 inches on DTOUR

have breakfast for dinner. Let your taste buds and your appetite be your guide! And don't worry about nailing your daily calorie budget exactly. It's okay to be a little bit over or a little bit under. The calories will balance out over time.

Throughout the book, you'll see "Make It a Meal" boxes, in which we offer our own suggestions for recipe pairings. Beginning on page 305, you'll find 14 full days of menus, featuring the DTOUR recipes. They're another good resource for ideas and planning.

A note about the beverages: You needn't stick with the recipes that begin on page 288. Any of the following is an acceptable substitute for any meal; just be sure to count the calories toward your daily total.

◆ Coffee or tea—with a splash of fat-free milk or a sprinkle of sugar-free sweetener, if you wish

GETTING ENOUGH D

Few nutrients have garnered more attention lately than vitamin D. Recent research has tagged the vitamin as a potential therapeutic agent for conditions ranging from diabetes and obesity to autism. In fact, if the latest findings are any indication, the current government recommendations for vitamin D intake—which range from 200 to 600 IU a day—might fall way short.

The human body can make all of the vitamin D that it requires with a daily 10-minute dose of sunshine—without sunscreen. (If you're going to be outside for longer than that, then definitely slather on sunscreen of SPF 15 or higher.) The thing is, many of us don't get outside for even that short amount of time on a daily basis. Where we live is a factor, too: Those of us who reside at more northern latitudes are less likely to get adequate sun exposure, especially during the winter months.

So it's a good idea to support your body's natural vitamin D production with foods and supplements. The best food sources by far are fortified milk and cereals. Fish that are rich in omega-3 fatty acids, such as salmon, tuna, mackerel, and sardines, supply more modest amounts of the nutrient.

Since vitamin D isn't all that plentiful in our food supply, you might want to consider adding a supplement, too. Most brand-name multivitamins provide adequate amounts of vitamin D, as well as calcium. Combination calcium-vitamin D products also are available, as are single supplements. Whichever you choose, your goal is to get a total of 200 IU to 600 IU per day from a combination of foods, supplements, and sun.

- Fat-free milk or low-fat soy or rice beverage fortified with calcium and vitamin D
- Reduced-calorie beverage that provides no more than 20 calories per serving
- Sparkling water

3. TRACK THE FAT-FIGHTING 4

As you'll see, every DTOUR recipe shows which of the Fat-Fighting 4 nutrients it contains and in what amounts. You'll want to keep an eye on these as you're making your food choices on any given day. These four supernutrients—fiber, calcium, vitamin D, and omega-3s—are important to the effectiveness of the DTOUR plan, with each one doing its part to help melt away pounds, rein in blood sugar, and reduce insulin resistance. The goal for each nutrient varies with calorie intake, but generally, you should be aiming for the following benchmarks:

- Fiber: 25 to 30 grams
- Calcium: 1,200 milligrams
- Vitamin D: 155 IU (from foods; remember that your body can make its own vitamin D with adequate sun exposure)
- Omega-3s: 2,500 to 2,700 milligrams (or 2.5 to 2.7 grams)

BEST BETS FOR OMEGA-3S

Mention omega-3s and most people immediately think fish—especially fatty fish such as salmon, tuna, herring, and mackerel. These are the best sources of omega-3s because the fats are in a form that your body can readily use.

But what if you aren't crazy about fish? You can get omega-3s from plant sources such as walnuts and flaxseed. The catch is that your body must take the extra step to convert this form of omega-3, known as alpha-linolenic acid (ALA), to eicosapentaenoic acid (EPA) and docosahexaenoic acid (DHA). These are the forms that your body can readily use.

Still, it's better to get ALA than to get no omega-3s at all. If you choose flaxseed as your omega-3 food source, just be sure to grind it before adding it to your cereal or smoothie. The seeds are more digestible when ground.

MIND YOUR MACROS

With all of the attention to the Fat-Fighting 4, we shouldn't lose sight of the so-called macronutrients: carbohydrates, proteins, and fats. Your body relies on this trio of nutrients for energy, structure, and function. They are essential to life.

If you have high blood sugar, you may already be tuned in to your carbohydrate intake. That's because the breakdown of carbohydrates has the most direct impact on your blood sugar level and on insulin, which is responsible for escorting all that sugar (or glucose) out of your bloodstream and into cells. Effectively managing your blood sugar and insulin largely boils down to watching your carbohydrate intake.

The DTOUR recipes average about 40 grams of carbohydrate per meal and about 20 grams of carbohydrate per snack.

This should help keep your blood sugar within a fairly tight range. Also, the recipes rely heavily on complex carbohydrates, the kind that break down and enter your bloodstream slowly. (Simple or refined carbs, by contrast, break down quickly and can send your blood sugar on a roller coaster ride.)

We've designed the DTOUR recipes so that no matter how you combine them, you should be getting a healthy mix of the macronutrients: about 40 percent of calories from carbohydrates, 25 percent from protein, and 35 percent from fats. Keep in mind that the percentages apply to an entire meal rather than to the individual dishes. Depending on the ingredients, certain dishes may seem high or low in a particular macronutrient. What's most important is getting the proper mix over the course of a day.

We talked about fiber earlier in the chapter. It adds bulk to food, and that bulk is responsible for satiety—the pleasantly full sensation that turns off the hunger switch in your brain and keeps you from overeating. What's more, when you eat soluble fiber from foods like whole grains, nuts, and fresh fruits and vegetables, they form a gummy material that helps to block the absorption of carbohydrates in the small intestine. In this way, fiber may play a direct role in lowering blood sugar and insulin resistance.

As for calcium and vitamin D, this nutritional dynamic duo seems to work best in tandem—which makes sense, considering one of the primary functions of vitamin D is to enhance the absorption of calcium. According to the landmark Nurses' Health Study, which tracked the health status of more than 83,000 women, those getting

1,200 milligrams of calcium and 800 IU of vitamin D a day were 33 percent less likely to develop type 2 diabetes.

Rounding out our Fat-Fighting 4 is, ironically enough, fat—or, more precisely, omega-3 fatty acids, the beneficial fats found mostly in fish. (Walnuts and flaxseed contain alpha-linolenic acid, or ALA, which your body can convert to omega-3s.) The omega-3s are best known for their heart-protective effects, but more recent research is exploring whether they might help banish belly fat, the unhealthiest kind of body fat. For one study, two groups of women followed identical diets, with one exception: One group took 1.8 grams of omega-3s in supplement form every day, while the other took a placebo. After 2 months, the women in the omega-3 group had lost 3 pounds of belly fat, compared with just $\frac{1}{2}$ pound for the women in the placebo group.

Every DTOUR recipe delivers a generous amount of at least one of the Fat-Fighting 4, with many doubling or tripling on these supernutrients. So as you mix and match recipes over the course of a day, you should cover your nutritional bases quite easily.

STAYING ON TRACK

The true test of any eating plan is how well it holds up in real life. Sure, it may look good on paper. But if it doesn't take into account individual preferences and lifestyle factors, sticking with it may be next to impossible.

One of the reasons that we recruited a test panel for a trial run of DTOUR was to see if our volunteers found the plan easy to follow and use. Their feedback was top of mind when we set out to develop the recipes for this cookbook.

Here you'll find something to please every palate and appetite: from our take on classics such as shepherd's pie, New England clam chowder, and French toast to dishes

DTOUR WINNER

"I've learned that if I choose the right foods, I really don't need to eat as much. I feel full with less. I'm staying away from the sugary breakfast foods that I used to be in love with. They don't taste as good as I feel right now!"

–THERESE CIESINSKI
Lost 7 pounds and 5½ inches on DTOUR

with an exotic flair, such as grilled tandoori chicken with cucumber sauce and chilaquiles; from fast-food favorites such as tacos and chili fries to slow-cooked meals such as pot roast and chicken stew. And we have desserts—lots of creamy, gooey, chocolaty desserts! With so many choices, we can guarantee that you'll never get bored on this plan.

Almost all of the DTOUR recipes can be made to go, so they're perfect for packing for work or wherever you might be off to. Watch for the "Make It Ahead" boxes; they identify recipes that can be prepared even days in advance and then refrigerated or frozen until mealtime.

Because many of the recipes serve two to four people (or more!), you may find yourself with leftovers on occasion. You can refrigerate them for another meal the next day, or you can fashion them into a whole new dish. The "Make It Again" box will show you how.

Perhaps the biggest challenge to following any eating plan is time. Eating health-fully takes thought and preparation. And let's be honest: After putting in an 8-hour day at work, you probably don't want to spend another hour (or more) standing at the kitchen sink julienning carrots, no matter how much you love cooking. This is why we've included the prep time and total time at the start of each DTOUR recipe. A special "Make It Fast" symbol tells you at a glance which dishes come together in 30 minutes or less, from start to finish.

If you're really in a pinch, be sure to check out DTOUR On the Go on page 320. Here you'll find lists of frozen foods and fast foods that fit the DTOUR nutritional guidelines.

DTOUR YOUR WAY

As you get accustomed to cooking and eating DTOUR-style, feel free to experiment with the recipes and adjust as you wish. Below, we've provided a short list of sugges-

EASY INGREDIENT SUBSTITUTIONS

One of the beauties of DTOUR is its flexibility. In many cases, you can swap different kinds of poultry or fish, different fruits or vegetables (depending on what's in season), even different beans or nuts and still stay on course nutritionally. So be inventive as you put together your menus; if you feel like making a change, do it! Here are a few suggestions to get started.

INSTEAD OF . . .	TRY . . .
Spinach	Collard greens, mustard greens, or Swiss chard
Salmon	Tuna
Hummus	Peanut butter
Blueberries	Blackberries or raspberries
Walnuts	Pecans
Chicken in stir-fry	Fish or tofu
Fresh fruits	Dried fruits

tions for ingredient substitutions. They're very simple, but they can completely change the flavor and texture of a dish. They'll add variety to your diet without dramatically altering the nutritional value of the original dish.

Many fruits and vegetables, for example, offer similar health benefits for a comparable number of calories. Try Swiss chard or collard greens instead of spinach, or mix and match any number of berries, beans, and nuts.

Once you're ready to start improvising, be sure to make ample use of your tools of the trade: measuring spoons and cups and a kitchen scale. These will help you monitor your portion sizes, which is a must for staying within your calorie budget. Also, read nutrition labels on any packaged ingredients to ensure that you're within the ballpark for the macronutrients as well as the Fat-Fighting 4.

With just this sort of mindfulness, you can customize DTOUR to your food preferences and lifestyle. We want it to be a plan that you feel good about. DTOUR isn't a temporary fix; it's a permanent solution to weight gain and high blood sugar. And as those pounds melt away and your blood sugar comes into balance, you'll feel so good that you won't imagine cooking—or eating—any other way.

PART
2

LET'S GET COOKING!

200 Irresistible Recipes Brimming with the Fat-Fighting 4

CHAPTER 4

APPETIZERS

Mexicana Deviled Eggs

PREP TIME: 15 MINUTES

6 omega-3-enriched eggs, hard-cooked

2 tablespoons light omega-3-enriched mayonnaise

¼ teaspoon chili powder + more for garnish

1 scallion, finely sliced

1 tablespoon chopped cilantro

FAT-FIGHTING 4

0 g fiber

21 mg calcium

3.5 IU vitamin D

200 mg omega-3s

MAKE IT FAST

1 Shell the eggs. Place 2 eggs in a shallow bowl. Cut the remaining 4 eggs into halves lengthwise. Remove the yolks and add to the eggs in the bowl. With a fork or pastry blender, mash the eggs and yolks in the bowl. Add the mayonnaise and ¼ teaspoon chili powder. Stir to mix.

2 Place the egg white halves on a plate, hollow side up. Dollop the yolk mixture into the hollows. Scatter the scallion and cilantro on top. Dust the plate with chili powder.

Makes 8 servings

PER SERVING: 69 calories, 5 g protein, 2 g carbohydrates, 4 g fat (1 g saturated fat), 136 mg cholesterol, 84 mg sodium

Herbed Cheese Ball with Crudités

PREP TIME: 20 MINUTES + CHILLING TIME

6 ounces fat-free soft cream cheese (tub-style)
³⁄₄ cup (6 ounces) shredded reduced-fat (2%) extra-sharp Cheddar cheese
1 tablespoon prepared horseradish
2 teaspoons Worcestershire sauce

¹⁄₄ cup walnuts, very finely chopped
16 fat-free plain rice cakes
4 ribs celery, cut into 2" pieces
4 carrots, cut into sticks
1 large cucumber, diagonally cut into ¹⁄₄" slices

1 Combine the cream cheese, Cheddar, horseradish, and Worcestershire sauce in a blender or food processor. Pulse until just blended. Place in a bowl and refrigerate for at least 1 hour. Remove and shape into a ball.

2 Place the walnuts on a plate and roll the cheese ball in the nuts, pressing to adhere.

3 Place the cheese ball on a serving plate with a canapé knife and surround with the rice cakes, celery, carrots, and cucumber.

Makes 8 servings

PER SERVING: 210 calories, 13 g protein, 22 g carbohydrates, 7 g fat (4 g saturated fat), 17 mg cholesterol, 396 mg sodium

MAKE IT AHEAD
If tightly wrapped, the cheese ball will keep in the refrigerator for up to 1 week or in the freezer for up to 1 month.

FAT-FIGHTING 4

2 g fiber

234 mg calcium

0 IU vitamin D

290 mg omega-3s

Cheese-and-Nut Stacks

PREP TIME: 15 MINUTES ◆ TOTAL TIME: 20 MINUTES

24 walnut halves
1 tablespoon maple syrup
Pinch of salt

12 dried Calimyrna figs, halved
$\frac{1}{2}$ cup low-fat goat cheese, softened

1 Line a baking sheet with parchment paper.

2 Heat a medium nonstick skillet over medium-high heat. Add the walnuts, maple syrup, and salt. Cook, stirring constantly, for 4 minutes or until coated. Spread onto parchment paper, separating the nuts, until cooled.

3 Arrange the figs on a serving plate. Top each with 1 level teaspoon of the cheese and 1 walnut.

Makes 4 servings (6 stacks per serving)

PER SERVING: 200 calories, 7 g protein, 22 g carbohydrates, 11 g fat (2 g saturated fat), 5 mg cholesterol, 141 mg sodium

FAT-
FIGHTING
4

3 g fiber

96 mg
calcium

0 IU
vitamin D

1,090 mg
omega-3s

MAKE IT
FAST

Spicy Sweet Potato "Fries" with Creole Mustard Dipping Sauce

PREP TIME: 10 MINUTES ◆ TOTAL TIME: 35 MINUTES

2 medium sweet potatoes
1 teaspoon canola oil
1 teaspoon Cajun seasoning
3 tablespoons light omega-3-enriched mayonnaise

1½ teaspoons coarse-grain mustard
1½ teaspoons prepared horseradish
1 scallion, finely sliced

1 Preheat the oven to 375°F. Coat a large baking sheet with cooking spray.

2 Peel the potatoes and cut in half through the middle. Cut each potato half into ½"-thick sticks. Heap onto the baking sheet. Drizzle the oil over the potato sticks. Sprinkle with the Cajun seasoning. Toss to coat. Spread out the sticks so they don't touch. Bake for 25 minutes, or until browned and tender.

3 Meanwhile, combine the mayonnaise, mustard, horseradish, and scallion in a bowl.

4 Serve the fries with the mustard sauce for dipping.

Makes 4 servings

PER SERVING: 100 calories, 1 g protein, 13 g carbohydrates, 5 g fat (0 g saturated fat), 4 mg cholesterol, 295 mg sodium

FAT-FIGHTING
4

2 g fiber

14 mg calcium

0 IU vitamin D

380 mg omega-3s

Salmon Sliders

PREP TIME: 20 MINUTES ◆ TOTAL TIME: 40 MINUTES + CHILLING TIME

1 egg white
¼ cup thick salsa
½ teaspoon dried oregano
¼ teaspoon smoked paprika
1 pouch (6 ounces) salmon, patted dry
¼ cup whole wheat bread crumbs

2 tablespoons ground flaxseed
2 plum tomatoes, each cut crosswise into
    3 slices
3 slices whole wheat bread
¼ cup chopped cilantro

FAT-FIGHTING 4

2 g fiber
----
24 mg calcium
----
0 IU vitamin D
----
270 mg omega-3s

1 Coat a baking sheet with cooking spray. Whisk the egg white in a medium bowl. Stir in the salsa, oregano, and paprika. Add the salmon, bread crumbs, and flaxseed and gently fold just until combined. Use 2 scant tablespoons of the mixture to form a ball, and place onto the baking sheet. Press slightly to form a 1½" patty. Repeat to make 6 patties in all. Chill for at least 30 minutes.

2 Preheat the oven to 375° F. Bake for 20 minutes, turning once, or until browned and crisp.

3 Meanwhile, cut the bread slices into 4 squares each. Place 6 squares on a serving plate. Top each with a patty, a tomato slice, and 1 tablespoon of the cilantro leaves. Top with the remaining bread slices.

Makes 6 servings

PER SERVING: 111 calories, 9 g protein, 13 g carbohydrates, 3 g fat (0.5 g saturated fat), 10 mg cholesterol, 300 mg sodium

Asian Lollipops with Peanut Dipping Sauce

PREP TIME: 10 MINUTES ◆ TOTAL TIME: 15 MINUTES

¼ cup omega-3-enriched peanut butter
3 tablespoons boiling water
2 tablespoons reduced-sodium soy sauce
1 tablespoon rice wine vinegar
1 teaspoon toasted sesame oil

½ teaspoon ground ginger
4 scallions, cut into 8 (2") pieces
1 package (8 ounces) Asian-flavored
     baked tofu, cut into 8 pieces

1 Soak 8 wooden skewers in water for 30 minutes. Coat a grill rack or broiler pan with cooking spray. Preheat the grill or broiler. Whisk together the peanut butter, water, soy sauce, vinegar, oil, and ginger in a small bowl. The mixture may look curdled. Keep whisking until smooth. Divide among small bowls on 4 plates.

2 Thread 1 piece of scallion and 1 piece of tofu onto each of the skewers. Place on a grill or under the broiler and cook, turning once, for 5 minutes, or until browned.

3 Place the skewers around the peanut sauce.

Makes 4 servings (2 tablespoons dipping sauce per serving)

PER SERVING: 182 calories, 10 g protein, 7 g carbohydrates, 13 g fat (2 g saturated fat), 0 mg cholesterol, 507 mg sodium

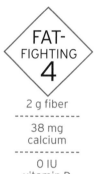

FAT-FIGHTING
4

2 g fiber

38 mg calcium

0 IU vitamin D

500 mg omega-3s

MAKE IT FAST

Asian Salmon Bites

PREP TIME: 20 MINUTES ◆ TOTAL TIME: 32 MINUTES + 1 HOUR CHILLING TIME

1 pouch (6 ounces) salmon, patted dry
1/3 cup dried bread crumbs
1 carrot, shredded
2 scallions, finely chopped
1 tablespoon reduced-sodium (light)
    soy sauce

2 teaspoons finely grated fresh ginger
4 tablespoons fat-free Greek-style yogurt
1/3 cup sesame seeds
1 teaspoon wasabi paste
1/4 cup drained pickled ginger

FAT-FIGHTING 4

3 g fiber
----
187 mg
calcium
----
0 IU
vitamin D
----
460 mg
omega-3s
----

1 Combine the salmon, bread crumbs, carrot, scallions, soy sauce, grated ginger, and 2 tablespoons of the yogurt, 1/4 cup of the sesame seeds, and 1/2 teaspoon of the wasabi paste in a medium bowl. Stir until well blended. Chill.

2 Stir together the remaining 2 tablespoons yogurt and 1/2 teaspoon wasabi paste until combined. Chill.

3 Preheat the oven to 400°F. Coat a baking sheet with cooking spray. Place the sesame seeds on a plate. Form 1 tablespoon of the salmon mixture into a patty and repeat, making 20 patties. Working one at a time, press into the sesame seeds to coat.

4 Place the patties on the prepared baking sheet. Spray the tops of the patties with cooking spray. Bake for 10 to 12 minutes, turning twice, or until browned.

5 Place the salmon bites on a serving plate. Top each with a generous teaspoon of the yogurt mixture and a small piece of the pickled ginger. Sprinkle with the remaining sesame seeds.

Makes 4 servings (5 bites per serving)

PER SERVING: 191 calories, 13 g protein, 14 g carbohydrates, 10 g fat (2 g saturated fat), 15 mg cholesterol, 478 mg sodium

MAKE IT AHEAD

These bites are a great portable snack. Prepare them up through step 4. Refrigerate the bites separately from the wasabi-yogurt sauce and assemble before eating.

Mediterranean Fish Crisps

PREP TIME: 10 MINUTES

1 can (3.75 ounces) sardines packed in
olive oil

2 tablespoons fat-free ricotta cheese

1 tablespoon lemon juice

1½ tablespoons finely chopped celery

1½ tablespoons finely chopped onion

1½ tablespoons finely chopped tomato

Ground black pepper

4 rye crisp crackers (7 g each), cut into
halves

Drain the sardines and pat dry with paper towels. Place in a shallow bowl with the ricotta and lemon juice. Mash coarsely with a fork to create a chunky mixture. Stir in the celery, onion, and tomato. Season to taste with the pepper. Spread on the crackers.

Makes 4 servings (2 crisps per serving)

PER SERVING: 190 calories, 8 g protein, 13 g carbohydrates, 3 g fat (0.5 g saturated fat), 33 mg cholesterol, 166 mg sodium

FAT-
FIGHTING
4

3 g fiber

120 mg
calcium

63 IU
vitamin D

350 mg
omega-3s

MAKE IT
FAST

Pickled Shrimp Salad

PREP TIME: 10 MINUTES ◆ TOTAL TIME: 13 MINUTES + MARINATING TIME

20 medium shrimp, peeled
½ cup thinly sliced carrot
½ cup thinly sliced zucchini
½ cup thinly sliced onion
2 bay leaves
¼ teaspoon dried thyme

1 tablespoon flaxseed oil
Pinch of salt
2-3 teaspoons white wine vinegar
1 cup baby spinach
Ground black pepper

FAT-
FIGHTING
4

1 g fiber

---

30 mg
calcium

---

46 IU
vitamin D

1,970 mg
omega-3s

---

1 Combine the shrimp, carrot, zucchini, onion, bay leaves, and thyme in a nonstick skillet. Cover and set over medium-high heat. Cook for 2 to 3 minutes, or until the shrimp are opaque. Remove from the heat and set aside, uncovered.

2 Combine the oil, salt, and 2 teaspoons of the vinegar in a bowl. Add the reserved shrimp and vegetables. Toss. Cover tightly and refrigerate for at least 12 hours, tossing occasionally.

3 To serve, divide the spinach among 4 salad plates. Remove the bay leaves from the shrimp and discard. Season to taste with the pepper and 1 teaspoon more vinegar, if desired. Spoon the shrimp mixture over the spinach.

Serves 4

PER SERVING: 77 calories, 7 g protein, 4 g carbohydrates, 4 g fat (0.5 g saturated fat), 46 mg cholesterol, 133 mg sodium

MAKE IT A MEAL
**Serve with the Mushroom Ragout
(page 248).**

Shredded Thai Vegetable Salad in Lettuce Cups

PREP TIME: 15 MINUTES

1 head Boston lettuce
1 tablespoon flaxseed oil
$\frac{1}{2}$ tablespoon reduced-sodium soy sauce
1 teaspoon white or red wine vinegar
Pinch of salt
6 ounces soft silken tofu, drained and cut
   in small cubes

$\frac{3}{4}$ cup shredded green or napa cabbage
$\frac{1}{2}$ cup shredded carrot
$\frac{1}{2}$ cup thinly sliced red onion
2 tablespoons cilantro
Pinch of red-pepper flakes

1 Wash and dry the lettuce. Select 16 equal-size leaves and place curved side up on a platter. (Reserve any remaining leaves for another recipe.)

2 Whisk the oil, soy sauce, vinegar, and salt in a mixing bowl. Add the tofu, cabbage, carrot, onion, cilantro, and red-pepper flakes. Toss to combine. Spoon equal amounts of the mixture onto each leaf. Serve immediately.

Makes 8 servings (2 bundles each)

PER SERVING: 44 calories, 2 g protein, 3 g carbohydrates, 3 g fat (0.5 g saturated fat), 0 mg cholesterol, 83 mg sodium

MAKE IT AGAIN
This recipe can also be served as a main-course salad for 4. Shred the lettuce and divide among 4 plates, then top with the tofu mixture.

FAT-FIGHTING
4

1 g fiber
26 mg calcium
0 IU vitamin D
930 mg omega-3s

MAKE IT FAST

Savory Artichoke Tomato Tart

PREP TIME: 20 MINUTES ◆ TOTAL TIME: 1 HOUR + COOLING TIME

3 tablespoons ground flaxseed
1 tablespoon canola oil
6 canned artichokes, rinsed, drained, and quartered
1/2 cup sliced grape tomatoes
2 cups fat-free ricotta cheese
3 omega-3-enriched eggs, beaten

1/4 cup grated Romano cheese
2 tablespoons chopped parsley
1 tablespoon cornstarch
1/2 teaspoon dried oregano
1/2 teaspoon ground black pepper
1/4 teaspoon salt

FAT-FIGHTING 4

1 g fiber
----
257 mg calcium
----
7 IU vitamin D
----
40 mg omega-3s
----

1 Position an oven rack in the bottom third of the oven. Preheat the oven to 325°F. Coat the bottom and sides of an 8" springform pan with cooking spray. Combine the flaxseed and oil with a fork in a small bowl. Sprinkle the mixture evenly over the pan bottom. (There may be some bare patches.) Set aside.

2 Place the artichokes and tomatoes, cut side down, on several layers of paper towels. Pat dry with paper towels.

3 Whisk the ricotta in a mixing bowl until smooth. Gradually add the eggs, whisking until smooth. Add the Romano, parsley, cornstarch, oregano, pepper, and salt. Whisk just until combined. Dollop the mixture into the prepared pan. Spread to smooth. Place the artichokes and tomatoes, cut side up, on top. Press with the back of a spatula to embed the vegetables.

4 Bake for about 35 minutes, or until set. Remove and allow to cool for at least 1 hour before serving. Or, cover and refrigerate for up to 24 hours.

5 To serve, cut into 10 slices.

Makes 10 servings

PER SERVING: 128 calories, 12 g protein, 7 g carbohydrates, 5 g fat (1 g saturated fat), 75 mg cholesterol, 301 mg sodium

MAKE IT AGAIN

For an easy lunch, place a serving of the leftover tart on a bed of baby spinach.

Roasted Asparagus Spears with Mustard Sauce

PREP TIME: 10 MINUTES ◆ TOTAL TIME: 25 MINUTES

20 spears asparagus, trimmed if necessary
1 teaspoon canola oil
½ cup fat-free ricotta cheese

2 tablespoons nonfat dry milk
2 tablespoons grated Parmesan cheese
2 teaspoons whole grain mustard
1 teaspoon prepared horseradish

1 Preheat the oven to 425°F. Place the asparagus on a baking sheet (with sides) large enough to hold them in a single layer. Drizzle with the oil and toss to coat the spears.

2 Bake for 15 to 17 minutes, or until the asparagus is crisp-tender. (Baking time will vary, depending upon thickness.)

3 Meanwhile, combine the ricotta, dry milk, Parmesan, mustard, and horseradish in a bowl.

4 Place 5 asparagus spears on each of 4 appetizer plates. Dollop the sauce on the spears.

Makes 4 servings (5 spears with sauce)

PER SERVING: 68 calories, 8 g protein, 6 g carbohydrates, 2 g fat (0.5 g saturated fat), 5 mg cholesterol, 128 mg sodium

MAKE IT A MEAL
Serve the asparagus as a side dish to the Chili-Rub Haddock Baked with Sweet Potatoes (page 228).

FAT-FIGHTING **4**

2 g fiber

177 mg calcium

0.11 IU vitamin D

10 mg omega-3s

MAKE IT FAST

Spinach, Cheese, and Red Pepper Pinwheels

PREP TIME: 15 MINUTES ◆ TOTAL TIME: 17 MINUTES

8 cups baby spinach
2 tablespoons blanched almonds
1 clove garlic
¼ cup drained roasted red peppers, patted dry
3 tablespoons part-skim ricotta cheese
2 tablespoons grated pecorino cheese
1 tablespoon nonfat dry milk
Pinch of salt
Dash of hot-pepper sauce
2 (8") omega-3-enriched whole wheat flour tortillas

1 Heat 1 tablespoon water in a nonstick skillet. Add the spinach. Cover and cook over medium-high heat for 2 minutes, or until the spinach is wilted. Drain and squeeze dry with paper towels. Chop finely and set aside.

2 Combine the almonds and garlic in a mini food processor or blender. Pulse until coarsely ground. Add the peppers, ricotta, pecorino, dry milk, salt, and hot-pepper sauce. Process or blend to a paste.

3 Lay the tortillas on a work surface. Spread the pepper paste on the tortillas. Scatter the spinach over top. Roll each tortilla into a tube. Holding each tube one at a time, seam side down, cut into 8 equal pieces. Set pinwheel side up, on a platter. Secure with wooden picks, if desired.

Makes 8 servings (2 pinwheels each)

PER SERVING: 74 calories, 3 g protein, 10 g carbohydrates, 3 g fat (1 g saturated fat), 3 mg cholesterol, 178 mg sodium

FAT-FIGHTING 4

2 g fiber

153 mg calcium

0 IU vitamin D

130 mg omega-3s

MAKE IT FAST

Endive Cheese Pitas

PREP TIME: 20 MINUTES

8 sun-dried tomato halves
1 cup soft fat-free cream cheese
   (tub-style)
1/4 cup shredded Parmesan cheese
1/3 cup loosely packed fresh basil,
   chopped

1/2 teaspoon lemon zest
1/4 teaspoon cracked black pepper
4 small pitas (4" diameter), halved
1 carrot, shredded
1 large head endive, chopped

FAT-FIGHTING 4

4 g fiber

198 mg
sodium

0 IU
vitamin D

50 mg
omega-3s

MAKE IT FAST

1 Place the tomatoes in a small bowl and cover with boiling water. Let stand for 10 minutes, or until soft. Drain and finely chop the tomatoes.

2 Combine the cream cheese, Parmesan, basil, lemon zest, pepper, and tomatoes in a medium bowl. Stir until well blended.

3 Divide the cheese mixture between the pita halves. Stuff with the carrot and endive.

Makes 4 servings

PER SERVING: 177 calories, 14 g protein, 25 g carbohydrates, 3 g fat (2 g saturated fat), 8 mg cholesterol, 655 mg sodium*

＊ Limit sodium to less than 2,300 mg per day.

Pea Pods with Feta-Herb Filling

PREP TIME: 15 MINUTES

½ cup fat-free ricotta cheese
½ cup reduced-fat feta cheese
1½ tablespoons finely chopped dill
½ teaspoon grated orange rind

Coarsely ground black pepper
30 Chinese snow pea pods
1 tablespoon finely chopped walnuts

1 Combine the ricotta, feta, dill, and orange rind in a bowl. Season liberally with the pepper. Mash with a fork to combine.

2 Slit open the straighter side of the pea pods with a small, sharp knife. Fill each pod with some of the cheese mixture, using a small spoon or knife. Place on a serving plate, sitting each pod upright like a rowboat. Sprinkle the walnuts over the pea pods.

Makes 10 servings (3 pods each)

PER SERVING: 33 calories, 3 g protein, 2 g fat (1 g saturated fat), 3 mg cholesterol, 110 mg sodium

MAKE IT AHEAD
Tightly cover the stuffed pods with plastic wrap and refrigerate for up to 3 days.

FAT-FIGHTING
4

0.5 g fiber
- - - - - - - - - - - - -
66 mg
calcium
- - - - - - - - - - - - -
0 IU
vitamin D
- - - - - - - - - - - - -
70 mg
omega-3s
- - - - - - - - - - - - -

MAKE IT
FAST

Edamame Crostini

PREP TIME: 10 MINUTES ◆ TOTAL TIME: 35 MINUTES

1 cup fresh or frozen shelled edamame
½ teaspoon dried thyme
1 teaspoon lemon juice
¼ teaspoon salt
4 ounces whole wheat French baguette,
    cut into thin slices

2 cloves garlic, peeled and cut in half
¼ cup loosely packed fresh basil, cut into
    thin strips

FAT-FIGHTING 4

3 g fiber

----

33 mg
calcium

----

0 IU
vitamin D

----

560 mg
omega-3s

----

1 Bring 1 cup water to a boil in a medium saucepan. Add the edamame and thyme. Reduce the heat to medium; cover and cook for 25 to 30 minutes, or until the edamame are very soft. Transfer to a blender or food processor with the lemon juice, salt, and some cooking water, if necessary. Puree until smooth.

2 Meanwhile, preheat the broiler. Place the bread slices on a baking sheet and toast for 3 minutes, turning once, or until browned. Remove and rub the garlic cloves onto the bread slices. Divide the edamame mixture among the bread slices and place on a serving plate. Sprinkle with the basil.

Makes 4 servings

PER SERVING: 114 calories, 6 g protein, 18 g carbohydrates, 2 g fat (0 g saturated fat), 0 mg cholesterol, 302 mg sodium

Mini Black-Bean Cakes

PREP TIME: 15 MINUTES ◆ TOTAL TIME: 30 MINUTES

1 cup no-salt-added canned black beans,
    rinsed and drained
2 tablespoons ground flaxseed
2 tablespoons chopped cilantro + extra
    leaves (optional)
1 tablespoon chopped onion

1 egg white, beaten
1 teaspoon canola oil
$\frac{1}{8}$ teaspoon chili powder
$\frac{1}{8}$ teaspoon salt
3 tablespoons low-fat plain yogurt
6 grape tomatoes, cut in half

1 Preheat the oven to 375°F. Coat a baking sheet with cooking spray.

2 Combine the beans, flaxseed, cilantro, onion, egg white, oil, chili powder, and salt in a blender or food processor. Blend or process, scraping down sides as needed, for 1½ minutes, or until the mixture comes together. Rinse your hands with cold water, shaking off excess. Shape the mixture into 12 patties, each about 2" wide and ¼" thick. Place on the prepared baking sheet.

3 Bake for 15 minutes, or until heated through.

4 Remove the cakes to a platter. Top each with a dollop of the yogurt, half a grape tomato, and a cilantro leaf (if using).

Makes 4 servings (3 patties each)

PER SERVING: 99 calories, 6 g protein, 12 g carbohydrates, 3 g fat (0.5 g saturated fat), 1 mg cholesterol, 105 mg sodium

MAKE IT AHEAD
These cakes can be baked in advance and refrigerated for up to 3 days or frozen for up to 3 months in an airtight container. To reheat, microwave on medium power for 1 to 2 minutes.

MAKE IT AGAIN
The bean cakes can be served as a main course. Shape the mixture into 4 larger cakes and bake for 18 minutes, or until heated through.

FAT-FIGHTING
4

4 g fiber

----

65 mg
calcium

----

0 IU
vitamin D

----

930 mg
omega-3s

MAKE IT
FAST

Borscht Dip with Belgian Endive

PREP TIME: 15 MINUTES

1 can (15 ounces) beets, drained

3 tablespoons fat-free plain yogurt

2 tablespoons nonfat dry milk

2 tablespoons chopped fresh dill + sprigs
   for garnish

2 tablespoons finely chopped scallions
   or chives

$\frac{1}{8}$ teaspoon salt

2-3 teaspoons prepared horseradish

Ground black pepper

2 heads Belgian endive (6 ounces each)

FAT-
FIGHTING
4

1 g fiber

33 mg
calcium

2 U
vitamin D

0 mg
omega-3s

MAKE IT
FAST

1 Combine the beets, yogurt, dry milk, chopped dill, scallions, salt, and 2 teaspoons of the horseradish in a blender or food processor. Pulse until the beets are finely chopped. Season with the pepper and up to 1 teaspoon more horseradish to taste. Transfer to a serving dish set on a platter. Cut the ends from the endive and separate the leaves. Arrange 24 large leaves around the dip. (Reserve any leftover leaves for salads.) Garnish with dill sprigs.

2 To serve, scoop 1 tablespoon dip on the end of each leaf.

Makes 8 servings (3 leaves each, plus dip)

PER SERVING: 22 calories, 1 g protein, 5 g carbohydrates, 0 g fat (0 g saturated fat), 0 mg cholesterol, 126 mg sodium

MAKE IT AGAIN

Pack any leftover dip in a tightly closed plastic storage container. Pack leftover endive in a plastic bag. Serve with 2 ounces sliced grilled chicken breast for lunch.

Clam Dip with Crudités

PREP TIME: 20 MINUTES ◆ TOTAL TIME: 26 MINUTES

1 can (10 ounces) baby clams,
    rinsed and drained
$\frac{1}{2}$ cup fat-free ricotta cheese
$\frac{1}{4}$ cup grated Parmesan cheese
2 tablespoons nonfat dry milk
4 scallions, sliced
1 teaspoon salt-free seasoning blend

$\frac{1}{8}$ teaspoon hot-pepper sauce
Paprika
2 cups mixed raw vegetables,
    such as celery sticks, baby carrots,
    broccoli florets, bell pepper strips,
    and zucchini strips

1 Coat an 8" square or round ceramic baking dish with cooking spray.

2 Combine the clams, ricotta, Parmesan, dry milk, scallions, seasoning blend, and hot-pepper sauce in a blender or food processor. Pulse several times, or until the clams are coarsely chopped and the ingredients are blended. Transfer to the prepared dish. Cover with plastic wrap, leaving a vent.

3 Place in the microwave. Cook on medium power for 5 minutes. Cook on high power for 1 minute, or until heated through.

4 Sprinkle the dip with the paprika. Serve with the vegetables for dipping.

Makes 6 servings

PER SERVING: 103 calories, 10 g protein, 12 g carbohydrates, 2 g fat (1 g saturated fat), 29 mg cholesterol, 357 mg sodium

FAT-FIGHTING 4

1 g fiber

173 mg calcium

0.07 IU vitamin D

20 mg omega-3s

MAKE IT FAST

MAKE IT AGAIN
Any leftover dip makes a tasty snack spread for whole grain crackers.

Mussels Rockefeller

PREP TIME: 10 MINUTES   ◆   TOTAL TIME: 18 MINUTES

24 mussels, scrubbed (1 pound)
3 cups baby spinach
1 clove garlic, finely chopped
Pinch of salt

1½ teaspoons ground flaxseed
Hot-pepper sauce
2 tablespoons grated Parmesan cheese

1 Preheat the broiler. Set out a 13" x 9" baking dish.

2 Place the mussels in a large nonstick skillet. Cover and set over high heat. Cook, tossing occasionally, for 2 to 3 minutes, or until the shells open. Discard any shells that don't open. With tongs, remove the mussels one at a time, tipping the shells to drain any juices into the pan. Set the mussels on a tray.

3 Add the spinach, garlic, and salt to the pan. Cover and set over medium-high heat. Cook for 2 minutes, or until wilted. Add the flaxseed and a couple of dashes of hot-pepper sauce. Stir with a fork to blend.

4 Remove and discard the empty shell half of each mussel. Place the shell halves with the mussel attached in the baking dish. Spoon some of the spinach mixture on each mussel. Sprinkle with the cheese.

5 Broil 6" from the heat for about 2 minutes, or until bubbling.

Makes 4 servings (6 mussels each)

PER SERVING: 108 calories, 13 g protein, 6 g carbohydrates, 3 g fat (1 g saturated fat), 29 mg cholesterol, 427 mg sodium

FAT-FIGHTING
4

1 g fiber

69 mg calcium

0 IU vitamin D

450 mg omega-3s

MAKE IT FAST

Citrus Seafood Cocktail

PREP TIME: 10 MINUTES ◆ TOTAL TIME: 22 MINUTES

1 tablespoon canola oil
6 ounces scallops
6 ounces skinless salmon fillet
1 navel orange
2 tablespoons chopped fresh cilantro

1 tablespoon flaxseed oil
$\frac{1}{8}$ teaspoon salt
1 cup baby spinach
2 tablespoons slivered, blanched almonds

1 Set a nonstick skillet over medium-high heat, add 1 teaspoon of the canola oil, and heat until hot. Spritz or brush the scallops and salmon very lightly with the remaining canola oil. Place the salmon in the pan, surrounded by the scallops. Cook for 4 minutes, or until browned on the bottom. Flip and cook for 4 to 6 minutes more, or until the fish is opaque. Cooking time will vary with the thickness of the seafood. Remove the seafood from the pan until cool enough to handle. Add 1 tablespoon water to the pan. Swirl to loosen any browned bits.

2 Remove about 1 tablespoon orange peel strips with a citrus zester to use for garnish.

Peel the orange and cut into small chunks. Place in a mixing bowl with the cilantro, flaxseed oil, salt, and pan juices. Cut the salmon and scallops into bite-size pieces. Add to the bowl. Toss.

3 Arrange the spinach on 4 appetizer plates or in shallow glass bowls. Top with the salad. Sprinkle with the almonds and the orange peel.

Makes 4 servings

PER SERVING: 220 calories, 17 g protein, 7 g carbohydrates, 14 g fat (2 g saturated fat), 39 mg cholesterol, 177 mg sodium

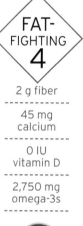

FAT-FIGHTING 4

2 g fiber
- - - - - - - - - - - -
45 mg calcium
- - - - - - - - - - - -
0 IU vitamin D
- - - - - - - - - - - -
2,750 mg omega-3s
- - - - - - - - - - - -

MAKE IT FAST

Spaghetti Carbonara

PREP TIME: 5 MINUTES ◆ TOTAL TIME: 25 MINUTES

¼ **cup finely chopped ham**
2 cloves garlic, finely chopped
1 tablespoon water
4 ounces whole grain spaghetti (such as Barilla Plus)

2 omega-3-enriched eggs, beaten
3 tablespoons grated Romano cheese
Ground black pepper

FAT-
FIGHTING
4

2 g fiber

82 mg
calcium

9 IU
vitamin D

150 mg
omega-3s

MAKE IT
FAST

❶ Set a covered saucepan of water over high heat.

❷ Place the ham, garlic, and water in a nonstick skillet (large enough to hold the pasta after it's cooked) over medium heat. Cook, stirring occasionally, for 5 minutes, or until the garlic is lightly golden. Reduce the heat if the mixture is browning too fast. Turn off the heat.

❸ When the water in the saucepan boils, add the pasta and stir. Return to a boil and cook, stirring occasionally, for 8 minutes, or until al dente. Reserve ¼ cup of the cooking water before draining the pasta. Transfer the pasta to the skillet. Pour about

2 tablespoons of the cooking water into the eggs. Add the egg mixture to the skillet. Toss to coat the pasta. Cook over medium-low heat, tossing constantly, for about 5 minutes, or just until the eggs thicken enough to make a creamy sauce. Remove the pan from the heat right away if the eggs start to curdle. Remove from the heat and add the cheese. Toss to combine. Season to taste with the pepper.

Makes 4 servings

PER SERVING: 174 calories, 11 g protein, 21 g carbohydrates, 5 g fat (2 g saturated fat), 97 mg cholesterol, 208 mg sodium

Stuffed Pasta Shells

PREP TIME: 20 MINUTES ◆ TOTAL TIME: 40 MINUTES

3 cups baby spinach
12 jumbo pasta shells
¾ cup part-skim ricotta cheese
1 small clove garlic, finely chopped
¼ teaspoon dried oregano
Pinch of salt
2 tablespoons grated pecorino cheese
2 tablespoons grated Parmesan cheese
Ground black pepper
1 tablespoon ground flaxseed

1 Preheat the oven to 400°F. Set out a 12-cup muffin tin or an 8" × 8" baking dish.

2 Place a covered medium saucepan filled with water over high heat. Bring to a boil. Add the spinach and boil for 1 minute. Remove with a skimmer to a clean kitchen towel. Set aside. Add the shells to the water and return to a boil. Stir. Boil for 10 minutes, or until cooked through but still firm. Drain and rinse with cold water. Turn upside down on a kitchen towel to dry.

3 Squeeze the spinach dry and chop finely. Place in a bowl with the ricotta, garlic, oregano, salt, 1 tablespoon of the pecorino, and 1 tablespoon of the Parmesan. Season to taste with the pepper.

4 Fill the reserved shells with the cheese mixture, using a teaspoon. Place open side up in the prepared tin or dish. Continue until all the shells are filled. (If using the baking dish, it may be necessary to twist small pieces of aluminum foil to use as props to hold the shells steady.) Combine the flaxseed and the remaining 1 tablespoon pecorino and 1 tablespoon Parmesan in a small bowl. Stir. Sprinkle atop the filling in each shell. Spritz lightly with olive oil spray.

5 Bake for 8 minutes, or until the crumbs are sizzling.

Makes 6 servings (2 shells per serving)

PER SERVING: 133 calories, 8 g protein, 14 g carbohydrates, 5 g fat (3 g saturated fat), 13 mg cholesterol, 132 mg sodium

FAT-
FIGHTING
4

1 g fiber
---
194 mg
calcium
---
0 IU
vitamin D
---
310 mg
omega-3s

Penne Pasta with Brussels Sprouts and Ham

PREP TIME: 10 MINUTES ◆ TOTAL TIME: 30 MINUTES

1 teaspoon canola oil
¼ cup finely chopped very lean ham
½ onion, halved and thinly sliced
2 cups thinly sliced Brussels sprouts
¼ cup water

4 ounces whole grain penne (such as Barilla Plus)
2 teaspoons flaxseed oil
¼ teaspoon red-pepper flakes

FAT-FIGHTING
4

4 g fiber
- - - - - - - - - - -
22 mg calcium
- - - - - - - - - - -
0 IU vitamin D
- - - - - - - - - - -
1,350 mg omega-3s
- - - - - - - - - - -

MAKE IT FAST

1 Set a covered saucepan of water over high heat.

2 Heat a nonstick skillet (large enough to hold the pasta after it's cooked) over medium heat. Add the oil and heat for 1 minute. Add the ham and onion. Toss. Cover and cook for 5 minutes, or until the onion starts to color. Add the Brussels sprouts and water and toss. Cover and cook, tossing occasionally, for 5 minutes, or until the sprouts are wilted and lightly charred. Set aside.

3 When the water in the saucepan boils, add the pasta and stir. Return to a boil and cook, stirring occasionally, for 6 minutes, or until al dente. Reserve ¼ cup of cooking water before draining the pasta. Transfer the pasta and reserved cooking water to the skillet. Add the flaxseed oil. Toss and serve with red-pepper flakes at the table.

Makes 4 servings

PER SERVING: 170 calories, 8 g protein, 25 g carbohydrates, 5 g fat (0.5 g saturated fat), 3 mg cholesterol, 98 mg sodium

BREAKFASTS

Farmers' Market Scrambled Eggs

PREP TIME: 15 MINUTES ◆ TOTAL TIME: 27 MINUTES

4 omega-3-enriched eggs
4 egg whites
2 ounces low-fat goat cheese (such as Coach Farm), crumbled
2 teaspoons chopped fresh tarragon
¼ teaspoon salt
¼ teaspoon ground black pepper

½ pound asparagus, trimmed and cut into 3" pieces
½ pound sugar snap peas, trimmed
10 radishes, trimmed and quartered
¼ cup fat-free, reduced-sodium chicken broth

FAT-FIGHTING 4

7 g fiber

513 mg calcium

118 IU vitamin D

110 mg omega-3s

MAKE IT FAST

1 Whisk together the eggs, egg whites, cheese, tarragon, salt, and pepper in a medium bowl. Set aside.

2 Coat a large nonstick skillet with cooking spray and heat over medium-high heat. Add the asparagus, peas, and radishes and cook, stirring, for 3 minutes. Add the broth, cover, and simmer for 5 minutes, or until tender. Remove to a platter; cover and keep warm.

3 Wipe the skillet clean and recoat with cooking spray. Heat the skillet over medium heat. Add the egg mixture and, using a rubber spatula, push the cooked eggs toward the center while tilting the pan to distribute the runny parts. Once the eggs are almost set, scramble them gently.

4 Place on the platter with the vegetables and serve immediately with 1 slice light whole grain toast and 1 cup fat-free milk.

Makes 4 servings

PER SERVING: 297 calories, 25 g protein, 36 g carbohydrates, 6 g fat (2 g saturated fat), 187 mg cholesterol, 544 mg sodium

NOTE
For the toast, we used Pepperidge Farm Light Style, at 45 calories per slice.

Egg and Tomato Sandwich

PREP TIME: 5 MINUTES ◆ TOTAL TIME: 15 MINUTES

1 omega-3-enriched egg
1 teaspoon water
1 whole grain light English muffin, split

1 thick slice tomato
1 slice (1 ounce) reduced-fat Cheddar cheese

1 Coat a nonstick skillet with cooking spray and heat over medium-high heat. Break and slip the egg into the skillet, gently pushing the white toward the center so the egg is about the size of an English muffin. Immediately reduce the heat to low. Cook for 1 minute, or until the edges turn white. Add the water. Tightly cover the skillet. Cook for 3 minutes, or until the white is completely set and the yolk begins to thicken but is not hard.

2 Meanwhile, toast the English muffin. Place 1 half on a plate and top with the tomato. Place the cheese on the other half and toast or broil until melted. Place the egg on the tomato. Top with the cheese-melted muffin half.

Makes 1 serving

PER SERVING: 270 calories, 20 g protein, 27 g carbohydrates, 12 g fat (5 g saturated fat), 204 mg cholesterol, 485 mg sodium

FAT-FIGHTING
4

8 g fiber

313 mg calcium

18 IU vitamin D

110 mg omega 3s

MAKE IT FAST

Spinach Frittata

PREP TIME: 10 MINUTES ◆ TOTAL TIME: 27 MINUTES

4 omega-3-enriched eggs
4 egg whites
¼ cup grated Asiago cheese
¼ teaspoon salt

1 small onion, minced
1 red bell pepper, cut into thin strips
¼ cup finely chopped Canadian bacon
4 cups baby spinach

1 Preheat the oven to 350°F. Whisk together the eggs, egg whites, cheese, and salt in a medium bowl.

2 Coat a large, ovenproof, nonstick skillet with cooking spray and heat over medium heat. Add the onion, pepper, and bacon and cook for 4 minutes, or until browned. Add the spinach and cook, stirring, for 1 minute, or until the spinach is wilted. Pour in the egg mixture and cook for 2 minutes, or until the bottom of the frittata is starting to set.

3 Place in the oven and bake for 10 minutes, or until set.

4 Serve with 1 slice whole grain toast and 1 cup fat-free milk.

Makes 4 servings

PER SERVING: 289 calories, 25 g protein, 30 g carbohydrates, 7 g fat (3 g saturated fat), 193 mg cholesterol, 610 mg sodium*

* Limit sodium to less than 2,300 mg per day.

FAT-FIGHTING 4

3 g fiber

373 mg calcium

118 IU vitamin D

140 mg omega-3s

MAKE IT FAST

> ### NOTE
> For the toast, we used Pepperidge Farm Light Style, at 45 calories per slice.

Italian Egg Sandwich

PREP TIME: 5 MINUTES ◆ TOTAL TIME: 13 MINUTES

2 omega-3-enriched eggs
½ cup (2 ounces) shredded part-skim
mozzarella cheese
1 teaspoon water

2 whole grain light English muffins, split
and toasted
¼ cup marinara sauce, heated

1 Coat a nonstick skillet with cooking spray and heat over medium-high heat. Break and slip the eggs into the skillet, gently pushing the white toward the center so the eggs are about the size of an English muffin. Top each egg with 2 tablespoons of the cheese. Immediately reduce the heat to low. Cook for 1 minute, or until the edges turn white. Add the water. Tightly cover the skillet. Cook for 3 minutes, or until the white is completely set and the yolk begins to thicken but is not hard.

2 Place half an English muffin on each of 2 plates. Top each with half of the sauce and the remaining 2 tablespoons cheese. Place 1 egg on each muffin. Top with the remaining muffin halves.

Makes 2 servings

PER SERVING: 264 calories, 20 g protein, 29 g carbohydrates, 11 g fat (4 g saturated fat), 202 mg cholesterol, 544 mg sodium

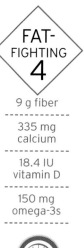

FAT-
FIGHTING
4

9 g fiber

335 mg
calcium

18.4 IU
vitamin D

150 mg
omega-3s

MAKE IT
FAST

Sweet Lemon-Ricotta Brunch Blintzes

PREP TIME: 20 MINUTES ◆ TOTAL TIME: 45 MINUTES

8 blintzes (6" diameter) (recipe follows)
1 cup part-skim ricotta cheese
2 tablespoons confectioners' sugar +
extra for garnish

¼ teaspoon lemon extract
1 cup fresh or frozen and thawed
raspberries

1 Preheat the oven to 350°F. Coat a 13" × 9" baking dish with cooking spray.

2 Meanwhile, combine the ricotta, sugar, and lemon extract in a bowl. Set aside.

3 Lay the blintzes on a work surface. Dollop some of the ricotta mixture in the center of each blintz. One at a time, fold 2 opposite sides of a blintz over the cheese to meet in the middle. Fold the opposite sides to the middle to make a bundle. Place seam side down in the baking dish. Continue until all the bundles are shaped. Cover the pan tightly with aluminum foil.

4 Bake for 25 to 30 minutes, or until heated through. Serve warm, garnished with raspberries and dusted with confectioners' sugar.

Makes 4 servings (2 blintzes each)

PER SERVING: 308 calories, 17 g protein, 33 g carbohydrates, 12 g fat (4 g saturated fat), 111 mg cholesterol, 181 mg sodium

NOTE
The times and nutrient values given here include the blintz preparation.

FAT-FIGHTING
4

5 g fiber

285 mg calcium

40 IU vitamin D

130 mg omega-3s

Blintzes

¾ cup white whole wheat flour
2 tablespoons ground flaxseed
Pinch of salt
2 omega-3-enriched eggs

1- 1¼ cups fat-free milk
1 tablespoon canola oil
1 teaspoon vanilla extract

1 Combine the flour, flaxseed, and salt in a mixing bowl. Stir to mix. Beat the eggs with a fork or whisk until very well blended, in another mixing bowl. Add 1 cup of the milk, the oil, and vanilla. Whisk to mix. Add gradually to the dry ingredients, whisking constantly, to create a smooth batter. Allow to sit for 5 minutes.

2 Stir the batter gently and let it run off of a spoon. It should be thinner than cake batter. Add 1 tablespoon more milk at a time until desired consistency is reached.

3 Heat a crepe pan or 8" nonstick skillet over medium-high heat. Pick up the pan with a mitt, and, holding it away from the heat, coat the pan lightly with cooking spray. Return to medium-high heat. Ladle a scant ¼ cup of batter into the pan. Swirl the pan quickly and evenly to cover the bottom with batter. Cook for 1 to 2 minutes, adjusting the heat higher or lower as

needed, or until the bottom is browned. Flip and cook for about 1 to 2 minutes, or until cooked through. Reduce the heat if the bottoms are browning too fast. Transfer to a tray. Off the heat, coat the pan with cooking spray. Return to the heat and cook another blintz. Continue until all the blintzes are cooked.

Makes 8 blintzes

NOTE
See page 77 for times and nutrient values.

MAKE IT AHEAD
If you want, you can make your blintzes several days or even weeks in advance of when you need them. Cool them and stack between small sheets of waxed paper, then place in an airtight container or resealable plastic bag. Refrigerate for up to 3 days or freeze for up to 3 weeks. Allow to thaw before filling and baking.

Breakfast Burritos

PREP TIME: 20 MINUTES ◆ TOTAL TIME: 34 MINUTES

1 package (14 ounces) Nasoya brand light tofu packed in calcium sulfate
3 (8") omega-3-enhanced whole wheat tortillas
1 red bell pepper, chopped
1 small onion, chopped
¼ teaspoon cumin
1 cup salsa
¼ cup cilantro
1 cup (4 ounces) shredded reduced-fat Cheddar cheese
3 cups baby spinach

1 Remove the tofu from the package and place in a colander in the sink. Place a flat plate on top of the tofu and a heavy can of vegetables on the plate for 5 minutes to drain. Preheat the oven to 350°F.

2 Wrap the tortillas in foil and place in the oven to heat.

3 Coat a large nonstick skillet with cooking spray and heat over medium heat. Cook the pepper, onion, and cumin for 5 minutes, or until tender. Crumble the tofu into the pan and cook for 2 minutes, or until lightly browned. Add the salsa and cilantro and cook for 5 minutes, stirring frequently, or until heated through. Top with the cheese and cook for 2 minutes to melt.

4 Lay 1 tortilla on a flat surface. Top with ½ cup of the spinach and approximately ½ cup of the tofu mixture. Roll to seal, then cut in half. Repeat with the remaining tortillas, spinach, and tofu mixture.

Makes 6 servings

PER SERVING: 181 calories, 13 g protein, 19 g carbohydrates, 7 g fat (2 g saturated fat), 13 mg cholesterol, 655 mg sodium

FAT-FIGHTING **4**

4 g fiber

558 mg calcium

100 IU vitamin D

250 mg omega-3s

MAKE IT AHEAD

Drain the tofu the night before by placing the colander in a bowl and topping it with a plate and a heavy can of vegetables. Then chop the vegetables and place in a sealed container. Refrigerate both overnight.

MAKE IT AGAIN

This recipe stores well for future use. If you won't use all of the tofu mixture, store it in a covered container in the refrigerator for up to 3 days. Heat in the microwave on 50% heat for 1 minute, or until warm. Don't overcook.

Chilaquiles

PREP TIME: 15 MINUTES ◆ TOTAL TIME: 52 MINUTES

3 (6") corn tortillas, cut into thin strips
1 cup baby spinach, coarsely chopped
1 cup canned black beans, rinsed and
 drained
½ cup canned, drained diced tomatoes
1 can (4.5 ounces) chopped green chiles

2 scallions, sliced
3 omega-3-enriched eggs
2 tablespoons nonfat dry milk
½ teaspoon chipotle hot sauce
¼ cup shredded 75% reduced-fat
 Cheddar cheese (such as Cabot)

FAT-FIGHTING 4

6 g fiber

123 mg calcium

14 IU vitamin D

80 mg omega-3s

1 Preheat the oven to 350°F. Coat an 8" round or square baking dish with cooking spray. Place the tortilla strips in the pan. Scatter the spinach, beans, tomatoes, chiles, and scallions over the tortillas.

2 Beat the eggs, dry milk, and hot sauce in a bowl with a fork until smooth. Pour into the baking dish. Press the mixture with the fork to submerge. Sprinkle with the cheese. Cover the pan with foil.

3 Bake for 25 minutes. Uncover the dish and bake for 12 minutes more, or until the cheese bubbles.

Makes 4 servings

PER SERVING: 202 calories, 13 g protein, 24 g carbohydrates, 5 g fat (1 g saturated fat), 135 mg cholesterol, 506 mg sodium

MAKE IT AHEAD

The chilaquiles can be prepared and refrigerated for up to 24 hours before baking.

MAKE IT AGAIN

Any leftover cooked chilaquiles can be cooled and refrigerated in an airtight container. To reheat a serving, place on a microwaveable plate, cover loosely with waxed paper, and microwave on medium power for 2 to 3 minutes, or until hot.

Southern Shrimp and Grits

PREP TIME: 10 MINUTES   ◆   TOTAL TIME: 30 MINUTES

2 cups fat-free milk
2 tablespoons nonfat dry milk
½ cup dry white grits
¼ cup grated Parmesan cheese

2 teaspoons canola oil
¾ pound medium shrimp, peeled
4 scallions, sliced
1 teaspoon Cajun seasoning

1 Combine the milk and dry milk in a saucepan. Bring to a simmer over medium heat. Whisk in the grits. Bring the mixture just to a boil, stirring occasionally. Cover partially and reduce heat. Simmer, stirring occasionally, for 12 to 15 minutes, or until very thick. Remove the saucepan from the heat. Stir in the Parmesan.

2 Heat a nonstick skillet over medium-high heat. Add the oil and swirl to coat the pan.

Add the shrimp, scallions, and Cajun seasoning. Toss for 5 minutes, or until the shrimp are opaque.

3 Divide the grits among 4 plates. Top with the shrimp mixture.

Makes 4 servings

PER SERVING: 262 calories, 26 g protein, 25 g carbohydrates, 6 g fat (1 g saturated fat), 135 mg cholesterol, 417 mg sodium

FAT-FIGHTING
4

1 g fiber
----
264 mg
calcium
----
179 IU
vitamin D
----
650 mg
omega-3s

MAKE IT
FAST

Seattle Salmon Hash

PREP TIME: 20 MINUTES ◆ TOTAL TIME: 40 MINUTES

½ cup fat-free, reduced-sodium chicken broth

2 turnips, peeled and cut into small dice

1 large red-skinned potato, cut into small dice

¾ teaspoon dried thyme

1 tablespoon flaxseed oil

1 bunch scallions, sliced

2 pouches (6 ounces each) boneless, skinless wild salmon

2 cups packed baby spinach, chopped

2 tablespoons ground flaxseed

¾ teaspoon paprika

FAT-FIGHTING 4

4 g fiber

67 mg calcium

0 IU vitamin D

3,580 mg omega-3s

1 Bring the broth to a boil in a large nonstick skillet over medium-high heat. Add the turnips, potatoes, and thyme. Cover and cook at a brisk simmer for 10 minutes, or until the potatoes are very tender. Remove from the heat. Smash the turnips and potatoes with a potato masher or pancake turner. Return to medium heat. Add the oil to the pan and heat.

2 Add the scallions. Cook, stirring occasionally, for 3 minutes. Add the salmon, spinach, flaxseed, and paprika. Cook for 5 to 7 minutes, flipping the mixture frequently, until the spinach is wilted and the mixture is lightly browned.

Makes 4 servings

PER SERVING: 198 calories, 18 g protein, 14 g carbohydrates, 8 g fat (2 g saturated fat), 30 mg cholesterol, 553 mg sodium

Breakfast Oats with Pears

PREP TIME: 10 MINUTES ◆ TOTAL TIME: 25 MINUTES

1 cup water
½ cup old-fashioned rolled oats
⅛ teaspoon ground cinnamon
Pinch of salt

1 red pear (such as red Bartlett), halved,
　cored, and cut into 1" pieces
1 tablespoon sugar-free maple syrup
4 tablespoons chopped walnuts

1 Heat the water in a small saucepan over high heat until just boiling. Add the oats, cinnamon, and salt. Reduce the heat to low, cover, and simmer for 20 minutes, or until the liquid is absorbed.

2 Meanwhile, coat a small nonstick skillet with butter-flavored cooking spray and heat over medium-high heat. Add the pear and cook, stirring, for 4 minutes, or until browned. Add the syrup and cook, stirring, until thickened. Top with the walnuts.

3 Divide the oats into 2 bowls. Divide the pear mixture over each.

Makes 2 servings

PER SERVING: 224 calories, 6 g protein, 29 g carbohydrates, 11 g fat (1 g saturated fat), 0 mg cholesterol, 94 mg sodium

NOTE
Compare the labels on sugar-free syrups, and choose the one that provides the fewest carbohydrates per serving.

FAT-FIGHTING
4

5 g fiber

36 mg calcium

0 IU vitamin D

1,330 mg omega-3s

MAKE IT FAST

Coconut Cream of Wheat with Strawberries and Pistachios

PREP TIME: 5 MINUTES ◆ TOTAL TIME: 8 MINUTES

½ cup canned fat-free evaporated milk
2 tablespoons Wheatena or whole grain cream of wheat cereal
½ teaspoon coconut extract

¼ cup sliced fresh or frozen and thawed strawberries
1 tablespoon chopped pistachios
1 teaspoon honey

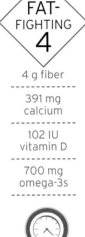

FAT-FIGHTING 4

4 g fiber

391 mg calcium

102 IU vitamin D

700 mg omega-3s

MAKE IT FAST

1 Combine the milk and cereal in a 4-cup microwaveable bowl or mixing cup. Whisk with a fork. Microwave on high power for 1 minute. Whisk with a fork. Microwave in 30-second intervals, whisking after each interval, for 90 seconds, or until thickened.

2 Remove and stir in the coconut extract. Spoon into a serving bowl. Top with the strawberries and pistachios. Drizzle on the honey.

Makes 1 serving

PER SERVING: 248 calories, 14 g protein, 39 g carbohydrates, 5 g total fat (1 g saturated fat), 5 mg cholesterol, 151 mg sodium

Morning Fried Rice

PREP TIME: 15 MINUTES ◆ TOTAL TIME: 25 MINUTES

2 teaspoons canola oil
1/2 cup Chinese pea pods, cut into thirds
1/4 cup shredded carrot
1/4 cup thinly sliced roasted red bell peppers (from a jar)

1/4 cup thinly sliced onion
2 omega-3-enriched eggs
1 tablespoon reduced-sodium soy sauce
1 teaspoon grated fresh ginger
1 1/2 cups cold cooked brown rice

FAT-FIGHTING 4

2 g fiber

28 mg calcium

9 IU vitamin D

60 mg omega-3s

MAKE IT FAST

① Heat a large nonstick skillet over medium-high heat for 1 minute. Add the oil and swirl to coat the pan bottom. Add the pea pods, carrot, peppers, and onion. Stir. Cover and cook for 5 minutes, or until the onion is wilted.

② Meanwhile, beat the eggs, soy sauce, and ginger in a bowl with a fork.

③ Uncover the vegetables and add the rice. Toss for 1 to 2 minutes, or until the rice

is hot. Reduce the heat to medium. Scrape the rice mixture to the sides of the pan. Add the egg mixture in the center. Stir the eggs to scramble lightly. Toss with the rice for 1 to 2 minutes, or until the eggs are cooked.

Makes 4 servings

PER SERVING: 154 calories, 6 g protein, 21 g carbohydrates, 5 g fat (1 g saturated fat), 90 mg cholesterol, 203 mg sodium

Oat Griddle Cakes with Melted Cheddar

PREP TIME: 10 MINUTES + STANDING TIME ◆ TOTAL TIME: 23 MINUTES

$\frac{1}{4}$ **cup + 2 tablespoons regular oats**
$\frac{1}{4}$ **cup white whole wheat flour**
2 tablespoons nonfat dry milk
1 tablespoon ground flaxseed
$\frac{1}{2}$ **teaspoon baking soda**
$\frac{1}{2}$ **teaspoon baking powder**
$\frac{1}{4}$ **teaspoon ground nutmeg**

Pinch of salt
1 omega-3-enriched egg
3 tablespoons low-fat plain yogurt
$1\frac{1}{2}$ **tablespoons canola oil**
$\frac{1}{4}$ **cup shredded reduced-fat Cheddar cheese**

1 Combine the oats, flour, dry milk, flaxseed, baking soda, baking powder, nutmeg, and salt in a bowl. Stir to mix well. Beat the egg with a fork in a small bowl. Add the yogurt and oil. Whisk with a fork to blend. Add to the dry ingredients. Stir just until mixed. Set aside for 5 minutes.

2 Set a griddle or nonstick skillet over medium-high heat for 1 minute. Turn off the heat and coat the griddle or skillet with cooking spray. Turn the heat back on. Dollop the batter in 8 portions onto the griddle or skillet. Cook for about 2 minutes, or until the griddle cakes are browned on the bottom. Flip and press down with the back of a pancake turner to flatten each into a $\frac{1}{2}$"-thick disk. Cook for 2 to 3 minutes, or until cooked through. Turn off the heat. Sprinkle the cheese on the oat cakes. Cover with a lid or sheet of aluminum foil. Allow to sit for 2 minutes, or until the cheese melts.

Makes 4 servings (2 cakes each)

PER SERVING: 165 calories, 7 g protein, 14 g carbohydrates, 9 g fat (2 g saturated fat), 51 mg cholesterol, 376 mg sodium

MAKE IT AHEAD

Since your time is worth money, it pays to double this recipe and freeze the extras. You'll have nutritious breakfast fare in the freezer without convenience-food prices. Cool the cakes and lay them on a tray. Place in the freezer for 24 hours, or until frozen solid. Pack into zip-top freezer bags. To serve, remove the number you need and thaw at room temperature or in the microwave. Place on a piece of aluminum foil. Top each cake with cheese. Place in a toaster oven for 1 minute, or until the cheese melts.

FAT-FIGHTING
4

2 g fiber

196 mg calcium

5 IU vitamin D

490 mg omega-3s

MAKE IT FAST

Baked French Toast

PREP TIME: 10 MINUTES ◆ TOTAL TIME: 25 MINUTES

2 slices whole wheat bread, toasted crisp and cut into ½"-wide strips
2 omega-3-enriched eggs
2 egg whites
½ cup fat-free evaporated milk

2 tablespoons light brown sugar
1 teaspoon pure vanilla extract
¼ teaspoon ground cinnamon
Confectioners' sugar

FAT-FIGHTING 4

1 g fiber

129 mg calcium

35 IU vitamin D

60 mg omega-3s

MAKE IT FAST

1 Preheat the oven to 350°F. Coat an 8" × 8" ovenproof pan with cooking spray.

2 Place the toast strips in the pan. Beat the eggs and egg whites in a bowl with a fork. Add the evaporated milk, brown sugar, vanilla, and cinnamon. Stir to mix. Pour over the bread. Press the bread down with a fork until it is soaked.

3 Bake for about 15 minutes, or until puffed and set. Serve lightly dusted with confectioners' sugar.

Makes 4 servings

PER SERVING: 136 calories, 9 g protein, 18 g carbohydrates, 3 g fat (1 g saturated fat), 91 mg cholesterol, 167 mg sodium

Peanutty Pocket

PREP TIME: 5 MINUTES

½ whole wheat pita (6" diameter)
1 tablespoon omega-3-enriched peanut
   butter
1 teaspoon honey

1 teaspoon ground flaxseed
Dash of ground cinnamon
¼ apple, thinly sliced
2 tablespoons blueberries

Toast the pita. Combine the peanut butter, honey, flaxseed, and cinnamon in a small bowl. Stir to mix. Spread the peanut butter mixture evenly in the pita. Slide in the apple slices. Scatter the blueberries inside.

Makes 1 serving

PER SERVING: 256 calories, 7 g protein, 36 g carbohydrates, 11 g fat (2 g saturated fat), 0 mg cholesterol, 227 mg sodium

FAT-
FIGHTING
4

6 g fiber
----
19 mg
calcium
----
0 IU
vitamin D

1,150 mg
omega-3s

MAKE IT
FAST

Carrot-Walnut Muffins

PREP TIME: 12 MINUTES ◆ TOTAL TIME: 32 MINUTES

MUFFINS
1 jar (4 ounces) pureed carrots baby food
1/3 cup honey
2 omega-3-enriched eggs
2 tablespoons canola oil
1 1/4 cups whole wheat pastry flour
1 teaspoon baking soda
1/2 teaspoon ground ginger
1/2 teaspoon salt
1/4 teaspoon ground cloves
1 1/2 cups shredded carrots
3/4 cup chopped walnuts

ICING
1/4 cup fat-free cream cheese
1/2 teaspoon honey

FAT-FIGHTING 4

2 g fiber

28 mg calcium

3 IU vitamin D

680 mg omega-3s

1 Preheat the oven to 350°F. Coat a 12-cup muffin pan with cooking spray or fill with paper cupcake liners.

2 To make the muffins, whisk together the pureed carrots, honey, eggs, and oil in a small bowl.

3 Whisk together the flour, baking soda, ginger, salt, and cloves in a large bowl. Make a well in the center and add the carrot mixture, stirring just until blended. Stir in the shredded carrots and walnuts.

4 Evenly divide the batter into the muffin cups. Bake for 20 minutes, or until a wooden pick inserted in the center comes out clean. Remove to a rack and cool for

10 minutes. Remove the muffins from the pan to the rack and cool completely.

5 To make the icing, stir together the cream cheese and honey until smooth. Spread a scant teaspoon on the center of each muffin.

Makes 12

PER MUFFIN: 169 calories, 4 g protein, 21 g carbohydrates, 8 g fat (1 g saturated fat), 30 mg cholesterol, 254 mg sodium

MAKE IT AHEAD
Freeze the muffins without icing in a zip-top freezer bag. They'll keep for up to 3 months.

Banana-Peanut Bread

PREP TIME: 15 MINUTES ◆ TOTAL TIME: 1 HOUR + COOLING TIME

3 medium very ripe bananas, mashed
$1/3$ cup omega-3-enriched peanut butter
$1/4$ cup honey
2 omega-3-enriched eggs
2 tablespoons canola oil
1 teaspoon pure vanilla extract

2 cups whole wheat pastry flour
2 teaspoons baking powder
$1/2$ teaspoon baking soda
$1/2$ teaspoon salt
$1/2$ cup golden raisins

FAT-FIGHTING 4

4 g fiber

50 mg calcium

3 IU vitamin D

250 mg omega-3s

1 Preheat the oven to 350°F. Coat a 9" × 5" loaf pan with cooking spray.

2 Combine the bananas, peanut butter, honey, eggs, oil, and vanilla in a medium bowl.

3 Whisk together the flour, baking powder, baking soda, salt, and raisins in a large bowl. Make a well in the center of the flour mixture and add the banana mixture. Stir just until moistened. Place in the prepared pan.

4 Bake for 40 to 50 minutes, or until a wooden pick inserted in the center comes out clean. Cool on a rack in the pan for 5 minutes. Remove from the pan and cool completely.

Makes 12 servings

PER SERVING: 220 calories, 5 g protein, 34 g carbohydrates, 7 g fat (1 g saturated fat), 30 mg cholesterol, 354 mg sodium

Maple-Walnut Scones

PREP TIME: 15 MINUTES ◆ TOTAL TIME: 30 MINUTES + COOLING TIME

2 cups whole grain pastry flour
¼ cup nonfat dry milk
2 tablespoons ground flaxseed
2 teaspoons baking powder
½ teaspoon baking soda
½ teaspoon salt

1 cup low-fat vanilla yogurt
2 tablespoons canola oil
¼ teaspoon maple flavoring (optional)
¼ cup maple syrup + 1 teaspoon for glaze
½ cup chopped walnuts
¼ cup light cream cheese

1 Preheat the oven to 400°F. Lightly coat a 9" round cake pan with cooking spray.

2 Whisk together the flour, dry milk, flaxseed, baking powder, baking soda, and salt in a large bowl.

3 Stir together the yogurt, oil, flavoring (if using), and ¼ cup maple syrup in a measuring cup.

4 Make a well in the center of the flour mixture and stir in the yogurt mixture. Add the walnuts and stir just until blended.

5 Spread the dough into the cake pan. It will be thick. Bake for 12 to 15 minutes, or until lightly browned and firm. Let cool on a rack.

6 When scones are almost completely cool, make the glaze. Place the cream cheese and 1 teaspoon maple syrup in a microwaveable bowl. Cook on medium power (50%) for 30-second intervals, or until warm enough to stir together. Using a spoon, drizzle the glaze over the scones in the pan.

7 Let cool completely before cutting into wedges and removing from pan.

Makes 10 servings

PER SERVING: 190 calories, 6 g protein, 24 g carbohydrates, 9 g total fat (1 g saturated fat), 14 mg cholesterol, 312 mg sodium

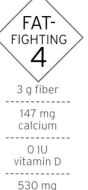

FAT-
FIGHTING
4

3 g fiber

147 mg
calcium

0 IU
vitamin D

530 mg
omega-3s

MAKE IT AHEAD
Freeze the scones in a zip-top freezer bag for up to 3 months.

Berry Fruit Salad

PREP TIME: 10 MINUTES

½ cup low-fat vanilla yogurt
½ teaspoon lime zest
½ cup blueberries
½ cup raspberries

½ cup halved strawberries
1 tablespoon chopped fresh mint
2 teaspoons chopped crystallized ginger
2 tablespoons chopped walnuts

1 Combine the yogurt and lime zest in a small bowl.

2 Combine the blueberries, raspberries, strawberries, mint, and ginger in a serving bowl. Toss to coat well. Top with the yogurt mixture and sprinkle with the walnuts.

Makes 1 serving

PER SERVING: 278 calories, 9 protein, 37 g carbohydrates, 12 g fat (2 g saturated fat), 8 mg cholesterol, 85 mg sodium

FAT-FIGHTING
4

9 g fiber
- - - - - - - - - - - -
238 mg
calcium
- - - - - - - - - - - -
0 IU
vitamin D
- - - - - - - - - - - -
1,520 mg
omega-3s
- - - - - - - - - - - -

MAKE IT
FAST

Breakfast "Banana Split"

PREP TIME: 10 MINUTES ◆ TOTAL TIME: 11 MINUTES

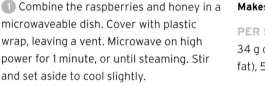

⅓ cup frozen raspberries
2 teaspoons honey
¼ cup fat-free ricotta cheese
½ small banana, halved lengthwise

1 teaspoon nonfat dry milk
½ teaspoon unsweetened cocoa powder
2 teaspoons chopped peanuts

1 Combine the raspberries and honey in a microwaveable dish. Cover with plastic wrap, leaving a vent. Microwave on high power for 1 minute, or until steaming. Stir and set aside to cool slightly.

2 Place the ricotta on an oval serving dish. Surround with the banana. Sprinkle on the dry milk and then the cocoa. Drizzle on the raspberries. Sprinkle with the peanuts.

Makes 1 serving

PER SERVING: 195 calories, 11 g protein, 34 g carbohydrates, 3 g fat (0.5 g saturated fat), 5 mg cholesterol, 89 mg sodium

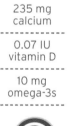

FAT-FIGHTING
4

4 g fiber

235 mg calcium

0.07 IU vitamin D

10 mg omega-3s

MAKE IT FAST

Creamy Gazpacho with Peppered Scallops

PREP TIME: 25 MINUTES ◆ TOTAL TIME: 40 MINUTES

3 plum tomatoes, seeded and chopped
2 yellow bell peppers, chopped
1 cucumber, peeled, seeded, and chopped
1 small red onion, chopped
2 cloves garlic, minced
3 cups low-sodium vegetable juice
1½ cups low-fat plain yogurt

3 tablespoons chopped fresh basil
1 tablespoon white wine vinegar
36 sea scallops (about 1¾ pounds)
½ teaspoon salt
¼ teaspoon cracked black pepper
⅛ teaspoon ground red pepper

FAT-FIGHTING 4

3 g fiber

416 mg calcium

100 IU vitamin D

230 mg omega-3s

1 Combine one-quarter (about 1¼ cups total) of the tomatoes, peppers, cucumber, onion, and garlic in a blender or food processor. Pulse until smooth. Add the vegetable juice, yogurt, basil, and vinegar and pulse to blend. Pour into a large bowl. Reserving about ¾ cup for garnish, fold the remaining vegetables into the mixture.

2 Divide the gazpacho among 6 shallow bowls. Set aside.

3 Place the scallops on a plate and sprinkle with the salt, black pepper, and red pepper, tossing to coat.

4 Coat a large nonstick skillet with cooking spray and heat over medium-high heat.

Working in batches, cook the scallops, turning once, for 5 to 6 minutes, or until opaque. Place 6 scallops in each bowl of gazpacho. Garnish with the reserved chopped vegetables.

5 Serve each bowl with 2 whole wheat bread sticks and 1 cup fat-free milk.

Makes 6 servings

PER SERVING: 310 calories, 31 g protein, 39 g carbohydrates, 3 g fat (1 g saturated fat); 36 mg cholesterol, 665 mg sodium

Minestrone with Parmesan Crisps

PREP TIME: 20 MINUTES ◆ TOTAL TIME: 45 MINUTES

2 tablespoons canola oil
1 onion, chopped
1 red bell pepper, chopped
1 carrot, sliced
$\frac{1}{2}$ teaspoon oregano
2 cloves garlic, minced
3 cups fat-free, low-sodium vegetable broth

1 can (14$\frac{1}{2}$ ounces) no-salt-added diced tomatoes
1 cup frozen shelled edamame
8 ounces green beans, snapped and cut in half
$\frac{3}{4}$ cup whole grain elbow noodles
$\frac{1}{2}$ cup shredded Parmesan cheese

1 Preheat the oven to 375°F. Line a baking sheet with parchment paper.

2 Heat the oil in a large saucepan over medium-high heat. Add the onion, pepper, carrot, and oregano. Cook, stirring, for 5 minutes, or until lightly browned. Add the garlic and cook, stirring, for 2 minutes.

3 Add the broth and tomatoes and bring to a boil. Add the edamame and green beans. Reduce the heat to low and simmer for 15 minutes, or until the edamame are tender, adding the pasta after 5 minutes.

4 Meanwhile, place 2 tablespoons of the cheese onto the parchment paper. Spread into a 4" circle. Repeat with the remaining cheese to make 4 circles. Bake for 6 minutes, or until lightly browned around the edges.

5 Carefully remove the crisps to a rack to cool. Top each serving of soup with a crisp.

Makes 4 servings

PER SERVING: 304 calories, 13 g protein, 34 g carbohydrates, 12 g fat (3 g saturated fat), 9 mg cholesterol, 556 mg sodium

FAT-FIGHTING
4

8 g fiber
- - - - - - - -
241 mg calcium
- - - - - - - -
0 IU vitamin D
- - - - - - - -
690 mg omega-3s
- - - - - - - -

Beef Noodle Soup

PREP TIME: 15 MINUTES ◆ TOTAL TIME: 40 MINUTES

6 ounces whole grain spaghetti (such as
   Barilla Plus)
1 tablespoon cornstarch
2 teaspoons reduced-sodium soy sauce
1 tablespoon canola oil
8 ounces top-round beef steak,
   thinly sliced
1 red bell pepper, cut into thin strips

6 scallions, diagonally sliced
1 tablespoon grated fresh ginger
2 cloves garlic, minced
$\frac{1}{8}$ teaspoon ground cinnamon
4 cups reduced-sodium beef
   or mushroom broth
1 tablespoon rice wine vinegar

◆ FAT-
FIGHTING
4

7 g fiber

51 mg
calcium

0 IU
vitamin D

70 mg
omega-3s

1 Prepare the pasta according to package directions and drain. Stir together the cornstarch and soy sauce in a small bowl and set aside.

2 Coat a large saucepan with cooking spray. Add the oil and heat over medium-high heat. Cook the beef in batches, turning once, for 3 minutes, or until browned. Remove to a bowl.

3 Recoat the pot with cooking spray. Add the pepper, scallions, ginger, garlic, and

cinnamon and cook, stirring, for 4 minutes. Add the broth and vinegar and bring to a boil. Stir in the soy sauce mixture and cook for 3 minutes, or until thickened.

4 Divide the beef, noodles, and broth mixture among 4 bowls.

Makes 4 servings

PER SERVING: 316 calories, 23 g protein, 38 g carbohydrate, 9 g fat (2 g saturated fat), 23 mg cholesterol, 594 mg sodium

New England Clam Chowder

PREP TIME: 20 MINUTES ◆ TOTAL TIME: 46 MINUTES

2 cans (6¹/₂ ounces each) chopped clams
1 bottle (8 ounces) clam juice
2 cups 2% milk
2 tablespoons all-purpose flour
1-2 tablespoons canola oil
1 onion, chopped

1 rib celery, chopped
1 large carrot, chopped
1 red bell pepper, chopped
1 clove garlic, minced
¹/₂ teaspoon dried thyme
2 red potatoes, cubed

1 Drain the clams, reserving the juice in a measuring cup. Add the bottled clam juice. Whisk together the milk and flour in another measuring cup. Set the clams, juice, and milk mixture aside.

2 Heat the oil in a large saucepan over medium-high heat. Cook the onion, celery, carrot, pepper, garlic, and thyme, stirring, for 6 minutes, or until browned and tender. Add the potatoes and reserved clam juice and bring to a simmer. Reduce the heat to low, cover, and simmer for 15 minutes, or until the potatoes are tender.

3 Stir the reserved milk mixture and add it and the reserved clams to the pot. Cook, stirring, for 5 minutes, or until thickened and the flavors meld.

Makes 4 servings

PER SERVING: 193 calories, 10 g protein, 25 g carbohydrates, 6 g fat (2 g saturated fat), 20 mg cholesterol, 583 mg sodium

FAT-FIGHTING **4**

3 g fiber

184 mg calcium

52 IU vitamin D

30 mg omega-3s

MAKE IT A MEAL
Serve with the Spinach and Fennel Salad (page 139).

Curried Coconut Shrimp Soup

PREP TIME: 20 MINUTES ◆ TOTAL TIME: 32 MINUTES

1 carton (32 ounces) fat free, low-sodium
    vegetable broth
2 cups water
3 carrots, julienned
8 ounces snow peas, cut into thin strips
1½ tablespoons reduced-sodium
    soy sauce
1 tablespoon grated fresh ginger

1 clove garlic, minced
6 ounces soba (100% buckwheat) noodles
    or whole wheat angel hair,
    broken in half
1 pound large shrimp, peeled and deveined
1 cup light coconut milk
¼ teaspoon green curry paste
4 scallions, diagonally sliced

FAT-
FIGHTING
4

2 g fiber

75 mg
calcium

86 IU
vitamin D

290 mg
omega-3s

1 Bring the broth, water, carrots, snow peas, soy sauce, ginger, and garlic to a boil in a large saucepan over high heat. Add the noodles and boil for 6 minutes, or until al dente.

2 Add the shrimp, coconut milk, and curry paste and cook for 2 minutes, or until the shrimp are opaque.

3 Divide among 8 bowls. Top with the scallions.

Makes 8 servings (12 cups)

PER SERVING: 190 calories, 16 g protein, 24 g carbohydrates, 3 g fat (2 g saturated fat), 86 mg cholesterol, 466 mg sodium

Hot-and-Sour Soup

PREP TIME: 25 MINUTES ◆ TOTAL TIME: 43 MINUTES

4 cups fat-free, reduced-sodium
   chicken broth
2 teaspoons reduced-sodium soy sauce
1/8 teaspoon hot red-pepper sauce
4 ounces shiitake mushrooms, sliced
1 cup snow peas, trimmed and thinly
   sliced lengthwise
1 carrot, julienned

2 tablespoons grated fresh ginger
3 tablespoons rice wine vinegar
2 tablespoons cornstarch
1 omega-3-enriched egg, slightly beaten
7 ounces firm tofu with calcium sulfate,
   drained and cut into 1/4" cubes
2 scallions, diagonally sliced

1 Heat the broth, soy sauce, and hot-pepper sauce in a large saucepan over medium-high heat. Bring to a boil. Add the mushrooms, snow peas, carrot, and ginger. Reduce the heat to low and simmer for 10 minutes, or until the vegetables are tender.

2 Whisk together the vinegar and cornstarch in a small bowl. Stir into the soup, then continue to stir for 1 minute, or until thickened. Slowly drizzle the egg into the pan, stirring constantly. Stir in the tofu. Heat gently for another minute. Remove from the heat and let stand, covered, for 1 minute. Top with the scallions.

Makes 4 servings

PER SERVING: 146 calories, 12 g protein, 14 g carbohydrates, 6 g fat (1 g saturated fat), 45 mg cholesterol, 594 mg sodium

FAT-
FIGHTING
4

3 g fiber

364 mg
calcium

90 IU
vitamin D

320 mg
omega-3s

Edamame Miso Soup

PREP TIME: 15 MINUTES ◆ TOTAL TIME: 35 MINUTES

3 cups fat-free, low-sodium vegetable broth

2 cups water

1 cup shelled edamame

3 scallions, sliced

2 teaspoons grated fresh ginger

1 clove garlic, minced

2 tablespoons red miso

1 carrot, shredded

4 ounces extra-firm tofu, drained and cut into $1/2$" cubes

2 teaspoons reduced-sodium soy sauce

4 cups baby spinach

2 cups hot cooked brown rice

FAT-FIGHTING 4

7 g fiber

118 mg calcium

0 IU vitamin D

10 mg omega-3s

1 Bring the broth, water, edamame, scallions, ginger, and garlic to a boil in a large saucepan over medium-high heat. Reduce the heat to low, cover, and simmer for 10 minutes.

2 Place the miso in a small bowl and stir in some of the hot broth to dissolve the miso. Pour into pan. Add the carrot, tofu, and soy sauce and cook for 5 minutes for the flavors to blend. Stir in the spinach. Remove from the heat and cover for 3 minutes, or until wilted.

3 Spoon $1/2$ cup rice into each of 4 bowls. Divide the soup among the bowls.

Makes 4 servings

PER SERVING: 233 calories, 12 g protein, 36 g carbohydrates, 5 g fat (0.5 g saturated fat), 0 mg cholesterol, 650 mg sodium*

✳ Limit sodium to less than 2,300 mg per day.

NOTE
You can find red miso in the natural foods section of your supermarket and in health food stores.

Smoky Black Bean Soup

PREP TIME: 25 MINUTES ◆ TOTAL TIME: 6-8 HOURS

1 pound black beans, picked over, rinsed,
    and soaked overnight
5 cups water
3 ribs celery, chopped
2 carrots, chopped
1 onion, chopped
1 red bell pepper, chopped

3 cloves garlic, smashed
1 dried chipotle chile pepper
2 teaspoons ground cumin
1½ teaspoons dried oregano
½ cup chopped cilantro + extra leaves, if
    desired
4 ounces queso blanco cheese, shredded

1 Place the beans, water, celery, carrots, onion, red pepper, garlic, chipotle, cumin, and oregano in a slow cooker.

2 Cook on low for 6 to 8 hours, or until the beans are very tender. Transfer the soup from the slow cooker to a large bowl. Remove and discard the chipotle pepper. Transfer the soup to a blender or food processor. Blend or process until smooth, working in batches. As you complete each batch, return the soup to the slow cooker. When you're finished, stir in the chopped cilantro.

3 Serve in bowls topped with the cilantro leaves (if desired) and cheese.

Makes 8 servings

PER SERVING: 252 calories, 16 g protein, 37 g carbohydrates, 5 g fat (3 g saturated fat), 15 mg cholesterol, 123 mg sodium

NOTE
An alternative to soaking the beans overnight is to use a quick-soak method. Place the beans in a large saucepan and cover with water. Bring to a boil over high heat and boil for 3 minutes. Remove from the heat, cover, and let stand for 1 hour. Drain and use as directed.

MAKE IT AGAIN
This soup freezes very well. Prepare this full batch and freeze in serving sizes for a quick lunch or light dinner in no time. If you'd rather, you may prepare just half the recipe.

MAKE IT A MEAL
Serve with the Cilantro Jicama Salad (page 137) and Garden of Eatin' Baked Blue Chips, which are made with flaxseed and have 300 milligrams of omega-3s per serving.

FAT-FIGHTING 4

13 g fiber
- - - - - - - - - - - -
160 mg calcium
- - - - - - - - - - - -
0 IU vitamin D
- - - - - - - - - - - -
20 mg omega-3s
- - - - - - - - - - - -

Updated Chicken Noodle Soup

PREP TIME: 25 MINUTES ◆ TOTAL TIME: 50 MINUTES

2 tablespoons canola oil

¾ pound boneless, skinless chicken breast, cut into 1" strips

1 large onion, chopped

2 cloves garlic, chopped

5 cups fat-free, reduced-sodium chicken broth

1 cup water

3 cups broccoli florets

2 carrots, julienned

2 teaspoons grated fresh ginger

8 ounces whole grain rotini

1 Heat the oil in a large saucepan over medium-high heat. Add the chicken and cook, stirring, for 5 minutes, or until browned. Remove to a bowl with a slotted spoon. Keep warm.

2 Add the onion and cook for 5 minutes, or until lightly browned. Add the garlic and cook for 1 minute. Pour in the broth and water. Add the broccoli, carrots, and ginger and bring to a boil. Stir in the pasta and cook for 11 minutes, or until tender. Add the chicken back to the soup during the last 2 to 3 minutes of cooking.

Makes 6 servings (9 cups)

PER SERVING: 276 calories, 22 g protein, 31 g carbohydrates, 8 g fat (1 g saturated fat), 33 mg cholesterol, 447 mg sodium

FAT-FIGHTING
4

7 g fiber

58 mg calcium

0 IU vitamin D

720 mg omega-3s

Moroccan Lentil Soup

PREP TIME: 25 MINUTES ◆ TOTAL TIME: 1 HOUR 5 MINUTES

1¹/₂ tablespoons canola oil
2 ribs celery, chopped
2 carrots, chopped
1 red bell pepper, chopped
1 large onion, chopped
2 cloves garlic, chopped
1 teaspoon ground ginger
¹/₂ teaspoon ground cinnamon
¹/₈ teaspoon ground cardamom

1 cup red lentils
2 cups fat-free, low-sodium
    vegetable broth
3 cups water
4 slices light whole grain bread
    (40-45 calories per slice)
4 ounces reduced-fat feta cheese,
    crumbled
1 teaspoon crushed anise seed

FAT-FIGHTING
4

14 g fiber

- - - - - - - - - - - - -

178 mg
calcium

- - - - - - - - - - - - -

0 IU
vitamin D

- - - - - - - - - - - - -

10 mg
omega-3s

- - - - - - - - - - - - -

1 Heat the oil in a large saucepan over medium-high heat. Add the celery, carrots, pepper, and onion and cook for 5 minutes, stirring, or until lightly browned. Add the garlic, ginger, cinnamon, and cardamom and cook for 1 minute.

2 Stir in the lentils, broth, and water and bring to a boil. Reduce the heat to low, cover, and simmer for 30 minutes, or until the lentils are very tender.

3 Preheat the oven to broil. Place the bread on a rack in a broiler pan and broil for

1 to 2 minutes, or until toasted. Turn and top each with 1 ounce of the cheese and one-quarter of the anise seed. Broil for 2 minutes, or until the feta is lightly browned and melted.

Makes 4 servings

PER SERVING: 367 calories, 22 g protein, 50 g carbohydrates, 11 g fat (3 g saturated fat), 8 mg cholesterol, 632 mg sodium

NOTE
Like other bean dishes, this one may seem high in carbs. Bear in mind, though, that beans are very high in fiber. So in this case, you're getting 36 grams of digestible carbs—right in line with the DTOUR carb goals.

Chickpea and Spinach Soup

PREP TIME 10 MINUTES ◆ COOK TIME 15 MINUTES

2 tablespoons canola oil

1 large onion, chopped

2 cloves garlic, chopped

1 teaspoon cumin

$\frac{1}{2}$ teaspoon smoked paprika

4 cups fat-free, reduced-sodium
chicken broth

1 can (15-19 ounces) no-salt-added
chickpeas, rinsed and drained

2 tablespoons tomato paste

1 bag (6 ounces) baby spinach

1 Heat the oil in a large saucepan over medium-high heat. Add the onion and cook, stirring, for 5 minutes, or until lightly browned. Add the garlic, cumin, and paprika and cook for 2 minutes.

2 Stir in the broth, chickpeas, and tomato paste and cook for 5 minutes for the flavors to blend. Add the spinach and cook for 3 minutes, or until the spinach is wilted.

Makes 4 servings

PER SERVING: 191 calories, 7 g protein, 25 g carbohydrates, 8 g fat (1 g saturated fat), 0 mg cholesterol, 604 mg sodium*

✳ Limit sodium to less than 2,300 mg per day.

FAT-
FIGHTING
4

6 g fiber

81 mg
calcium

0 IU
vitamin D

0 mg
omega-3s

MAKE IT
FAST

Carrot-Fennel Bisque

PREP TIME: 15 MINUTES ◆ TOTAL TIME: 1 HOUR 5 MINUTES

4 large carrots, halved lengthwise
1 large fennel bulb, trimmed, with fronds
reserved and cut into slices
1 large onion, cut into wedges
1 clove garlic, minced

2 tablespoons canola oil
3 cups fat-free, reduced-sodium
chicken broth
1 can (12 ounces) fat-free evaporated
milk

FAT-
FIGHTING
4

4 g fiber

309 mg
calcium

68 IU
vitamin D

680 mg
omega-3s

1 Preheat the oven to 400°F. Coat a baking sheet with sides with cooking spray. Place the carrots, fennel, onion, and garlic on the baking sheet and drizzle with the oil, turning the vegetables to coat them. Roast for 45 minutes, or until browned and very tender.

2 Combine the vegetables in a blender or food processor with 2 cups of the broth. Blend or process until smooth.

3 Place the vegetable mixture in a saucepan with the milk and the remaining 1 cup broth. Heat over medium heat for 5 minutes, stirring occasionally, or until the flavors meld and the soup is hot. Ladle into 4 bowls and top each with the fennel fronds.

Makes 4 servings

PER SERVING: 194 calories, 9 g protein, 25 g carbohydrates, 8 g fat (1 g saturated fat), 3 mg cholesterol, 517 mg sodium

Creamy Asparagus Soup

PREP TIME: 10 MINUTES ◆ TOTAL TIME: 35 MINUTES

1 tablespoon canola oil
4 shallots, chopped
$\frac{1}{2}$ teaspoon dried thyme
2 cups fat-free, reduced-sodium
   chicken broth

1 russet potato, peeled and chopped
$1\frac{1}{2}$ pounds asparagus, trimmed and cut
   into 1" pieces
1 can (12 ounces) fat-free evaporated milk
$\frac{1}{4}$ cup grated Parmesan cheese

FAT-FIGHTING 4

3 g fiber
----
346 mg
calcium
----
68 IU
vitamin D
----
30 mg
omega-3s
----

1 Heat the oil in a 4- to 6-quart pot over medium heat. Add the shallots and thyme and cook for 3 minutes, or until lightly browned. Add the broth and potato. Bring to a boil, reduce the heat to low, cover, and simmer for 15 minutes, or until the potato is very tender.

2 Add the asparagus and cook for 4 minutes, or until the asparagus is bright green and tender. Place the mixture in a food processer fitted with a metal blade and process until smooth. Return to the pot with the milk. Heat for 5 minutes to blend the flavors.

3 Top each serving with 1 tablespoon of the cheese.

Makes 4 servings

PER SERVING: 183 calories, 13 g protein, 23 g carbohydrates, 5 g fat (1 g saturated fat), 8 mg cholesterol, 403 mg sodium

Caribbean Tofu and Veggie Sandwich

PREP TIME: 10 MINUTES ◆ TOTAL TIME: 35 MINUTES

1 onion, quartered
1 red bell pepper, quartered
¼ cup fat-free Greek-style yogurt
1 teaspoon orange peel
1 teaspoon honey
8 slices light, high-fiber, whole wheat bread (40–45 calories per slice)

2 cups mesclun or baby romaine
1 package (8 ounces) Caribbean-flavored smoked tofu (such as SoyBoy), each half cut into 6 slices

1 Preheat the oven to 400°F. Place the onion and pepper on a baking sheet coated with cooking spray and coat the tops of the vegetables with cooking spray. Roast for 15 minutes, turning once, or until tender and browned.

2 Meanwhile, stir together the yogurt, orange peel, and honey in a small bowl.

3 Place the bread slices on a flat surface. Layer the greens, roasted vegetables, and tofu onto each of 4 bread slices. Top with the yogurt spread and remaining bread slices.

Makes 4 servings

PER SERVING: 230 calories, 17 g protein, 30 g carbohydrates, 6 g fat (1 g saturated fat), 0 mg cholesterol, 482 mg sodium

FAT-FIGHTING
4

7 g fiber
- - - - - - - - - - - -
192 mg calcium
- - - - - - - - - - - -
0 IU vitamin D
- - - - - - - - - - - -
50 mg omega-3s
- - - - - - - - - - - -

NOTE
Baked tofu is much more dense and flavorful than water-packed tofu. Available in a variety of flavors, it's great in sandwiches or salads.

Grilled Vegetable Stack

PREP TIME: 10 MINUTES ◆ TOTAL TIME: 23 MINUTES

**1 small eggplant (about 1 pound), cut
    diagonally into 8 slices**
**1 medium zucchini (about 8 ounces),
    cut diagonally into 8 slices**
**1 yellow bell pepper, cut lengthwise
    into 4 slices**

2-3 tablespoons prepared basil pesto
2 tablespoons balsamic vinegar
4 slices whole wheat Italian bread
1 clove garlic
**4 ounces fresh mozzarella,
    cut into 4 slices**

1 Preheat the grill or broiler. Coat the eggplant, zucchini, and pepper with cooking spray. Grill or broil for 10 minutes, turning once, or until tender and browned.

2 Meanwhile, stir together the pesto and vinegar in a small bowl. Set aside.

3 Place the bread slices on the grill or under the broiler for 2 minutes, turning once, or until toasted. Remove and rub the garlic over 1 side of each slice.

4 Place 1 slice of bread on each of 4 plates. Top with the cheese and grilled vegetables. Drizzle with the pesto mixture.

Makes 4 servings

PER SERVING: 240 calories, 12 g protein, 24 g carbohydrates, 11 g fat (5 g saturated fat), 23 mg cholesterol, 297 mg sodium

FAT-
FIGHTING
4

7 g fiber
----
225 mg
calcium
----
0 IU
vitamin D
----
50 mg
omega-3s

MAKE IT
FAST

Portobello and Caramelized-Onion Wrap

PREP TIME: 15 MINUTES ◆ TOTAL TIME: 37 MINUTES

4 large portobello mushrooms,
  cut into ½" slices
¼ cup reduced-fat Italian salad dressing
1 teaspoon olive oil
1 large onion, thinly sliced
1 tablespoon balsamic vinegar

4 whole grain omega-3-enriched wraps or
  tortillas (8" diameter)
4 ounces low-fat goat cheese, softened
1 cup baby spinach
1 carrot, julienned

1 Place the mushrooms in a shallow bowl. Pour the dressing over the mushrooms, turning to coat. Set aside.

2 Coat a nonstick skillet with cooking spray and heat over medium heat. Add the onion and cook, stirring, for 5 minutes, or until browned. Add the vinegar, cover, and cook for 10 minutes more, or until very tender. Remove the onion from the pan and set aside.

3 Add the reserved mushrooms and any dressing from the bowl to the same pan and cook on medium heat, turning once, for 5 to 7 minutes, or until well browned.

4 Place 1 wrap on each of 4 plates. Divide the cheese among the wraps and spread down the center of each wrap. Top with the spinach, carrot, mushrooms, and reserved onion.

Makes 4 servings

PER SERVING: 216 calories, 8 g protein, 29 g carbohydrates, 6 g fat (2 g saturated fat), 5 mg cholesterol, 665 mg sodium*

✻ Limit sodium to less than 2,300 mg per day.

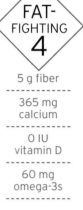

FAT-FIGHTING **4**

5 g fiber

365 mg calcium

0 IU vitamin D

60 mg omega-3s

Chipotle Grilled Cheese Sandwich

PREP TIME: 7 MINUTES ◆ TOTAL TIME: 11 MINUTES

1 tablespoon light omega-3-enriched
  mayonnaise
1 tablespoon adobo sauce from canned
  chipotle chiles
8 slices light extra-fiber whole wheat
  bread (40-45 calories each)

4 thin slices red onion
¼ cup cilantro
1½ cups (6 ounces) shredded reduced-fat
  extra-sharp Cheddar cheese

FAT-FIGHTING 4

2 g fiber

346 mg calcium

0 IU vitamin D

130 mg omega-3s

MAKE IT FAST

❶ Stir together the mayonnaise and adobo sauce in a small bowl.

❷ Place 4 bread slices on a work surface. Spread the mayonnaise on the bread slices. Layer with the onion, cilantro, and cheese and top with the remaining bread slices.

❸ Coat the top bread slice of each sandwich with cooking spray. Place the coated side down on the grill pan or skillet. Coat the remaining bread slice of each sandwich with cooking spray. Place a heavy pan over the top of the sandwiches. Cook for 2 minutes, then turn and repeat.

Makes 4 servings

PER SERVING: 248 calories, 15 g protein, 21 g carbohydrates, 11 g fat (6 g saturated fat), 32 mg cholesterol, 473 mg sodium

NOTE
A panini or sandwich press works well for making these sandwiches, although an indoor grill (George Foreman) also will do the trick. Place the sandwiches (coated with cooking spray) on the press or grill, close the lid, and press slightly. There's no need to turn the sandwiches.

MAKE IT A MEAL
Serve with the Cilantro Jicama Salad (page 137).

Buffalo Chicken Salad Sandwich

PREP TIME: 15 MINUTES

½ cup fat-free Greek-style yogurt
¼ cup crumbled blue cheese
2-6 drops hot-pepper sauce
2 cups chopped cooked chicken breast

3 ribs celery, diagonally sliced
2 whole wheat pitas (6" diameter), halved
4 green lettuce leaves
½ small red onion, sliced

1 Stir together the yogurt, cheese, and hot sauce in a medium bowl. Stir in the chicken and celery.

2 Fill each pita half with one-quarter of the lettuce, onion, and chicken salad.

Makes 4 servings

PER SERVING: 256 calories, 29 g protein, 21 g carbohydrates, 6 g fat (2 g saturated fat), 66 mg cholesterol, 410 mg sodium

FAT-
FIGHTING
4

3 g fiber

112 mg
calcium

0 IU
vitamin D

90 mg
omega-3s

MAKE IT
FAST

Open-Faced Sweet-and-Spicy Chicken Sandwich

PREP TIME: 15 MINUTES ◆ TOTAL TIME: 25 MINUTES

4 chicken cutlets (3 ounces each)
5 teaspoons reduced-sodium soy sauce
2 tablespoons rice wine vinegar
1 clove garlic, minced
3 teaspoons honey
¼ teaspoon red chili sauce

2 carrots, shredded
1 small cucumber, peeled, halved, seeded, and cut into thin slices (1 cup)
¼ cup cilantro
4 slices whole grain Italian bread
⅓ cup fat-free Greek-style yogurt

1 Coat a grill rack or broiler pan with cooking spray. Preheat the grill or broiler. Brush each chicken cutlet with 1 teaspoon of the soy sauce and grill or broil the cutlets, turning once, for 10 to 12 minutes, or until no longer pink and the juices run clear.

2 Whisk together the vinegar, garlic, chili sauce, and 2 teaspoons of the honey in a small bowl. Toss together the carrots, cucumber, and half of the cilantro in a medium bowl. Toss with half of the vinegar mixture. Set aside.

3 Add the remaining 1 teaspoon soy sauce and 1 teaspoon honey to the remaining vinegar mixture.

4 Place 1 bread slice on each of 4 plates. Top each with a chicken breast and one-quarter of the carrot mixture. Drizzle with 2 tablespoons of the soy mixture. Top each with 2 tablespoons of the yogurt and sprinkle with the remaining cilantro.

Makes 4 servings

PER SERVING: 211 calories, 26 g protein, 21 g carbohydrates, 2 g fat (0.5 g saturated fat), 49 mg cholesterol, 447 mg sodium

FAT-FIGHTING
4

3 g fiber
- - - - - - - - - - - - -
76 mg calcium
- - - - - - - - - - - - -
0 IU vitamin D
- - - - - - - - - - - - -
80 mg omega-3s
- - - - - - - - - - - - -

MAKE IT FAST

Knife-and-Fork Turkey Reuben

PREP TIME: 5 MINUTES ◆ TOTAL TIME: 9 MINUTES

2 cups cole slaw mix from bagged salad
⅓ cup reduced-fat Thousand Island
    dressing
4 slices whole grain bread
4 tablespoons mustard

8 ounces lower-sodium deli turkey breast
4 slices (1 ounce each) Jarlsberg light
    cheese

1 Preheat the oven to broil. Stir together the cole slaw mix and salad dressing in a small bowl.

2 Place the bread slices on a baking sheet. Spread each with 1 tablespoon of the mustard. Top with the turkey, cole slaw mixture, and cheese.

3 Place 4" to 6" from the heat and broil for 4 minutes, or until the cheese is melted.

Makes 4 servings

PER SERVING: 236 calories, 24 g protein, 20 g carbohydrates, 7 g fat (2 g saturated fat), 31 mg cholesterol, 772 mg sodium*

✳ Limit sodium to less than 2,300 mg per day.

FAT-
FIGHTING
4

7 g fiber

---

323 mg
calcium

---

0 IU
vitamin D

---

50 mg
omega-3s

MAKE IT
FAST

Indian-Spiced Chicken Salad

PREP TIME: 15 MINUTES

½ cup fat-free Greek-style yogurt
1 tablespoon mango chutney
1 teaspoon curry powder
2 cups chopped cooked chicken breast
1 carrot, shredded

¼ cup currants
¼ cup sunflower seeds
2 cups mesclun
2 whole wheat pitas (6" diameter), halved

1 Stir together the yogurt, chutney, and curry powder in a medium bowl.

2 Add the chicken, carrot, currants, and sunflower seeds.

3 Divide the mesclun among the pita halves. Fill with the chicken mixture.

Makes 4 servings

PER SERVING: 316 calories, 30 g protein, 31 g carbohydrates, 9 g fat (2 g saturated fat), 61 mg cholesterol, 256 mg sodium

FAT-FIGHTING
4

5 g fiber

86 mg
calcium

0 IU
vitamin D

70 mg
omega-3s

MAKE IT
FAST

Cubano Panini

PREP TIME: 5 MINUTES ◆ TOTAL TIME: 13 MINUTES

8 small slices whole grain bread (60 calories and 2-4 grams fiber per slice)

4 sandwich-slice dill pickles

4 ounces sliced deli roast pork

4 ounces sliced lower-sodium deli ham

4 slices (½ ounce each) Jarlsberg light cheese

1 tablespoon *mojo criollo* marinade or yellow mustard

1 Arrange 4 of the bread slices on a cutting board. Place 1 slice of pickle on each bread slice. Divide the pork, ham, and cheese among the slices. Spread the remaining bread slices with the marinade and place marinade side down on the cheese.

2 Coat the tops of the sandwiches with cooking spray and place coated side down in a grill pan or skillet. Coat the remaining top slices of bread with cooking spray. Place a heavy pan over the top of the sandwiches. Cook for 2 minutes, then flip and repeat.

Makes 4 servings

PER SERVING: 244 calories, 21 g protein, 25 g carbohydrates, 6 g fat (2 g saturated fat) 38 mg cholesterol, 992 mg sodium*

✳ Limit sodium to less than 2,300 mg per day.

> ### NOTE
> A panini or sandwich press works well for making these sandwiches, although an indoor grill (George Foreman) also does the trick. Place the sandwiches coated with cooking spray on the press or grill. Then, instead of using the heavy pan, close the lid and press slightly. There's no need to turn over the sandwiches.

FAT-FIGHTING 4

4 g fiber

157 mg calcium

0 IU vitamin D

120 mg omega-3s

MAKE IT FAST

Curry Fish Sandwiches

PREP TIME: 10 MINUTES ◆ TOTAL TIME: 15 MINUTES

¼ cup fat-free Greek-style yogurt
2 tablespoons mango chutney
1 teaspoon lime juice
1 teaspoon curry powder
¾ pound snapper fillet, cut into 4 pieces
½ teaspoon salt

1 teaspoon olive oil
4 whole wheat hamburger rolls
2 cups baby spinach
2 roasted red peppers (from a jar),
    drained and patted dry, cut in half

FAT-FIGHTING 4

5 g fiber

103 mg calcium

0 IU vitamin D

320 mg omega-3s

MAKE IT FAST

1 Stir together the yogurt, chutney, lime juice, and ½ teaspoon of the curry powder in a small bowl. Set aside. Lightly coat both sides of the snapper with cooking spray. Sprinkle with the salt and remaining ½ teaspoon curry powder.

2 Coat a nonstick skillet with cooking spray. Add the oil and heat over medium heat. Add the fish and cook, turning once, for 3 minutes, or until opaque.

3 Place the bottom of 1 roll on each of 4 plates. Top each with ½ cup of the spinach and a pepper slice. Top with the snapper and drizzle with the yogurt mixture, then cover with the top half of a roll.

Makes 4 servings

PER SERVING: 242 calories, 23 g protein, 29 g carbohydrates, 4 g fat (1 g saturated fat), 31 mg cholesterol, 592 mg sodium

Grilled Salmon with Wasabi Aioli Sandwich

PREP TIME: 15 MINUTES ◆ TOTAL TIME: 23 MINUTES

**1 tablespoon omega-3-enriched
light mayonnaise**
1 tablespoon fat-free Greek-style yogurt
1/2 teaspoon wasabi paste
1 tablespoon chopped cilantro
2 teaspoons grated fresh ginger
1/4 teaspoon salt
4 salmon fillets (4 ounces each)
2 cups mesclun
4 whole wheat rolls

1 Preheat the broiler. Combine the mayonnaise, yogurt, and wasabi paste in a small bowl. Combine the cilantro, ginger, and salt in another small bowl.

2 Press the cilantro mixture onto the salmon fillets. Coat a broiler pan with cooking spray. Place the fillets on the pan and broil 6" from the heat for 6 to 8 minutes, or until the fish is opaque.

3 Place the bottom of 1 roll on each of 4 plates. Top each with 1/2 cup of the mesclun, a salmon fillet, and one-quarter of the wasabi aioli, then cover with the top half of a roll.

Makes 4 servings

PER SERVING: 406 calories, 29 g protein, 35 g carbohydrates, 17 g fat (3 g saturated fat), 70 mg cholesterol, 579 mg sodium

FAT-FIGHTING
4

5 g fiber

101 mg
calcium

0 IU
vitamin D

2,480 mg
omega-3s

MAKE IT
FAST

Tuscan Tuna Salad Wrap

PREP TIME: 20 MINUTES

2 tablespoons fat-free Greek-style yogurt

1 tablespoon chopped fresh basil

1 teaspoon lemon juice

1/4 teaspoon lemon zest

1 can (6 ounces) white tuna packed in water, drained

1/2 cup canned white beans (such as cannellini or great Northern), rinsed and drained

1/2 cup chopped celery

2 tablespoons chopped red onion

4 whole grain omega-3-enriched wraps (8" diameter)

8 teaspoons prepared tapenade (olive spread)

2 cups baby arugula

1 Stir together the yogurt, basil, lemon juice, and lemon zest in a medium bowl. Stir in the tuna, beans, celery, and onion.

2 Lay the wraps on a flat surface and spread each with 1/2 tablespoon of the tapenade. Top with the arugula and tuna mixture. Roll.

Makes 4 servings

PER SERVNG: 219 calories, 21 g protein, 24 g carbohydrates, 7 g fat (1 g saturated fat), 16 mg cholesterol, 665 mg sodium*

✳ Limit sodium to less than 2,300 mg per day.

FAT-FIGHTING
4

10 g fiber

65 mg calcium

0 IU vitamin D

380 mg omega-3s

MAKE IT FAST

CHAPTER 7

SALADS & SIDES

Citrus Arugula Salad with Grilled Chicken

PREP TIME: 20 MINUTES ◆ TOTAL TIME: 40 MINUTES + MARINATING TIME

¼ cup orange juice
2 tablespoons lemon juice
2 tablespoons lime juice
1 tablespoon honey
3 cloves garlic, minced
1 teaspoon dried thyme

4 boneless, skinless chicken breast halves
  (4 ounces each)
2 tablespoons canola oil
½ cup fat-free Greek-style yogurt
8 cups arugula
2 beets, peeled and shredded

FAT-FIGHTING 4

2 g fiber

114 mg calcium

0 IU vitamin D

750 mg omega-3s

1 Whisk together the orange juice, lemon juice, lime juice, honey, garlic, and thyme in a shallow covered dish. Add the chicken, turning to coat. Cover and refrigerate for 1 to 2 hours, turning occasionally. (Chicken can marinate up to 12 hours, if desired.)

2 Coat a broiler pan or grill rack with cooking spray. Preheat the broiler or grill. Place the chicken on the broiler pan or grill rack, reserving the marinade. Cook for 15 minutes, or until a thermometer inserted in the thickest portion registers 160°F and the juices run clear.

3 Meanwhile, place the marinade in a small saucepan over high heat. Bring to a boil and boil for 3 minutes. Remove from

the heat and whisk in the oil. Gently whisk in the yogurt.

4 Divide the arugula and beets among 4 plates. Slice the chicken, place on the salads, and drizzle with the marinade.

Makes 4 servings

PER SERVING: 258 calories, 31 g protein, 15 g carbohydrates, 9 g fat (1 g saturated fat), 66 mg cholesterol, 128 mg sodium

NOTE
Shredding the beets in the food processor or with a mandoline keeps your hands and kitchen a bit cleaner than shredding by hand.

Chicken Souvlaki Salad

PREP TIME: 20 MINUTES ◆ TOTAL TIME: 25 MINUTES + MARINATING TIME

3 tablespoons lemon juice

2 tablespoons canola oil

1 teaspoon dried oregano

1 clove garlic, minced

¼ teaspoon salt

1 pound boneless, skinless chicken
   breasts, cut into 1½" cubes

½ cup fat-free Greek-style yogurt

½ pound romaine, coarsely chopped

2 tomatoes, chopped

1 cucumber, peeled, halved, seeded,
   and sliced

2 whole wheat pitas (6" diameter), halved

1 Combine the lemon juice, oil, oregano, garlic, and salt in a small bowl. Pour half of the mixture in a zip-top bag. Add the chicken and toss to coat. Seal and refrigerate for 4 to 24 hours. Cover and refrigerate the remaining lemon mixture.

2 Coat a grill rack or broiler pan with cooking spray. Preheat the grill or broiler pan. Skewer the chicken onto 6 (10") skewers. Grill or broil the chicken for 5 minutes, turning once, or until browned and no longer pink.

3 Whisk together the yogurt and the reserved lemon mixture. Add the lettuce, tomatoes, and cucumber and toss to coat. Divide among 4 plates. Top with the chicken. Serve each with a pita half.

Makes 4 servings

PER SERVING: 316 calories, 33 g protein, 25 carbohydrates, 10 g fat (1 g saturated fat), 66 mg cholesterol, 409 mg sodium

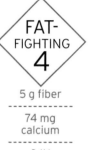

FAT-
FIGHTING
4

5 g fiber

----

74 mg
calcium

----

0 IU
vitamin D

----

130 mg
omega-3s

Creamy Italian Pasta Salad

PREP TIME: 10 MINUTES ◆ TOTAL TIME: 23 MINUTES

2 cups whole grain rotini
1/2 cup fat-free Greek-style yogurt
2 tablespoons Parmesan cheese
2 tablespoons chopped fresh basil
1 tablespoon red wine vinegar
1/2 teaspoon dried mustard

1 clove garlic, minced
1 can (6 ounces) solid white tuna packed
   in water, drained and flaked
4 cups chopped romaine
1 cup cherry tomatoes, halved

FAT-FIGHTING 4

6 g fiber

98 mg calcium

0 IU vitamin D

470 mg omega-3s

MAKE IT FAST

1 Prepare the pasta according to package directions. Rinse under cold water and drain.

2 Meanwhile, stir together the yogurt, cheese, basil, vinegar, mustard, and garlic in a large bowl. Add the tuna, romaine, tomatoes, and pasta. Toss to coat well.

Makes 4 servings

PER SERVING: 281 calories, 22 g protein, 44 g carbohydrates, 3 g fat (1 g saturated fat), 20 mg cholesterol, 219 mg sodium

MAKE IT AGAIN

If you won't be using all of the salad immediately, keep the lettuce separate, and then serve the pasta mixture over a bed of lettuce.

Garbanzo and Roasted Tomato Salad

PREP TIME: 10 MINUTES ◆ TOTAL TIME: 20 MINUTES

8 plum tomatoes, halved and cored
8 scallions, cut into 2" pieces
2 tablespoons canola oil
¼ teaspoon salt

1 bag (6 ounces) baby spinach
1 can (15-19 ounces) chickpeas,
 rinsed and drained
2 tablespoons balsamic vinegar

1 Preheat the oven to 425°F.

2 Place the tomatoes and scallions on a large baking sheet with sides. Drizzle with the oil and salt. Toss to coat. Roast for 10 minutes, or until browned and tender.

3 Meanwhile, place the spinach and chickpeas in a large bowl. Top with the tomato mixture and drizzle all with the vinegar. Toss to coat. Serve immediately.

Makes 4 servings

PER SERVING: 170 calories, 6 g protein, 23 g carbohydrates, 8 g fat (0.5 g saturated fat), 0 mg cholesterol, 306 mg sodium

FAT-FIGHTING
4

7.1 g fiber
- - - - - - - - - - - - -
89 mg
calcium
- - - - - - - - - - - - -
0 IU
vitamin D
- - - - - - - - - - - - -
0 mg
omega-3s
- - - - - - - - - - - - -

MAKE IT
FAST

Warm Sweet Potato and Onion Salad with Goat Cheese

PREP TIME: 25 MINUTES ◆ COOK TIME: 60 MINUTES

FAT-FIGHTING 4

6 g fiber

---

171 mg calcium

---

0 IU vitamin D

2,880 mg omega-3s

---

2 large sweet potatoes (about 2 pounds), peeled and cut into 1" pieces
2 large red onions, cut into wedges
½ teaspoon herbes de Provence
¼ teaspoon salt
¼ teaspoon ground black pepper
5 ounces low-fat goat cheese

6 tablespoons chopped toasted walnuts
1 tablespoon balsamic vinegar
1 teaspoon honey
½ teaspoon Dijon mustard
1 tablespoon flaxseed oil
5 cups baby arugula

1 Preheat the oven to 400°F. Coat a baking sheet with cooking spray.

2 Place the potatoes and onions on the baking sheet and sprinkle with the herbes de Provence, salt, and pepper. Roast for 30 minutes, turning once, or until tender and browned.

3 Meanwhile, place the cheese in the freezer for 10 minutes. Remove and slice into 8 rounds. Place the walnuts on a small plate. Press each cheese round into the nuts and place on a small baking sheet. Place in the oven with the vegetables during the last 5 minutes of cooking.

4 Whisk together the vinegar, honey, and mustard in a large bowl. Whisk in the oil. Add the arugula and toss to coat. Toss in the vegetables.

5 Place on 4 plates and top each with 2 slices of the cheese.

Makes 4 servings

PER SERVING: 301 calories, 10 g protein, 35 g carbohydrates, 15 g fat (3 g saturated fat), 6 mg cholesterol, 373 mg sodium

---

MAKE IT A MEAL
Serve with Creamy Asparagus Soup (page 112) and whole wheat bread sticks.

Field Greens with Pear and Walnuts

PREP TIME: 10 MINUTES ◆ TOTAL TIME: 14 MINUTES

1 teaspoon Dijon mustard
1 teaspoon honey
2 tablespoons white balsamic vinegar
⅛ teaspoon salt
⅛ teaspoon ground black pepper
4 teaspoons canola oil

1 ripe pear, halved, cored, and sliced
1 bag (7 ounces) mesclun or mixed greens
¼ cup walnuts, toasted
2 tablespoons crumbled reduced-fat
   blue cheese

1 Whisk together the mustard, honey, vinegar, salt, and pepper in a large bowl. Whisk in the oil. Set aside.

2 Coat a nonstick skillet with cooking spray and heat over medium-high heat. Add the pear and cook, turning once, for 4 minutes, or until browned. Remove from the heat.

3 Add the greens to the bowl and toss to coat. Top with the pear, walnuts, and cheese.

Makes 4 servings

PER SERVING: 139 calories, 3 g protein, 12 g carbohydrates, 10 g fat (1 g saturated fat), 2 mg cholesterol, 165 mg sodium

FAT-
FIGHTING
4

3 g fiber

59 g
calcium

0 IU
vitamin D

61 mg
omega-3s

MAKE IT
FAST

Cilantro Jicama Salad

PREP TIME: 15 MINUTES

2 tablespoons freshly squeezed lime juice

4 teaspoons canola oil

$1/2$ teaspoon honey

$1/4$ teaspoon ground cumin

1 medium jicama (about $1^1/_2$ pounds), peeled and julienned

2 carrots, julienned

$1/4$ cup chopped cilantro

Whisk together the lime juice, oil, honey, and cumin in a medium bowl. Add the jicama, carrots, and cilantro and toss to coat well.

Makes 4 servings

PER SERVING: 95 calories, 1 g protein, 13 g carbohydrates, 5 g fat (0.5 g saturated fat), 0 mg cholesterol, 26 mg sodium

MAKE IT A MEAL

Serve with 3 ounces grilled pork tenderloin or shrimp and a serving of Sweet Potato Crisps (page 157).

FAT-FIGHTING
4

1 g fiber

25 mg
calcium

0 IU
vitamin D

10 mg
omega-3s

MAKE IT
FAST

Spiced-Up Spinach Salad

PREP TIME: 10 MINUTES ◆ TOTAL TIME: 18 MINUTES

1/2 cup walnuts, coarsely chopped

1 teaspoon ground peppercorn medley or black pepper

1 tablespoon balsamic vinegar

2 teaspoons Dijon mustard

2 teaspoons honey

1/8 teaspoon salt

1/8 teaspoon ground black pepper

1/3 cup fat-free Greek-style yogurt

1 bag (6 ounces) baby spinach

1/4 cup dried cranberries

FAT-FIGHTING 4

3 g fiber

60 mg calcium

0 IU vitamin D

1,330 mg omega-3s

MAKE IT FAST

1 Preheat the oven to 400°F. Coat a small baking sheet with cooking spray. Place the walnuts on the baking sheet and coat with cooking spray. Sprinkle with the peppercorn medley and bake for 8 minutes, or until toasted.

2 Meanwhile, whisk together the vinegar, mustard, honey, salt, and 1/8 teaspoon pepper. Stir in the yogurt.

3 Combine the spinach, cranberries, walnuts, and yogurt mixture in a large bowl. Toss to coat well.

Makes 4 servings

PER SERVING: 164 calories, 5 g protein, 18 g carbohydrates, 10 g fat (1 g saturated fat), 0 mg cholesterol, 226 mg sodium

MAKE IT AGAIN

Not sure what to do with leftover shrimp, salmon, or chicken breast? Add a 4-ounce serving to this salad!

Spinach and Fennel Salad

PREP TIME: 15 MINUTES

2 tablespoons white or red wine vinegar
4 teaspoons canola oil
1 tablespoon frozen orange juice
   concentrate

½ teaspoon Dijon mustard
1 bulb fennel
1 small red onion
1 bag (6 ounces) baby spinach

1 Whisk together the vinegar, oil, orange juice concentrate, and mustard in a large bowl.

2 Slice the fennel and onion in a food processor with the slicing blade or with a mandoline. (If you'd prefer, use a knife and cut into very thin slices.) Add to the vinaigrette and toss to coat well.

3 Divide the spinach among 4 plates. Top with the fennel mixture.

Makes 4 servings

PER SERVING: 73 calories, 1 g protein, 8 g carbohydrates, 5g fat (0.5 g saturated fat), 0 mg cholesterol, 46 mg sodium

FAT-FIGHTING
4

2 g fiber

34 mg
calcium

0 IU
vitamin D

0 mg
omega-3s

MAKE IT
FAST

Smoked Salmon and Egg Salad

PREP TIME: 10 MINUTES ◆ TOTAL TIME: 15 MINUTES

2 tablespoons lemon juice
1 tablespoon flaxseed oil
1 clove garlic, minced
⅓ cup fat-free Greek-style yogurt
1 head frisée, torn into bite-size pieces

1 red bell pepper, cut into thin strips
4 ounces smoked salmon, cut into
    thin strips
4 omega-3-enriched eggs
1 teaspoon water

1 Whisk together the lemon juice, oil, and garlic in a large bowl. Stir in the yogurt. Add the frisée and pepper and toss to coat. Divide the salad among 4 plates. Divide the salmon over each.

2 Coat a nonstick skillet with cooking spray and heat over medium-high heat. Break and slip the eggs into the skillet, moving the whites toward the yolks. Reduce the heat to low. Cook for 1 minute, or until the edges turn white. Add the water. Cover the skillet. Cook for 3 minutes, or until the white is completely set and the yolk begins to thicken but is not hard. Place 1 egg over each salad. Serve immediately.

Makes 4 servings

PER SERVING: 229 calories, 26 g protein, 6 g carbohydrates, 11 g fat (2 g saturated fat), 224 mg cholesterol, 99 mg sodium

FAT-FIGHTING **4**

2 g fiber
- - - - - - - - - - - -
74 mg
calcium
- - - - - - - - - - - -
18 IU
vitamin D
- - - - - - - - - - - -
2,650 mg
omega-3s
- - - - - - - - - - - -

MAKE IT
FAST

Chinese Chopped Salad with Shrimp

PREP TIME: 15 MINUTES ◆ TOTAL TIME: 20 MINUTES

12 wonton sheets, each cut into 4 strips
2 tablespoons rice wine vinegar
½ teaspoon soy sauce
½ teaspoon dark sesame oil
¼ teaspoon ground ginger
⅓ cup fat-free Greek-style yogurt
3 cups shredded napa (Chinese) cabbage

3 carrots, julienned
1 cucumber, peeled, halved, seeded, and julienned
3 scallions, julienned
1 pound peeled and deveined cooked shrimp, chopped

1 Preheat the oven to 375°F. Coat a baking sheet with cooking spray. Place the wonton strips on the baking sheet and lightly coat with cooking spray. Bake for 5 minutes, or until lightly browned. Set aside.

2 Stir together the vinegar, soy sauce, oil, and ginger in a small bowl. Stir in the yogurt.

3 Arrange the cabbage on a serving dish. Stack the carrots, cucumber, and scallions over the cabbage. Top with the shrimp. Drizzle with the dressing and top with the reserved wontons.

Makes 4 servings

PER SERVING: 230 calories, 26 g protein, 24 g carbohydrates, 3 g fat (0.5 g saturated fat), 153 cholesterol, 358 mg sodium

FAT-
FIGHTING
4

3 g fiber

151 mg
calcium

151 IU
vitamin D

50 mg
omega-3s

MAKE IT
FAST

Asian Zucchini Slaw

PREP TIME: 15 MINUTES

¼ cup omega-3-enriched Asian sesame
    vinaigrette dressing
1 tablespoon frozen orange juice
    concentrate, thawed
2 zucchini, shredded

2 carrots, shredded
1 red bell pepper, cut into very thin strips
3 scallions, diagonally sliced
2 tablespoons sesame seeds, toasted

1 Whisk together the dressing and orange juice in a large bowl. Add the zucchini, carrots, pepper, and scallions and toss to coat well.

2 Just before serving, sprinkle with the sesame seeds.

Makes 4 servings

PER SERVING: 120 calories, 3 g protein, 15 g carbohydrates, 6 g fat (0.5 g saturated fat), 0 mg cholesterol, 198 mg sodium

FAT-
FIGHTING
4

3 g fiber
----
51 mg
calcium
----
0 IU
vitamin D
----
220 mg
omega-3s

MAKE IT
FAST

Sweet-and-Sour Cabbage

PREP TIME: 15 MINUTES ◆ TOTAL TIME: 37 MINUTES

1 tablespoon canola oil
1 red onion, cut into thin wedges
1 apple, halved, cored, and sliced
1 small head green cabbage
   (about 1 pound), thinly sliced
1/4 cup fat-free, reduced-sodium
   chicken broth

2 tablespoons white wine vinegar
1 tablespoon honey
1/4 teaspoon salt
1/4 cup chopped walnuts, toasted

FAT-FIGHTING 4

7 g fiber
- - - - - - - - - -
88 mg
calcium
- - - - - - - - - -
0 IU
vitamin D
- - - - - - - - - -
670 mg
omega-3s
- - - - - - - - - -

1 Heat the oil in a large nonstick skillet over medium heat. Add the onion and cook, stirring, for 4 minutes, or until tender. Add the apple and cook, stirring, for 2 minutes, or until browned.

2 Stir in the cabbage, tossing to coat. Add the broth and bring to a simmer. Reduce the heat to low, cover, and simmer for 10 to 15 minutes, or until the cabbage is tender. Remove from the heat.

3 Stir in the vinegar, honey, and salt. Top with the walnuts.

Makes 4 servings (6 cups)

PER SERVING: 176 calories, 5 g protein, 25 g carbohydrates, 9 g fat (1 g saturated fat), 0 mg cholesterol, 207 mg sodium

Sesame Broccoli

PREP TIME: 15 MINUTES ◆ TOTAL TIME: 27 MINUTES

1 pound broccoli, cut into florets
(about 4 cups)
2 tablespoons reduced-sodium soy sauce
2 teaspoons honey
1 teaspoon rice-wine vinegar
1 tablespoon canola oil

1 red onion, cut into wedges
1 clove garlic, minced
4 ounces Asian-style baked tofu,
at room temperature, cubed
1 tablespoon sesame seeds

1 Bring 6 cups of water to a boil in a large stockpot. Add the broccoli and cook for 2 minutes, or until crisp-tender. Drain.

2 Meanwhile, combine the soy sauce, honey, and vinegar in a small bowl. Heat the oil in a large nonstick skillet over medium-high heat. Add the onion and cook, stirring, for 5 minutes, or until lightly browned. Add the broccoli and garlic and cook, stirring, for 3 minutes. Stir the sauce mixture and add to the skillet, stirring, for 2 minutes.

3 Sprinkle with the tofu and sesame seeds.

Makes 4 servings

PER SERVING: 121 calories, 6 g protein, 11 g carbohydrates, 7 g fat (1 g saturated fat), 0 mg cholesterol, 397 mg sodium

> ## MAKE IT AGAIN
> Toss any leftover broccoli with mixed greens and fat-free Asian-style salad dressing.

FAT-FIGHTING
4

3 g fiber

77 mg calcium

0 IU vitamin D

10 mg omega-3s

MAKE IT FAST

Creamy Pasta and Broccoli

PREP TIME: 10 MINUTES ◆ TOTAL TIME: 25 MINUTES

6 ounces whole grain spaghetti
4 cups broccoli florets
1 small red onion, chopped
2 tablespoons all-purpose flour

1 cup milk
2 ounces fat-free cream cheese
1/3 cup chopped fresh basil
1/4 cup grated Parmesan cheese

1 Prepare the pasta according to package directions, adding the broccoli during the last 5 minutes of cooking. Drain. Place in a large serving bowl.

2 Meanwhile, coat a nonstick saucepan with cooking spray. Add the onion and heat over medium heat for 5 minutes. Add the flour and cook, stirring constantly with a wooden spoon, for 2 minutes, or until lightly browned. Gradually whisk in the milk. Cook,

whisking, for 5 minutes, or until thickened. Remove from the heat and stir in the cream cheese, basil, and Parmesan. Pour over the pasta and toss to coat well.

Makes 4 servings

PER SERVING: 267 calories, 16 g protein, 41 g carbohydrates , 5 g fat (2 g saturated fat), 13 mg cholesterol, 241 mg sodium

FAT-
FIGHTING
4

6 g fiber
----
245 mg
calcium
----
24 IU
vitamin D
----
160 mg
omega-3s

MAKE IT
FAST

Old-Fashioned Creamed Spinach

PREP TIME: 10 MINUTES ◆ TOTAL TIME: 45 MINUTES + STANDING TIME

3 tablespoons ground flaxseed
1 red onion, chopped
4 ounces mushrooms, sliced
1 clove garlic, minced
$\frac{1}{2}$ cup fat-free, reduced-sodium
 chicken broth

10 ounces baby spinach
3 ounces fat-free cream cheese
$\frac{1}{2}$ cup (2 ounces) shredded reduced-fat
 Cheddar cheese
1 teaspoon Dijon mustard

1 Preheat the oven to 350°F. Coat a 1½-quart baking dish with cooking spray and sprinkle the flaxseed over the bottom of the dish.

2 Coat a large nonstick skillet with cooking spray and heat over medium heat. Add the onion and mushrooms and cook, stirring, for 5 minutes, or until tender and the mushrooms have released their juices. Add the garlic and cook, stirring, for 2 minutes, or until lightly browned.

3 Stir in the broth and spinach and cook for 4 minutes, stirring, or until the spinach wilts. Stir in the cheeses and mustard. Stir until just melted and well blended.

4 Pour into a prepared dish. Bake for 20 minutes, or until set. Let stand for 5 minutes before serving.

Makes 4 servings

PER SERVING: 142 calories, 11 g protein, 15 g carbohydrates, 6 g fat (2 g saturated fat), 12 mg cholesterol, 432 mg sodium

FAT-
FIGHTING
4

6 g fiber

313 mg
calcium

5 IU
vitamin D

1,390 mg
omega-3s

Smoky Cauliflower

PREP TIME: 5 MINUTES ◆ TOTAL TIME: 25 MINUTES

1 small head cauliflower, cut into florets
2 tablespoons canola oil
1 teaspoon dried thyme

¼ teaspoon smoked paprika
¼ teaspoon salt

1 Preheat oven to 450°F.

2 Place the cauliflower on a large baking sheet with sides. Drizzle with the oil, thyme, paprika, and salt. Toss to coat. Roast for 20 minutes, turning once, or until browned and tender.

Makes 4 servings

PER SERVING: 79 calories, 1 g protein, 4 g carbohydrates, 4 g fat (0.5 g saturated fat), 0 mg cholesterol, 165 mg sodium

FAT-
FIGHTING
4

2 g fiber

19 mg
calcium

0 IU
vitamin D

670 mg
omega-3s

MAKE IT
FAST

Ginger Roasted Squash

PREP TIME: 15 MINUTES ◆ TOTAL TIME: 57 MINUTES

**1 butternut squash (2 pounds), peeled,
seeded, and cut into 1" pieces**
1 large red onion, cut into 1" pieces
2 tablespoons canola oil

1 tablespoon grated fresh ginger
1 teaspoon ground cinnamon
¼ teaspoon ground cloves
½ teaspoon salt

1 Preheat the oven to 400°F. Place the squash and onion in a large baking sheet with sides. Sprinkle with the oil, ginger, cinnamon, cloves, and salt, tossing to coat. Roast, turning occasionally, for 40 minutes, or until tender and browned.

Makes 4 servings

PER SERVING: 173 calories, 3 g protein, 29 g carbohydrates, 7 g fat (1 g saturated fat), 0 mg cholesterol, 301 mg sodium

FAT-
FIGHTING
4

5 g fiber

117 mg
calcium

0 IU
vitamin D

60 mg
omega-3s

MAKE IT AGAIN
Add any leftover squash to salad greens, and toss with crumbled reduced-fat goat cheese and fat-free balsamic vinaigrette for a delicious lunch.

Roasted Asparagus with Toasted Walnuts

PREP TIME: 5 MINUTES ◆ TOTAL TIME: 22-28 MINUTES

¼ **cup walnuts, chopped**
1 pound asparagus, trimmed
1 tablespoon canola oil

1 clove garlic, minced
¼ **teaspoon salt**
¼ **teaspoon ground black pepper**

1 Preheat the oven to 400°F.

2 Place the walnuts on a large baking sheet with sides and bake for 5 minutes, or until toasted. Place on plate.

3 Arrange the asparagus spears in the same baking sheet. Sprinkle with the oil, garlic, salt, and pepper and then turn to coat.

4 Roast for 12 to 15 minutes, depending on the thickness of the spears, or until lightly browned. Place on a serving plate and sprinkle with the toasted nuts.

Makes 4 servings

PER SERVING: 98 calories, 3 g protein, 5 g carbohydrates, 8 g fat (1 g saturated fat), 0 mg cholesterol, 147 mg sodium

FAT-FIGHTING
4

2 g fiber

31 mg
calcium

0 IU
vitamin D

670 mg
omega-3s

MAKE IT
FAST

Spring Vegetables and Quinoa

PREP TIME: 20 MINUTES ◆ TOTAL TIME: 50 MINUTES

1½ cups water
¾ cup quinoa, rinsed
¼ teaspoon salt
1 tablespoon canola oil
1 red onion, cut into wedges
8 ounces snow peas, trimmed
2 cloves garlic, minced

¼ cup fat-free, low-sodium
   vegetable broth
2 tablespoons apricot all-fruit spread
1 tablespoon balsamic vinegar
1 bunch red Swiss chard (about 1 pound),
   cut crosswise into ½" strips

1 In a medium saucepan, bring the water to a boil over high heat. Stir in the quinoa and salt and return to a boil. Reduce the heat to low, cover, and simmer for 20 minutes, or until all of the water is absorbed and the quinoa is tender.

2 Meanwhile, coat a large nonstick skillet with cooking spray and heat over medium-high heat. Add the onion and cook, stirring, for 3 minutes, or until tender. Stir in the snow peas and garlic and cook for 2 minutes. Add the broth, apricot spread, and vinegar and stir for 1 minute to deglaze the

pan. Add half of the chard, cover, and cook for 3 minutes. Add the remaining chard, cover, and cook for 2 minutes, stirring, or until the chard is wilted.

3 Serve the vegetable mixture in individual bowls, each topped with one-quarter of the quinoa.

Makes 4 servings

PER SERVING: 231 calories, 9 g protein, 38 g carbohydrates, 6 g fat (1 g saturated fat), 0 mg cholesterol, 424 mg sodium

FAT-FIGHTING
4

6 g fiber
----
110 mg
calcium
----
0 IU
vitamin D
----
430 mg
omega-3s

Whole Grain Pilaf with Artichokes

PREP TIME: 15 MINUTES ◆ TOTAL TIME: 1 HOUR 5 MINUTES

1 tablespoon canola oil
1 red or green bell pepper, diced
1 onion, chopped
1 carrot, chopped
$\frac{1}{2}$ cup barley
1 clove garlic, minced
$2\frac{1}{2}$ cups fat-free, reduced-sodium
    vegetable or chicken broth

$\frac{1}{2}$ cup water
$\frac{1}{4}$ cup bulgur
1 package (10-12 ounces) frozen
    artichoke hearts
$\frac{1}{2}$ teaspoon lemon zest
2 ounces crumbled low-fat feta cheese
    or ricotta salata

FAT-FIGHTING 4

8 g fiber

62 mg calcium

127 IU vitamin D

230 mg omega-3s

1 Heat the oil in a medium saucepan over medium-high heat. Cook the pepper, onion, and carrot over medium-high heat for 5 minutes, stirring, or until the vegetables soften. Add the barley and garlic and cook, stirring, for 3 to 5 minutes.

2 Stir in the broth and water and bring to a boil over high heat. Reduce the heat to low, cover, and simmer for 25 minutes. Stir in the bulgur and cook for 5 minutes. Stir in the artichokes and lemon zest and cook for 10 minutes, or until all of the broth is absorbed and the barley is al dente. Spoon the pilaf into a serving dish. Sprinkle with the cheese.

Makes 6 servings

PER SERVING: 166 calories, 7 g protein, 28 g carbohydrates, 4 g fat (1 g saturated fat), 3 mg cholesterol, 361 mg sodium

Fruited Rice Medley

PREP TIME: 10 MINUTES ◆ TOTAL TIME: 55 MINUTES

1 tablespoon canola oil

1 onion, chopped

1/2 small fennel bulb or 2 ribs celery, chopped

1 cup brown rice

2 cups water

1 tablespoon frozen orange juice concentrate

1/2 teaspoon salt

1/4 cup sliced almonds

2 tablespoons currants

1 Heat the oil in a small saucepan over medium heat. Add the onion and fennel and cook for 3 minutes. Stir in the rice and cook for 1 minute.

2 Add the water, orange juice concentrate, and salt and bring to a boil over high heat. Reduce the heat to low, cover, and simmer for 40 minutes, or until the water is absorbed and the rice is tender. Stir in the almonds and currants.

Make 4 servings

PER SERVING: 276 calories, 6 g protein, 47 g carbohydrates, 8 g fat (1 g saturated fat), 0 mg cholesterol, 314 mg sodium

FAT-FIGHTING

4

4 g fiber

- - - - - - - - - - - - -

56 mg calcium

- - - - - - - - - - - - -

0 IU vitamin D

- - - - - - - - - - - - -

20 mg omega-3s

- - - - - - - - - - - - -

Greek-Style Brown Rice

PREP TIME: 10 MINUTES ◆ TOTAL TIME: 1 HOUR 10 MINUTES

1 box (10 ounces) frozen chopped spinach,
    thawed and drained
³/₄ cup brown rice
3 plum tomatoes, cored, seeded, and
    chopped

1 onion, chopped
1 clove garlic, minced
¹/₂ teaspoon salt
1¹/₂ cups boiling water
¹/₂ cup crumbled reduced-fat feta cheese

FAT-FIGHTING 4

5 g fiber

165 mg
calcium

0 IU
vitamin D

80 mg
omega-3s

1 Preheat the oven to 375°F.

2 Stir together the spinach, rice, tomatoes, onion, garlic, and salt in a 1¹/₂-quart baking dish with a lid. Stir in the boiling water. Cover and bake for 1 hour, or until all the liquid is absorbed and the rice is tender. Sprinkle with the cheese.

Makes 4 servings

PER SERVING: 204 calories, 10 g protein, 35 g carbohydrates, 4 g fat (2 g saturated fat), 5 mg cholesterol, 587 mg sodium

MAKE IT AGAIN
Serve a portion of leftover rice on a bed of greens with 2 ounces of canned tuna and a drizzle of fat-free vinaigrette.

Sweet Potato Crisps

PREP TIME: 10 MINUTES ◆ TOTAL TIME: 28 MINUTES

2 large sweet potatoes, peeled
1 teaspoon lemon pepper

$\frac{1}{2}$ teaspoon dried thyme

1 Preheat the oven to 375°F. Lightly coat 2 baking sheets with cooking spray.

2 Thinly slice the potatoes in a food processor or with a mandoline, or slice with a sharp knife to $\frac{1}{8}$" thick

3 Arrange the slices in a single layer on the prepared baking sheets. Sprinkle with half of the lemon pepper and thyme. Turn

and sprinkle with the remaining lemon pepper and thyme. Bake for 20 to 25 minutes, turning once, or until lightly browned.

Makes 4 servings

PER SERVING: 122 calories, 2 g protein, 29 g carbohydrates, 0 g fat (0 g saturated fat), 0 mg cholesterol, 158 mg sodium

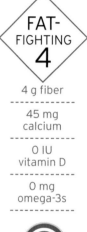

FAT-
FIGHTING
4

4 g fiber

45 mg
calcium

0 IU
vitamin D

0 mg
omega-3s

MAKE IT
FAST

Chili-Baked Fries

PREP TIME: 5 MINUTES ◆ TOTAL TIME: 47 MINUTES

½ teaspoon chili powder
¼ teaspoon ground cumin
¼ teaspoon dried oregano
**2 large Yukon gold potatoes, scrubbed,
each cut into 10 wedges**

1 tablespoon canola oil
**½ cup (2 ounces) shredded low-fat
Monterey Jack cheese**

1 Preheat the oven to 400°F. Combine the chili powder, cumin, and oregano in a small bowl.

2 Place the potatoes in a baking sheet with sides and sprinkle with the oil and chili powder mixture. Toss to coat. Bake for 40 minutes, turning occasionally, or until tender. Top with the cheese and bake for 2 minutes, or until melted.

Makes 4 servings

PER SERVING: 141 calories, 6 g protein, 16 g carbohydrates, 7 fat (2 g saturated fat), 10 mg cholesterol, 127 mg sodium

FAT-FIGHTING 4

1 g fiber

103 mg calcium

0 IU vitamin D

320 mg omega-3s

MEATS & POULTRY

Balsamic-Glazed Flank Steak with Broccoli Raab and Chickpea Puree

PREP TIME: 25 MINUTES ◆ TOTAL TIME: 50 MINUTES + MARINATING TIME

FAT-FIGHTING 4

4 g fiber

113 mg calcium

0 IU vitamin D

1,920 mg omega-3s

8 ounces flank steak
½ cup balsamic vinegar
½ small red onion, chopped
1 tablespoon finely chopped fresh rosemary
⅛ teaspoon salt
1 can (15-19 ounces) chickpeas, rinsed and drained
3 cloves garlic, quartered

1 tablespoon flaxseed oil
1 cup fat-free reduced-sodium chicken broth
Ground black pepper
4 cups coarsely chopped broccoli raab
½ teaspoon olive oil
1 tablespoon grated Parmesan cheese

1 Combine the steak, vinegar, onion, rosemary, and salt in a heavy zip-top bag. Marinate for at least 30 minutes at room temperature or for several hours in the refrigerator.

2 Simmer the chickpeas, garlic, flaxseed oil, and ¾ cup of the broth in a saucepan for 10 minutes, or until the garlic is very tender. Transfer the mixture to a blender or food processor. Blend or puree, scraping down sides as needed, until smooth. Season with plenty of the pepper. Return to the saucepan to simmer over low heat if the mixture is too runny.

3 Place a large nonstick skillet over medium-high heat. Add the remaining ¼ cup broth to the skillet and bring to a boil. Add the broccoli raab. Cook, tossing, for 3 minutes, until the broccoli raab wilts. Remove and cover to keep warm.

4 Wipe the skillet dry. Add the olive oil to the pan and heat on medium-high. Remove the steak from the marinade (reserving any left for a balsamic sauce). Sear the steak in the heated pan for 3 to 4 minutes, or until it's browned on the bottom. Flip and cook for 4 to 6 minutes, then remove the pan from the heat. Turn the heat down to medium. Remove the steak to a cutting board and let it rest for 5 minutes. Meanwhile, add the remaining marinade to the pan and return it to the heat. Scrape the bottom of the pan to remove the browned bits. Cook at a brisk simmer for 3 to 5 minutes, or until the mixture is sticky. Remove the pan from the heat and set aside.

5 Cut the steak across the grain into thin slices. Spoon the chickpea puree and the broccoli raab onto 4 dinner plates. Top the puree with the beef, then drizzle the beef with the balsamic sauce. Sprinkle the cheese on the broccoli raab.

Makes 4 servings

PER SERVING: 246 calories, 18 g protein, 19 g carbohydrates, 11 g fat (3 g saturated fat), 24 mg cholesterol, 340 mg sodium

Pepper Steak

PREP TIME: 15 MINUTES ◆ TOTAL TIME: 1 HOUR 20 MINUTES

1½ cups water
½ cup brown rice
¾ pound top round steak, thinly sliced
3 tablespoons reduced-sodium soy sauce
1 tablespoon rice wine vinegar
2 cloves garlic, minced
1 tablespoon grated fresh ginger

2½ teaspoons canola oil
2 red bell peppers, sliced
1 yellow bell pepper, sliced
6 scallions, cut into 2" pieces
½ cup reduced-sodium beef broth
2 teaspoons cornstarch

1 Bring the water to boiling in a small saucepan over high heat. Stir in the rice and reduce the heat to low, cover, and cook for 50 minutes, or until the rice is tender and the liquid is absorbed.

2 Meanwhile, combine the steak, soy sauce, vinegar, garlic, and ginger in a large bowl. Refrigerate for 30 minutes.

3 After 30 minutes, heat the oil in a large nonstick skillet or wok over medium-high heat. Add the peppers and cook, stirring, for 5 minutes. Add the scallions and cook for 3 minutes, or until the peppers and scallions are browned. Remove to a serving plate. Coat the skillet with cooking spray.

4 Remove the steak from the marinade. Place the marinade in a small bowl and whisk with the broth and cornstarch. Cook the steak in the same skillet over medium-high heat, stirring constantly, for 3 minutes, or until no longer pink. Stir the broth mixture, peppers, and scallions into the skillet and cook, stirring, for 1 minute, or until thickened.

5 Divide the rice among 4 plates. Top with the steak mixture.

Makes 4 servings

PER SERVING: 305 calories, 23 g protein, 28 g carbohydrates, 11 g fat (3 g saturated fat), 35 mg cholesterol, 567 mg sodium

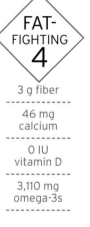

FAT-
FIGHTING
4

3 g fiber
- - - - - - - - - -
46 mg
calcium
- - - - - - - - - -
0 IU
vitamin D
- - - - - - - - - -
3,110 mg
omega-3s
- - - - - - - - - -

Slow Cooker Beef Pot Roast with Root Vegetables

PREP TIME: 15 MINUTES ◆ TOTAL TIME: 8-9 HOURS

5 medium carrots, coarsely chopped
2 large onions, coarsely chopped
3 turnips, coarsely chopped
1 cup tomato puree or sauce
1 cup fat-free, reduced-sodium
    chicken broth
2 teaspoons dried thyme
2 bay leaves

$\frac{1}{2}$ teaspoon salt
1 pound eye-of-round beef roast,
    trimmed of all visible fat
2 tablespoons canola oil
1 cup frozen baby peas
2 tablespoons flaxseed oil
Ground black pepper
Prepared horseradish

FAT-FIGHTING 4

5 g fiber

71 mg calcium

0 IU vitamin D

1,900 mg omega-3s

1 Combine the carrots, onions, turnips, tomato puree, broth, thyme, bay leaves, and salt in a medium oval slow cooker or large round slow cooker. Stir to mix. Heat the canola oil in a large nonstick skillet. Brown the beef on all sides for 3 to 4 minutes. Remove the roast and nestle into the vegetable mixture. Place the lid on the cooker and cook on low for 8 to 9 hours.

2 Remove the beef to a cutting board. Stir the peas into the slow-cooker mixture and allow to sit for 5 minutes. Remove and discard the bay leaves. Season to taste with the pepper. Cut the beef into serving pieces. Return the beef to the pot and stir into the vegetables. Stir in the flaxseed oil. Serve with the horseradish, if desired.

Makes 8 servings

PER SERVING: 251 calories, 16 g protein, 21 g carbohydrates, 12 g fat (3 g saturated fat), 23 mg cholesterol, 583 mg sodium

MAKE IT AHEAD
Because the slow cooker does all the work, it's easy to create enough for 2 meals at one time. After dinner, cool 4 servings and pack into a sturdy plastic freezer container. Label and freeze for up to 3 months.

Spaghetti Squash Bolognese

PREP TIME: 30 MINUTES ◆ TOTAL TIME: 1 HOUR 25 MINUTES

1 medium spaghetti squash
(about 3 pounds)
½ pound 95% fat-free ground beef
1 onion, finely chopped
2 carrots, finely chopped
1 rib celery, finely chopped
2 cloves garlic, minced

1 teaspoon dried oregano
1 teaspoon dried basil
½ cup beef broth
1 can (28 ounces) chopped tomatoes
in thick puree
1 cup fat-free evaporated milk

1 Preheat the oven to 400°F. Pierce the squash with a fork in several places. Place in a roasting pan. Bake for 55 minutes, or until tender and soft to the touch. When it is cool enough to handle, cut the squash in half, then scoop out and discard the seeds. Scrape the flesh, crosswise, with a fork to separate the spaghetti-like strands. Place in a large serving bowl. Set aside.

2 Meanwhile, cook the beef in a large saucepan over medium heat, stirring occasionally, for 10 minutes, or until no longer pink. Remove to a bowl; do not drain.

3 Coat the pan with cooking spray. Add the onion, carrots, celery, garlic, oregano,

and basil and cook, stirring, for 5 to 7 minutes, or until browned. Add the broth and reserved beef with any drippings and cook for 3 to 5 minutes.

4 Stir in the tomatoes, bring to a simmer, cover, and simmer over low heat for 1 hour for flavors to blend.

5 Remove the sauce from the heat and stir in the milk. Serve over the squash.

Makes 4 servings

PER SERVING: 279 calories, 22 g protein, 41 g carbohydrates, 7 g fat (2 g saturated fat), 38 mg cholesterol, 550 mg sodium

FAT-FIGHTING 4

4 g fiber
----
280 mg calcium
----
51 IU vitamin D
----
220 mg omega-3s

Shepherd's Pie

PREP TIME: 25 MINUTES ◆ TOTAL TIME: 1 HOUR 5 MINUTES

2½ pounds parsnips, peeled and cut into 1" pieces

1½ cups reduced-sodium chicken or mushroom broth

1½ tablespoons cornstarch

1 pound 99% fat-free ground turkey breast

2 tablespoons canola oil

1 onion, coarsely chopped

10 ounces baby bella mushrooms, quartered

2 carrots, sliced

½ teaspoon dried thyme

1 tablespoon Worcestershire sauce

1 cup frozen peas

1 tablespoon tomato paste

¼ cup fat-free Greek-style yogurt

3 tablespoons grated Parmesan cheese

FAT-FIGHTING 4

11 g fiber

- - - - - - - - - - - - -

120 mg calcium

- - - - - - - - - - - - -

0 IU vitamin D

- - - - - - - - - - - - -

450 mg omega-3s

- - - - - - - - - - - - -

1 Preheat the oven to 375°F. Place the parsnips in a medium saucepan and cover with water. Bring to a boil over high heat. Reduce the heat to low, cover, and simmer for 15 minutes, or until very tender.

2 Meanwhile, whisk together the broth and cornstarch in a measuring cup. Set aside.

3 Heat 1 tablespoon of the oil in a nonstick skillet over medium-high heat. Add the turkey and cook for 5 minutes, or until browned and no longer pink. Remove from the skillet. Cook the onion, mushrooms, carrots, and thyme in the remaining 1 tablespoon oil in the same skillet, stirring, for 5 minutes, or until lightly browned. Add the Worcestershire sauce and cook, stirring,

for 1 minute to loosen any brown bits. Stir in the peas, tomato paste, and reserved broth mixture and bring to a simmer. Add the turkey back to the skillet. Cook for 5 minutes.

4 Coat a 2½-quart baking dish with cooking spray. Drain the parsnips and place in a bowl. Mash with the yogurt and cheese. Place the turkey mixture in the prepared baking dish. Top with the parsnips. Bake for 15 minutes, or until heated through.

Makes 6 servings

PER SERVING: 325 calories, 26 g protein, 43 g carbohydrates, 7 g fat (1 g saturated fat), 32 mg cholesterol, 289 mg sodium

Roast Pork and Vegetables

PREP TIME: 15 ♦ TOTAL TIME: 1 HOUR 30 MINUTES

½ teaspoon salt
½ teaspoon ground cinnamon
¼ teaspoon ground ginger
¼ teaspoon ground allspice
1 butternut squash (about 2 pounds), peeled, seeded, and cut into 1" cubes

2 parsnips, peeled and cut into 1" cubes
2 large onions, cut into wedges
1½ pounds boneless pork loin roast, trimmed of all fat

FAT-FIGHTING 4

5 g fiber
---
109 mg calcium
---
0 IU vitamin D
---
50 mg omega-3s
---

❶ Preheat the oven to 400°F. Coat a large roasting pan with cooking spray. Combine the salt, cinnamon, ginger, and allspice in a small bowl.

❷ Combine the squash, parsnips, and onions in the prepared pan. Lightly coat the vegetables with cooking spray and sprinkle with half of the spice mixture. Toss to coat well. Roast for 15 minutes and remove the pan from the oven.

❸ While the vegetables are roasting, rub the remaining spice mixture over the pork roast and place the roast on a rack. Move the vegetables to the edges of the pan and place the roast in the center of the pan. Roast for 45 minutes, occasionally tossing the vegetables to brown them, or until a thermometer inserted in the center of the roast reaches 155°F and the juices run clear. Let the roast stand for 10 minutes before slicing.

Makes 6 servings

PER SERVING: 250 calories, 27 g protein, 26 g carbohydrates, 5 g fat (1 g saturated fat), 78 mg cholesterol, 270 mg sodium

Southern-Style Pork, Black-Eyed Peas, and Collard Greens

PREP TIME: 10 MINUTES ◆ TOTAL TIME: 30 MINUTES

¼ cup white vinegar

1 teaspoon red-pepper flakes

1 teaspoon canola oil

½ red onion, chopped

¾ pound pork tenderloin, cut into 8 slices

1 can (15.5 ounces) no-salt-added black-eyed peas, rinsed and drained

¼ cup fat-free, reduced-sodium chicken broth

½ teaspoon dried thyme

⅛ teaspoon salt

6 cups coarsely chopped collard greens

2 teaspoons flaxseed oil

1 Combine the vinegar and pepper flakes in a microwaveable cup. Microwave on high power for 30 seconds, or until hot. Remove and set aside.

2 Heat a large nonstick skillet over medium-high heat. Add the canola oil and swirl to coat the pan bottom. Add the onion. Cover and cook, stirring occasionally, for 2 minutes, or until the onion starts to wilt. Scrape the onion to one side. Place the pork in the pan. Cook for 4 minutes, or until browned on the bottom. Flip the pork and cook for 2 minutes, or until no longer opaque on the bottom. Add the black-eyed peas, broth, thyme, and salt. Cover and reduce the heat so the mixture simmers for 10 to 15 minutes for the flavors to blend.

3 Add the greens and stir to combine. Cover and cook, stirring occasionally, for 5 minutes, or until the greens wilt. Remove from the heat.

4 Stir the flaxseed oil into the mixture. Spoon onto 4 dinner plates. Drizzle with the reserved red-pepper vinegar at the table.

Makes 4 servings

PER SERVING: 201 calories, 23 g protein, 14 g carbohydrates, 6 g fat (1 g saturated fat), 55 mg cholesterol, 172 mg sodium

FAT-
FIGHTING
4

5 g fiber

107 mg calcium

0 IU vitamin D

1,400 mg omega-3s

MAKE IT FAST

MAKE IT AHEAD

Cooking dried legumes from scratch is cheaper than buying canned beans. As a bonus, they're sodium free. Cook 1 pound of legumes at a time, following the instructions on the bag. Freeze in labeled plastic containers in recipe-size portions (note that 1⅔ cups cooked beans is roughly equal to a 15-ounce can).

Pork-and-Vegetable Tostadas

PREP TIME: 25 MINUTES ◆ TOTAL TIME: 1 HOUR 10 MINUTES

³⁄₄ **pound pork tenderloin**
¹⁄₂ **cup cherry tomatoes, halved**
6 scallions, cut into 2" pieces
**2 jalapeño chile peppers (wear plastic
    gloves when handling), seeded and
    cut in strips**
2 teaspoons canola oil
1 teaspoon chili powder

¹⁄₈ **teaspoon salt**
2 cups shredded baby spinach
4 corn tortillas (6" diameter)
¹⁄₂ **cup canned fat-free refried beans**
¹⁄₂ **cup fat-free plain yogurt**
**4 tablespoons shredded reduced-fat
    Cheddar cheese**
4 tablespoons chopped cilantro

1 Preheat the oven to 375°F. Cover a small baking sheet with aluminum foil. Place the pork on the baking sheet. Surround with the tomatoes, scallions, and peppers. Drizzle evenly with the oil. Sprinkle with the chili powder and salt. Rub to coat the pork and vegetables evenly with seasonings.

2 Roast for 30 to 35 minutes, or until an instant-read thermometer inserted in the center of the pork tenderloin registers 155°F and the juices run clear. Remove the baking sheet from the oven and place the pork on a cutting board. Toss the spinach with the roasted vegetables. Let the pork stand for 10 minutes before slicing. Turn off the oven. Place the tortillas in a single layer directly on the oven rack to crisp while the pork rests.

3 Place the beans in a microwaveable bowl with 2 tablespoons water. Stir until smooth. Cover with plastic wrap, leaving a vent. Microwave on medium power for 2 minutes, or until hot.

4 Place each tortilla on a dinner plate. Spread with the beans. Thinly slice the pork and fan over the beans. Top with the roasted vegetables and juices, cheese, yogurt, and cilantro.

Makes 4 servings

PER SERVING: 308 calories, 26 g protein, 33 g carbohydrates, 8 g fat (2 g saturated fat), 61 mg cholesterol, 436 mg sodium

FAT-
FIGHTING
4

6 g fiber

180 mg
calcium

10 IU
vitamin D

100 mg
omega-3s

Chinese Barbecued Pork and Edamame

PREP TIME: 10 MINUTES ◆ TOTAL TIME: 1 HOUR 5 MINUTES + STANDING TIME

1 cup reduced-sodium tomato sauce
4 scallions, sliced
1 tablespoon molasses
1 tablespoon reduced-sodium soy sauce
2 teaspoons grated fresh ginger
3/4 pound pork tenderloin

1 cup fresh shelled edamame
4 ounces firm tofu with calcium sulfate, drained and cut into 1/2" chunks
1/4 cup quick brown rice
1/4 cup water

FAT-FIGHTING 4

4 g fiber

252 mg calcium

0 IU vitamin D

180 mg omega-3s

1 In a medium heavy saucepan, combine the tomato sauce, scallions, molasses, soy sauce, and ginger. Bring to a simmer. Add the pork and edamame. Cover and simmer gently for 40 minutes, or until a thermometer inserted in the center reaches 155°F and the juices run clear.

2 Remove the pork to a cutting board. Cut into very thin slices. Return to the pan. Add the tofu, rice, and water. Stir. Cover and simmer for 10 minutes, or until the rice is tender.

3 Remove from heat and let stand for 5 minutes before serving.

Makes 4 servings (3 cups)

PER SERVING: 255 calories, 28 g protein, 20 g carbohydrates, 7 g fat (2 g saturated fat), 55 mg cholesterol, 250 mg sodium

NOTE

If fresh shelled edamame are not available, replace with 1 bag (12 ounces) frozen edamame in the pod. Blanch the frozen pods in a pot of boiling water for about 3 minutes. Drain and rinse with cold water. Shell the beans and throw away the pods. Yield is 1 cup edamame.

Szechuan Stir-Fried Pork

PREP TIME: 20 MINUTES ◆ TOTAL TIME: 32-34 MINUTES

¾ cup fat-free, reduced-sodium
   chicken broth
2 tablespoons reduced-sodium soy sauce
1 tablespoon rice wine vinegar
1 tablespoon grated fresh ginger
¼ teaspoon ground red pepper

2½ teaspoons canola oil
¾ pound pork tenderloin, cut into
   ¼" slices
1 pound green beans, cut in half
2 carrots, julienned
1 red onion, cut into thin strips

1 Whisk together ½ cup of the broth, the soy sauce, vinegar, ginger, and pepper in a measuring cup. Set aside.

2 Heat the oil in a large nonstick skillet over medium-high heat. Cook the pork, turning, for 3 to 4 minutes, or until browned and no longer pink. Remove to a plate.

3 Add the green beans, carrots, onion, and remaining ¼ cup broth and cook, stirring, for 6 minutes, or until the beans are just crisp-tender. Stir the broth mixture and add to the skillet with the pork and any accumulated juices. Cook, stirring, for 3 minutes, or until the sauce is reduced by half.

Makes 4 servings

PER SERVING: 184 calories, 21 g protein, 14 g carbohydrates, 5 g fat (1 g saturated fat), 55 mg cholesterol, 461 mg sodium

FAT-
FIGHTING
4

5 g fiber
- - - - - - - - - - - -
63 g
calcium
- - - - - - - - - - - -
0 IU
vitamin D
- - - - - - - - - - - -
50 mg
omega-3s
- - - - - - - - - - - -

Quick Pork Chops with Green Salsa

PREP TIME: 15 MINUTES ◆ TOTAL TIME: 30 MINUTES

1½ cups frozen shelled edamame
4 boneless pork chops (3 ounces each), trimmed of all visible fat
1 teaspoon ground cumin
¼ teaspoon salt
1 tablespoon canola oil

6 tomatillos, cut into wedges
4 scallions, cut into ½" pieces
1 clove garlic, minced
½ cup fat-free, reduced-sodium chicken broth
¼ cup chopped cilantro

FAT-FIGHTING 4

5 g fiber

73 mg calcium

0 IU vitamin D

340 mg omega-3s

MAKE IT FAST

❶ Prepare the edamame according to package directions; drain.

❷ Meanwhile, rub the chops with the cumin and salt. Coat a large nonstick skillet with cooking spray and heat over medium-high heat. Add the chops and cook for 4 minutes, turning once, or until a thermometer inserted in the center of a chop registers 160°F and the juices run clear. Remove to a plate and keep warm.

❸ Heat the oil in the same skillet over medium-high heat. Cook the tomatillos, scallions, and garlic, stirring constantly, for 5 minutes, or until browned. Add the broth, cilantro, and edamame and cook for 3 minutes, or until the flavors meld. Serve with the chops.

Makes 4 servings

PER SERVING: 240 calories, 26 g protein, 11 g carbohydrates, 10 g fat (1 g saturated fat), 59 mg cholesterol, 278 mg sodium

Parmesan Turkey with Greens

PREP TIME: 15 MINUTES ◆ TOTAL TIME: 35 MINUTES

½ cup grated Parmesan cheese
¼ cup ground flaxseed
¼ teaspoon cracked black pepper
1 pound turkey breast cutlets

2 cloves garlic, minced
1 large bunch red Swiss chard, stemmed
   and chopped
2 tablespoons water

FAT-FIGHTING 4

4 g fiber
- - - - - - - - - - - - -
181 mg
calcium
- - - - - - - - - - - - -
0 IU
vitamin D
- - - - - - - - - - - - -
1,880 mg
omega-3s
- - - - - - - - - - - - -

1 Preheat the oven to 400°F. Coat a large baking sheet with cooking spray.

2 Combine the cheese, flaxseed, and pepper on a large plate. Dredge the cutlets into the mixture and place on the prepared baking sheet. Coat the cutlets with cooking spray. Bake for 20 minutes, turning once, or until no longer pink.

3 Meanwhile, coat a large nonstick skillet with cooking spray and heat over medium heat. Add the garlic and cook, stirring, for 2 minutes. Add the chard and cook, stirring, for 2 minutes. Add the water, cover, and cook for 2 minutes, or until the chard is wilted. Serve alongside the turkey.

Makes 4 servings

PER SERVING: 227 calories, 35 g protein, 7 g carbohydrates, 7 g fat (2 g saturated fat), 54 mg cholesterol, 447 mg sodium

Turkey with Cilantro Pesto

PREP TIME: 15 MINUTES ◆ TOTAL TIME: 40 MINUTES

1 bunch cilantro
¼ cup walnuts
2 cloves garlic
1 teaspoon lime juice

½ teaspoon lime peel
1 tablespoons canola oil
1½ pounds boneless turkey breast

1 Preheat the oven to 400°F. Coat a roasting pan with cooking spray.

2 Combine the cilantro, walnuts, garlic, lime juice, and lime peel in a blender or food processor. Pulse to puree. Add the oil with the processor running until well blended.

3 Place the turkey breast in the prepared roasting pan and spread the top and sides with the cilantro mixture. Roast for 25 to 30 minutes, or until a thermometer inserted in the thickest portion registers 170°F and the juices run clear.

Makes 6 servings

PER SERVING: 181 calories, 29 g protein, 1 g carbohydrate, 6 g fat (1 g saturated fat), 70 mg cholesterol, 58 mg sodium

FAT-
FIGHTING
4

1 g fiber
- - - - - - - - - - - -
22 mg
calcium
- - - - - - - - - - - -
0 IU
vitamin D
- - - - - - - - - - - -
450 mg
omega-3s
- - - - - - - - - - - -

MAKE IT AGAIN
Serve any leftover turkey breast over Spinach and Fennel Salad (page 139). Or cut up ½ pound of the turkey for the Enchiladas Suiza (page 194).

Turkey Cutlets with Jeweled Salsa

PREP TIME: 15 MINUTES ◆ TOTAL TIME: 20-22 MINUTES

1 cup shelled edamame
2 tomatoes, chopped
1 yellow bell pepper, chopped
3 scallions, diagonally sliced
2 tablespoons red wine vinegar
1 teaspoon minced fresh oregano
1 pound turkey cutlets
¼ teaspoon ground black pepper
⅛ teaspoon salt
2 teaspoons canola oil

1 Prepare the edamame according to package directions. Rinse under cold water and drain.

2 Meanwhile, combine the tomatoes, bell pepper, scallions, vinegar, and oregano in a bowl. Stir in the edamame.

3 Sprinkle the turkey with the black pepper and salt. Heat the oil in a nonstick skillet over medium-high heat. Cook the turkey, turning once, for 5 to 7 minutes, or until no longer pink. Place on a serving plate and top with the salsa.

Makes 4 servings

PER SERVING: 213 calories, 34 g protein, 9 g carbohydrates, 5 g fat (0 g saturated fat), 45 mg cholesterol, 181 mg sodium

FAT-
FIGHTING
4

3 g fiber

40 mg
calcium

0 IU
vitamin D

10 mg
omega-3s

MAKE IT
FAST

Old-Fashioned Chicken Stew

PREP TIME: 15 MINUTES ◆ TOTAL TIME: 1 HOUR

$\frac{1}{3}$ **cup dry yellow split peas**
1$\frac{1}{2}$ cups fat-free, reduced-sodium
   chicken broth
2 teaspoons canola oil
1 large onion, cut into 1" chunks
2 carrots, cut into $\frac{1}{2}$" chunks
2 ribs celery, cut into 1" pieces

$\frac{1}{4}$ **teaspoon salt**
$\frac{3}{4}$ **pound boneless, skinless chicken**
   breasts, cut into 1" chunks
1 tablespoon dried, crumbled sage
Ground black pepper
4 teaspoons flaxseed oil
1 tablespoon chopped parsley (optional)

1 Combine the split peas and 1 cup of the broth in a small saucepan. Bring to a boil, then reduce the heat so the mixture simmers for 30 minutes, or until the peas are very tender. Transfer the mixture to a blender or food processor. Blend or process, scraping sides of bowl as needed and adding 2 to 3 tablespoons of broth to loosen, until smooth.

2 Meanwhile, heat a large nonstick skillet over medium-high heat. Add 1 teaspoon of the canola oil and swirl to coat the pan bottom. Add the onion, carrots, celery, and $\frac{1}{8}$ teaspoon of the salt. Stir. Cover and cook, stirring occasionally, for 10 minutes, or until the vegetables start to brown. Transfer the vegetables to a plate.

3 Return the pan to medium-high heat. Add the remaining 1 teaspoon canola oil. Scatter the chicken into the pan. Season with the remaining $\frac{1}{8}$ teaspoon salt. Do not stir. Cook for 2 minutes, or until browned on the bottom. Toss and cook for about 2 minutes, or until no longer pink. Return the vegetables to the pan. Add the sage, split pea puree, and $\frac{1}{4}$ cup of the remaining broth. Stir.

4 Cover the pan and reduce the heat so the mixture simmers slowly. Cook for 10 minutes, or until the chicken is cooked through and the vegetables are very tender. If a thinner gravy is desired, stir in the remainder of the broth. Season generously with the pepper. Remove from the heat and stir in the flaxseed oil. Sprinkle with the parsley, if using.

Makes 4 servings

PER SERVING: 247 calories, 25 g protein, 18 g carbohydrates, 8 g fat (1 g saturated fat), 49 mg cholesterol, 408 mg sodium

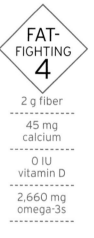

FAT-FIGHTING
4

2 g fiber

45 mg calcium

0 IU vitamin D

2,660 mg omega-3s

MAKE IT AHEAD

To save time and effort, cook the split peas and puree in advance, perhaps on a weekend or during an evening. (You can double or triple the amount to have on hand for future meals.) Store in an airtight container and refrigerate for up to 3 days or freeze for up to 3 months.

To thaw, microwave on medium power for 2 to 3 minutes.

Southern "Fried" Chicken Fingers with Mashed Sweet Potatoes

PREP TIME: 20 MINUTES ◆ TOTAL TIME: 45 MINUTES

1½ pounds sweet potatoes, peeled, cut into ½" chunks
3 large cloves garlic
5 tablespoons ground flaxseed
1½ teaspoons poultry seasoning
½ teaspoon salt
1 egg white
1 tablespoon water
¾ pound boneless, skinless chicken tenders

1 tablespoon white whole wheat flour
1 tablespoon canola oil
2 tablespoons nonfat dry milk
⅛ teaspoon grated nutmeg
½ teaspoon hot-pepper sauce + extra to taste
2 scallions, sliced

FAT-FIGHTING 4

8 g fiber
----
97 mg calcium

0.11 IU vitamin D

2,320 mg omega-3s
----

1 Preheat the oven to 375°F. Line a baking sheet with aluminum foil. Coat with cooking spray.

2 Place the sweet potatoes and garlic in an 8" round or square microwaveable baking dish. Cover with plastic wrap, leaving a small vent. Microwave on high power, tossing the mixture occasionally without removing the plastic, for 10 to 12 minutes, or until very soft. Remove and set aside, covered.

3 Meanwhile, combine the flaxseed, poultry seasoning, and ¼ teaspoon of the salt on a large sheet of waxed paper. Mix with fingers. Beat the egg white and water with a fork in a shallow bowl.

4 Lay the tenders in a single layer on a work surface. Place the flour in a small, fine sieve and sprinkle evenly and lightly on both sides of the tenders. Dip each tender into the egg white mixture, shaking off excess.

Dip into the flax mixture to coat evenly. Place on the prepared baking sheet. Press any remaining flaxseed mixture evenly on top of the chicken. Drizzle evenly with the oil. Bake for 10 minutes, or until no longer pink and the juices run clear.

5 Meanwhile, carefully remove the plastic from the sweet potatoes. Add the dry milk, nutmeg, ½ teaspoon of the hot-pepper sauce, and the remaining ¼ teaspoon salt. With a potato masher, smash the potatoes and garlic to reach the desired smoothness. (If a softer mash is desired, mix in 1 to 2 tablespoons hot water.) Spoon onto 4 dinner plates. Surround with the chicken fingers. Sprinkle with the scallions. Serve with hot-pepper sauce at the table.

Makes 4 servings

PER SERVING: 319 calories, 26 g protein, 37 g carbohydrates, 8 g fat (1 g saturated fat), 50 mg cholesterol, 452 mg sodium

Chicken-Vegetable Pot Pie

PREP TIME: 25 MINUTES ◆ TOTAL TIME: 1 HOUR 25 MINUTES

1 teaspoon olive oil
2 carrots, thinly sliced
2 ribs celery, thinly sliced
1 pound boneless, skinless chicken
breasts, cooked and cut into bite-size
pieces
1 can (15 ounces) fat-free chicken gravy

$\frac{1}{2}$ cup fresh or frozen peas
1 tablespoon ground flaxseed
1 tablespoon chopped parsley, or to taste
$\frac{1}{4}$ teaspoon salt
$\frac{1}{4}$ teaspoon ground black pepper
1 (9") refrigerated ready-to-roll, deep-
dish, double pie crust

FAT-FIGHTING 4

2 g fiber

30 mg calcium

0 IU vitamin D

340 mg omega-3s

① Preheat the oven to 350°F. Coat a 9" square or round baking dish with cooking spray.

② Heat the oil in a medium nonstick skillet over medium-high heat. Add the carrots and celery. Cook, stirring, for 7 minutes, or until tender. Place in a large bowl. Add the chicken, gravy, peas, flaxseed, parsley, salt, and pepper. Place the bottom pie crust in the prepared baking dish. Add the chicken

mixture and top with the second crust. Trim the edges and crimp.

③ Bake for 50 minutes, or until brown and bubbling.

Makes 6 servings

PER SERVING: 296 calories, 21 g protein, 26 g carbohydrates, 12 g fat (4 g saturated fat), 51 mg cholesterol, 319 mg sodium

Ranch Chicken Fingers

PREP TIME: 15 MINUTES ◆ TOTAL TIME: 27-30 MINUTES

⅓ cup light ranch salad dressing
½ cup fresh whole wheat bread crumbs
¼ cup ground flaxseed

1 pound boneless, skinless
   chicken tenders

1 Preheat the oven to 400°F. Coat a large baking sheet with cooking spray.

2 Place the salad dressing in a shallow bowl. Combine the bread crumbs and flaxseed in another shallow bowl. Dip the chicken into the dressing and dredge in the crumb mixture, then place it on the prepared baking sheet. Coat the tenders with cooking spray.

3 Bake for 12 minutes, turning once, or until the chicken is no longer pink and the juices run clear.

Makes 4 servings

PER SERVING: 237 calories, 29 g protein, 7 g carbohydrates, 10 g fat (1 g saturated fat), 71 mg cholesterol, 311 mg sodium

> ## MAKE IT A MEAL
> **Serve with Chili-Baked Fries (page 158) and carrot and celery sticks.**

FAT-FIGHTING
4

3 g fiber
- - - - - - - - - - - - -
46 g
calcium
- - - - - - - - - - - - -
0 IU
vitamin D
- - - - - - - - - - - - -
1,890 mg
omega-3s
- - - - - - - - - - - - -

MAKE IT
FAST

Swiss Cheese Chicken Fillets with Spinach-Leek Sauté

PREP TIME: 10 MINUTES ◆ TOTAL TIME: 30 MINUTES

4 boneless, skinless chicken tenders
2 teaspoons canola oil
1 leek, thinly sliced
3 tablespoons fat-free, reduced-sodium chicken broth
1 bag (6 ounces) baby spinach, coarsely chopped

½ cup part-skim ricotta cheese
¼ cup nonfat dry milk
⅛ teaspoon salt
⅛ teaspoon grated nutmeg
2 slices (¾ ounce each) reduced-fat Swiss cheese, halved

FAT-FIGHTING 4

2 g fiber

309 mg calcium

0.22 IU vitamin D

200 mg omega-3s

MAKE IT FAST

1 Place the chicken tenders on a cutting board. Cover with plastic wrap. Glide a smooth meat pounder over the chicken to flatten to ¼" thickness. Heat a large nonstick skillet over medium-high heat. Add 1 teaspoon of the oil and swirl to coat the pan bottom. Add the chicken and cook for 2 minutes, or until golden on the bottom. Flip and cook for 2 minutes, or until no longer pink. Remove to a plate.

2 Return the pan to medium-low heat. Add the remaining 1 teaspoon oil. Add the leek and 1 tablespoon of the broth. Toss. Cover the pan and cook, stirring occasionally, for 5 minutes, or until the leek browns lightly. Add the spinach and remaining

2 tablespoons broth. Toss. Cover and cook for 3 minutes, or until spinach is wilted.

3 Meanwhile, whisk the ricotta, dry milk, salt, and nutmeg in a bowl. Reduce the skillet heat to low. Add the ricotta mixture, stirring to incorporate. Return the chicken to the pan over the spinach mixture. Top each chicken fillet with a strip of Swiss cheese. Cover and cook for 2 minutes, or until the Swiss cheese is melted. Serve the chicken over the spinach-leek mixture.

Makes 4 servings

PER SERVING: 187 calories, 21 g protein, 13 g carbohydrates, 6 g fat (3 g saturated fat), 49 mg cholesterol, 407 mg sodium

Creamy Chicken and Snow Peas with Spaghetti

PREP TIME: 15 MINUTES ◆ TOTAL TIME: 26 MINUTES

¼ cup part-skim ricotta cheese
¼ cup grated Parmesan cheese
3 tablespoons nonfat dry milk
1 tablespoon canola oil
1 red onion, halved and thinly sliced
8 ounces Chinese pea pods

¼ teaspoon salt
8 ounces cooked chicken breast, cut in thin strips (about 2 cups)
3 ounces whole grain spaghetti (such as Barilla Plus)
Ground black pepper

1 Set a medium covered pot of water over high heat. Combine the ricotta, Parmesan, and dry milk in a small bowl. Stir until smooth. Set aside.

2 Heat the oil in a deep, wide skillet over medium heat for 1 minute. Add the onion. Cover and cook, tossing occasionally, for 5 minutes, or until golden. Add the pea pods and salt. Toss for 1 minute, or until the pods turn bright green. Add the chicken and toss for 1 minute. Turn off the heat.

3 Meanwhile, when the water boils, add the pasta. Stir and bring to a boil. Cook for 5 to 6 minutes, or until al dente. Reserve 1 cup of the cooking water. Drain the pasta

and transfer to the skillet. Toss to combine the ingredients. Add ¼ cup cooking water to the skillet, scraping the pan to remove any browned bits. Add ¼ cup cooking water to the ricotta mixture. Stir until smooth. Add the ricotta mixture to the skillet and toss with the spaghetti. Toss to coat. Add cooking water in small splashes, tossing, until the sauce is the desired consistency. Allow to sit for 1 minute for flavors to blend. Pass the pepper at the table.

Makes 4 servings (4 cups)

PER SERVING: 315 calories, 32 g protein, 24 g carbohydrates, 10 fat (3 g saturated fat), 69 mg cholesterol, 325 mg sodium

FAT-FIGHTING
4

3 g fiber
- - - - - - - - - - - - -
181 mg calcium
- - - - - - - - - - - - -
0.17 IU vitamin D
- - - - - - - - - - - - -
470 mg omega-3s
- - - - - - - - - - - - -

MAKE IT FAST

Chicken and Chickpea Couscous

PREP TIME: 20 MINUTES ◆ TOTAL TIME: 40 MINUTES

2 teaspoons canola oil
1 red or yellow bell pepper,
    cut into 1" chunks
1 red onion, cut into 1" chunks
1 carrot, cut into 1"chunks
1 teaspoon ground cumin
1/4 teaspoon salt
1 cup no-salt-added canned chickpeas,
    rinsed and drained

3 cloves garlic, finely chopped
3/4 pound boneless, skinless chicken
    breast, cut into 1" chunks
1/2 cup fat-free, reduced-sodium
    chicken broth
1/4 cup whole wheat couscous
1 tablespoon flaxseed oil
2 tablespoons chopped cilantro

FAT-
FIGHTING
4

5 g fiber

59 mg
calcium

0 IU
vitamin D

1,850 mg
omega-3s

1 Heat a large nonstick skillet over medium-high heat. Add 1 teaspoon of the canola oil and swirl to coat the pan bottom. Add the pepper, onion, carrot, 1/2 teaspoon of the cumin, and 1/8 teaspoon of the salt. Toss. Cover and cook, tossing occasionally, for 8 minutes, or until glossy and golden. Add the chickpeas and garlic. Cook, stirring, for 1 minute. Transfer to a plate and set aside.

2 Return the skillet to medium heat. Add the remaining 1 teaspoon canola oil and swirl to coat the pan bottom. Add the chicken. Season with the remaining 1/2 teaspoon cumin and 1/8 teaspoon salt. Cook without stirring for 2 minutes, or until the

chicken is lightly browned on the bottom. Toss and cook for 2 minutes, or until no longer pink. Add the reserved vegetables and chickpeas. Toss for 1 minute, or until fragrant. Add the broth and couscous.

3 Cover and reduce the heat so the mixture simmers gently. Cook for 5 minutes, or until the carrot is cooked through. Remove from the heat and stir in the flaxseed oil. Sprinkle the cilantro on the mixture. Serve in pasta bowls.

Makes 4 servings (5 cups)

PER SERVING: 268 calories, 25 g protein, 24 g carbohydrates, 8 g fat (1 g saturated fat), 49 mg cholesterol, 289 mg sodium

Chicken and Artichoke Cacciatora

PREP TIME: 10 MINUTES ◆ TOTAL TIME: 35 MINUTES + STANDING TIME

1 onion, diced

3 cloves garlic, finely chopped

1 tablespoon canola oil

1 can (14.5 ounces) no-salt-added diced tomatoes

1 can (14 ounces) water-packed artichoke hearts, rinsed and drained

2 tablespoons ground flaxseed

1 tablespoon dried oregano

1 pound boneless, skinless chicken tenders

1/4 teaspoon red-pepper flakes

1 Combine the onion, garlic, and oil in a deep, wide skillet. Cover and set over medium-high heat. Cook, stirring occasionally, for about 5 minutes, or until the onion starts to soften. Reduce the heat if the onion starts to brown. Add the tomatoes (with juice), artichokes, flaxseed, and oregano. Stir. Simmer for about 10 minutes to blend the flavors.

2 Add the chicken tenders to the pan, spooning some of the tomato-artichoke mixture on top. Cover and simmer for 8 minutes, or until the chicken is no longer pink. Allow to sit, covered, for 5 minutes before serving. Sprinkle with the red-pepper flakes and serve.

Makes 4 servings

PER SERVING: 227 calories, 30 g protein, 15 g carbohydrates, 6 g fat (0.5 g saturated fat), 67 mg cholesterol, 454 mg sodium

MAKE IT AGAIN

Any leftovers of this dish make a delicious soup for a quick lunch. Simply reheat one portion in a saucepan with 1 cup fat-free, reduced-sodium chicken broth.

FAT-FIGHTING
4

5 g fiber

33 mg calcium

0 IU vitamin D

960 mg omega-3s

Grilled Tandoori Chicken with Cucumber-Yogurt Sauce

PREP TIME: 25 MINUTES ◆ TOTAL TIME: 1 HOUR 10 MINUTES + MARINATING TIME

1 cup fat-free plain yogurt
3 large cloves garlic, finely chopped
1 teaspoon ground cumin
1 teaspoon ground coriander
Freshly grated zest of 1 lime
$\frac{1}{2}$ teaspoon ground red pepper
$\frac{1}{4}$ teaspoon salt

$\frac{3}{4}$ pound boneless, skinless chicken breast
2 tablespoons nonfat dry milk
1 tablespoon ground flaxseed
1 small English cucumber, thinly sliced
2 scallions, thinly sliced
2 tablespoons finely chopped fresh mint

FAT-FIGHTING 4

2 g fiber

135 mg calcium

20 IU vitamin D

30 mg omega-3s

1 Combine $\frac{1}{4}$ cup of the yogurt, the garlic, cumin, coriander, red pepper, lime zest, and $\frac{1}{8}$ teaspoon of the salt in a 1-gallon zip-top bag. Massage the bag to mix the ingredients. Add the chicken and massage the bag to evenly coat the chicken. Press out all the air and seal the bag. Refrigerate for at least 2 hours or as long as 8, turning the bag occasionally.

2 Combine the remaining $\frac{3}{4}$ cup yogurt, the dry milk, ground flaxseed, and remaining $\frac{1}{8}$ teaspoon salt in another container. Stir until smooth. Add the cucumber, scallions, and mint. Stir. Cover securely and refrigerate for up to 8 hours.

3 Preheat a charcoal or gas grill or a stove-top grill pan. Remove the chicken from the refrigerator 30 minutes before grilling. Brush the grill with a little oil and wipe off excess. Place the chicken on the grill and cook for about 4 minutes on each side, or until a thermometer inserted in the thickest portion registers 160°F and the juices run clear. Remove the chicken and allow it to sit for 5 minutes before cutting it into thin slices. Serve accompanied with the cucumber-yogurt sauce.

Makes 4 servings

PER SERVING: 152 calories, 24 g protein, 9 g carbohydrates, 2 g fat (0.5 g saturated fat), 51 mg cholesterol, 177 mg sodium

Chicken Jambalaya

PREP TIME: 20 MINUTES ◆ TOTAL TIME: 47 MINUTES + STANDING TIME

½ red bell pepper, chopped
4 scallions, sliced
3 cloves garlic, finely chopped
2 teaspoons Creole seasoning
1 teaspoon canola oil
1 can (14 ounces) no-salt-added diced tomatoes
1 cup no-salt-added canned small red beans, rinsed and drained

⅛ teaspoon salt
½ pound boneless, skinless chicken breast, cut into ¼"-thick strips across the grain
4 ounces reduced-fat Italian chicken or turkey sausage, cut into 8 pieces
3 tablespoons quick brown rice
Hot-pepper sauce

FAT-FIGHTING
4

5 g fiber
- - - - - - - - - - -
44 mg calcium
- - - - - - - - - - -
0 IU vitamin D
- - - - - - - - - - -
20 mg omega-3s
- - - - - - - - - - -

1 Combine the bell pepper, scallions, garlic, seasoning, and oil in a deep, wide nonstick skillet. Cover and set over medium heat. Cook, stirring occasionally, for 5 minutes, or until the pepper starts to soften. Reduce the heat if the pepper starts to brown. Add the tomatoes, beans, and salt. Stir. Simmer for 5 minutes to blend the flavors.

2 Add the chicken, sausage, and rice, spooning some of the tomatoes on top. Cover and simmer for 10 minutes, or until the chicken is no longer pink and the rice is tender. Remove from the heat and allow to sit, covered, for 5 minutes for flavors to blend. Serve with hot-pepper sauce at the table.

Makes 4 servings

PER SERVING: 220 calories, 24 g protein, 18 g carbohydrates, 5 g total fat (1 g saturated fat), 58 mg cholesterol, 634 mg sodium*

✳ Limit sodium to less than 2,300 mg per day.

Balsamic Chicken

PREP TIME: 10 MINUTES ◆ TOTAL TIME: 31 MINUTES

4 boneless, skinless chicken breast halves
   (about 1½ pounds)
½ teaspoon dried thyme
4 teaspoons canola oil
1 white onion, cut into wedges
1 red onion, cut into wedges
4 scallions, diagonally sliced into
   ½" pieces

2 tablespoons balsamic vinegar
¾ cup fat-free, reduced-sodium
   chicken broth
1 bag (6 ounces) baby spinach
½ cup crumbled reduced-fat feta cheese

1 Sprinkle the chicken with the thyme. Heat the oil in a large nonstick skillet over medium-high heat. Cook the chicken for 5 to 7 minutes, turning once, or until well browned. Remove to a plate.

2 Cook the onions and scallions in the same skillet, stirring, for 5 to 7 minutes, or until browned. Add the vinegar and cook for 1 minute, stirring to loosen any brown bits. Add the broth and bring to a boil. Return the chicken to the skillet, reduce the heat to medium-low, cover, and simmer for 10 minutes, or until a thermometer inserted in the thickest portion registers 160°F and the juices run clear.

3 Place the spinach on a serving platter. Top with the chicken-and-onion mixture and sprinkle with the cheese.

Makes 4 servings

PER SERVING: 315 calories, 45 g protein, 13 g carbohydrates, 9 g fat (2 g saturated fat), 104 mg cholesterol, 504 mg sodium

FAT-
FIGHTING
4

4 g fiber

127 mg
calcium

0 IU
vitamin D

50 mg
omega-3s

Chicken Normandy

PREP TIME: 15 MINUTES ◆ TOTAL TIME: 42 MINUTES

1 teaspoon dried thyme, crushed
¼ teaspoon salt
¼ teaspoon ground black pepper
¾ pound boneless, skinless chicken
    breast halves, cut to 3-ounce portions
4 ounces reduced-fat Jarlsberg cheese,
    cut into 4 pieces (each about
    3" x 1½" x ½")

4 apples, halved, cored, and sliced
3 leeks (white and tender portion of
    green), halved lengthwise, rinsed well,
    and cut into thin lengthwise strips
2 tablespoons white balsamic vinegar or
    apple juice

FAT-FIGHTING 4

6 g fiber

270 mg calcium

0 IU vitamin D

110 mg omega-3s

1 Preheat the oven to 375°F. Combine the thyme, salt, and pepper in a small bowl.

2 Place a chicken breast on a cutting board and, working parallel to the board, cut a pocket in the breast, being sure not to cut all the way through. Slide a piece of cheese in the pocket and seal with a wooden pick. Repeat with the remaining breasts and cheese. Rub the thyme mixture over the breasts.

3 Heat a large nonstick, ovenproof skillet coated generously with cooking spray over medium-high heat. Cook the chicken, turning once, for 5 to 6 minutes, or until browned. Remove to a plate. Recoat the skillet with cooking spray and place over medium-high heat. Add the apples and leeks and cook, stirring, for 6 minutes, or until well browned. Add the vinegar, stirring to break up any brown bits.

4 Place the chicken over the apples and bake for 15 minutes, or until the chicken is no longer pink and the juices run clear.

Makes 4 servings

PER SERVING: 308 calories, 30 g protein, 36 g carbohydrates, 5 g fat (2 g saturated fat), 59 mg cholesterol, 349 mg sodium

Santa Fe Chicken

PREP TIME: 10 MINUTES ◆ TOTAL TIME: 3 HOURS 30 MINUTES–8 HOURS

1 can (15 ounces) no-salt-added black beans, rinsed and drained
1 jar (16 ounces) fresh salsa, from the supermarket
1 teaspoon dried oregano
¾ pound boneless, skinless chicken breast halves, cut to 3-ounce portions
½ teaspoon ground cumin
¼ cup chopped cilantro
1 cup shredded reduced-fat Monterey Jack Cheese

1 Combine the beans, salsa, and oregano in a 3- to 6-quart slow cooker. Top with the chicken breasts and sprinkle with the cumin. Cover and cook on high for 3½ to 4 hours or on low for 7 to 8 hours.

2 Place 1 chicken portion on each of 4 plates. Stir the cilantro into the bean mixture. Divide over the chicken and sprinkle with the cheese.

Makes 4 servings

PER SERVING: 278 calories, 31 g protein, 20 g carbohydrates, 7 g fat (4 g saturated fat), 70 mg cholesterol, 714 mg sodium

MAKE IT A MEAL
Serve with Sweet Potato Crisps (page 157).

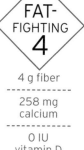

FAT-FIGHTING **4**

4 g fiber
- - - - - - - - -
258 mg calcium
- - - - - - - - -
0 IU vitamin D
- - - - - - - - -
40 mg omega-3s
- - - - - - - - -

Enchiladas Suiza

8 corn tortillas (6" each)
1 red bell pepper, chopped
1 zucchini, chopped
1 bunch scallions, chopped
2 cloves garlic, minced
8 ounces cooked, shredded chicken or
   turkey breast (about 1¼ cups)

1 cup shredded, reduced-fat Colby and
   Monterey Jack cheese
1 jar (16 ounces) salsa verde
½ cup fat-free Greek-style yogurt

FAT-FIGHTING 4

4 g fiber

498 mg calcium

0 IU vitamin D

70 mg omega-3s

1 Preheat the oven to 325°F. Coat a 13" × 9" baking dish with cooking spray. Wrap the tortillas in paper towels. Set aside.

2 Heat a large nonstick skillet coated with cooking spray over medium-high heat. Cook the pepper, zucchini, scallions, and garlic for 5 minutes, stirring, or until browned and tender. Stir in the chicken and cook for 2 minutes. Remove from the heat and stir in ½ cup of the cheese.

3 Spread ¼ cup of the salsa on the bottom of the baking dish. Microwave the tortillas on high for 30 seconds. Place ⅓ cup of the chicken mixture down the center of each

tortilla, then roll up. Place the tortillas, seam side down, in the baking dish. Pour the salsa over the tortillas and sprinkle with the remaining ½ cup cheese. Bake for 15 to 20 minutes, or until heated through and the cheese melts. Place 2 tortillas on each plate and top each with 1 tablespoon of the yogurt.

Makes 4 servings

PER SERVING: 351 calories, 32 g protein, 34 g carbohydrates, 9 g fat (4 g saturated fat), 63 mg cholesterol, 997 mg sodium*

∗ Limit sodium to less than 2,300 mg per day.

Southwest Pan-Seared Chicken with Pinto Beans

PREP TIME: 15 MINUTES ◆ COOK TIME: 45 MINUTES

3 teaspoons canola oil

1 teaspoon ground cumin

1 teaspoon dried oregano

1/8 teaspoon + pinch of salt

3/4 pound boneless, skinless chicken breast

1/2 red or yellow bell pepper, chopped

1/2 onion, chopped

3 cloves garlic, finely chopped

1 can (15 ounces) reduced-sodium pinto beans, rinsed and drained

3/4 cup fat-free, reduced-sodium chicken broth

4 wedges lime

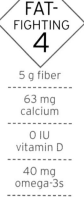

FAT-FIGHTING 4

5 g fiber

63 mg calcium

0 IU vitamin D

40 mg omega-3s

1 Combine 1 teaspoon of the oil, 1/2 teaspoon of the cumin, 1/2 teaspoon of the oregano, and a pinch of salt on a plate. Add the chicken and rub to coat evenly with the mixture.

2 Heat a large skillet over medium-high heat. Add the remaining 2 teaspoons oil and heat for 1 minute. Add the pepper, onion, garlic, 1/8 teaspoon salt, and the remaining 1/2 teaspoon cumin and 1/2 teaspoon oregano. Cover and cook, stirring occasionally, for 5 minutes, or until the vegetables are golden. Add the beans and 1/2 cup of the broth. Cover and reduce the heat so the mixture simmers. Cook for 10 minutes to flavor the beans.

3 Meanwhile, heat a nonstick skillet over high heat. Place the chicken in the skillet. Cook for 5 minutes, or until browned on bottom. Flip and cook, weighted with a bacon or panini press, for 4 to 5 minutes, or until a thermometer inserted in the thickest portion registers 160°F and the juices run clear. Remove to a cutting surface. Let rest for 5 minutes.

4 Add the remaining 1/4 cup broth to the chicken skillet and scrape up any browned particles in the pan. Add to the bean mixture. Bring to a simmer. Smash some of the beans with the back of a large spoon to thicken the mixture. Spoon the beans onto 4 dinner plates. Cut the chicken into thin, diagonal slices across the grain. Fan out over the beans. Place a lime wedge on each plate for squeezing at the table.

Makes 4 servings

PER SERVING: 204 calories, 24 g protein, 15 g carbohydrates, 5 g fat (1 g saturated fat), 49 mg cholesterol, 224 mg sodium

MAKE IT AGAIN

For a tasty lunch, reheat a half portion in the microwave. Spoon it into a heated 6" corn tortilla and top with a tablespoon of fat-free plain yogurt.

Slow-Cooked Chili Verde

PREP TIME: 25 MINUTES ◆ TOTAL TIME: 4-8 HOURS

1 pound boneless, skinless
    chicken breasts
1 large onion, chopped
1 green bell pepper, chopped
2 ribs celery, chopped
2 cloves garlic, minced
1 teaspoon ground cumin
1 teaspoon dried oregano

1 jar (16 ounces) salsa verde
1 cup frozen shelled edamame, thawed
12 (6") corn tortillas, each cut into 6
    wedges
$\frac{1}{2}$ cup chopped cilantro
8 ounces shredded, reduced-fat, white
    Cheddar or Monterey Jack cheese

1 Place the chicken, onion, pepper, celery, and garlic in a 4- to 6-quart slow cooker. Sprinkle with the cumin and oregano and top with the salsa verde. Cover and cook on high for 4 to 5 hours or on low for 6 to 8 hours.

2 During the last 20 minutes of cooking, remove the chicken to a cutting board and add the edamame (if cooking on low, increase the heat to high). Shred the chicken with two forks. Stir into the chili.

3 Meanwhile, preheat the oven to 400°F. Coat a baking sheet with cooking spray. Place the tortillas on the baking sheet and coat with cooking spray. Bake for 3 minutes, or until crisp and lightly browned.

4 Finish the chili by stirring in the cilantro. Spoon into 6 bowls and top with the cheese. Serve with the tortillas.

Makes 6 servings

PER SERVING: 302 calories, 23 g protein, 40 g carbohydrates, 4 g fat (0.5 g saturated fat), 44 mg cholesterol, 391 mg sodium

FAT-
FIGHTING
4

5 g fiber

53 mg
calcium

0 IU
vitamin D

30 mg
omega-3s

NOTE
Using frozen chicken breasts in the slow cooker keeps them from overcooking.

Stir-Fry Chicken with Pineapple and Red Peppers

PREP TIME: 25 MINUTES ◆ TOTAL TIME: 35 MINUTES

1 tablespoon cornstarch
½ cup fat-free, reduced-sodium chicken broth
1 tablespoon reduced-sodium soy sauce
2 teaspoons grated fresh ginger
3 teaspoons canola oil
½ large onion, chopped into 1" pieces
½ large red or yellow bell pepper, cut into thin slices

3 cloves garlic, finely chopped
3 cups chopped broccoli raab
¾ pound boneless, skinless chicken breast, cut into thin strips
½ cup canned pineapple chunks, drained
1 tablespoon ground flaxseed

FAT-FIGHTING 4

2 g fiber

---

56 mg calcium

---

0 IU vitamin D

---

850 mg omega-3s

---

1 Place the cornstarch in a bowl. While whisking, gradually add the broth until the cornstarch is dissolved. Stir in the soy sauce and ginger and set aside.

2 Heat a nonstick wok or large skillet over medium-high heat. Add 1 teaspoon of the oil and heat until the oil shimmers. Add the onion and pepper. Cook, tossing, for 2 to 3 minutes, or until crisp-tender. Add the garlic. Toss until fragrant. Add the broccoli raab. Toss for 2 minutes, or until the broccoli raab is wilted. Transfer the vegetables to a platter.

3 Return the pan to the heat. Add the remaining 2 teaspoons oil and heat.

Add the chicken. Cook, without tossing, for 1 minute, or until browned on the bottom. Toss and cook for 1 to 2 minutes, or until most of the pink is gone. Add the sauce. Cook, stirring constantly, for 1 minute, or until thickened. Add the pineapple, reserved vegetables, and flaxseed to the pan. Toss just to combine.

Makes 4 servings

PER SERVING: 177 calories, 22 g protein, 9 g carbohydrates, 6 g total fat (1 g saturated fat), 49 mg cholesterol, 275 mg sodium

CHAPTER 9

SEAFOOD

Veracruz Shrimp Tacos

PREP TIME 15 MINUTES ◆ TOTAL TIME 35 MINUTES

¾ pound medium shrimp, peeled
12 scallions, cut in 1½" pieces
2 teaspoons canola oil
1 teaspoon dried oregano
¾ cup grape tomatoes, halved
½ ripe avocado, sliced

¼ cup chopped cilantro
2 tablespoons ground flaxseed
Juice of 1 lime
Pinch of salt
8 corn tortillas (6" diameter)
Hot-pepper sauce

FAT-FIGHTING 4

10 g fiber

---

98 mg
calcium

---

129 IU
vitamin D

1,400 mg
omega-3s

---

1 Toss the shrimp, scallions, oil, and oregano in a bowl. Set aside for 15 minutes.

2 Combine the tomatoes, avocado, cilantro, flaxseed, lime juice, and salt in another bowl. Set aside.

3 Preheat a perforated grill rack set over a grill. Wearing a protective mitt, brush the grill rack with a little oil and wipe off the excess. Place the reserved shrimp and scallions on the grill rack. Cook for 2 minutes more, or until the shrimp are browned on the bottom. Flip and cook for 2 minutes more, or until opaque. Remove to a plate.

4 Meanwhile, place the tortillas directly on the grill. Cook for about 1 minute on each side, or until warm and starting to puff. Place 2 tortillas on each of 4 plates. Divide the shrimp and scallions evenly on the tortillas. Top evenly with the reserved salsa. Pass the hot-pepper sauce at the table.

Makes 4 servings

PER SERVING: 423 calories, 26 g protein, 53 g carbohydrates, 12 g fat (1 g saturated fat), 129 mg cholesterol, 360 mg sodium

Shrimp Provençal

PREP TIME: 15 MINUTES ◆ TOTAL TIME: 43 MINUTES

1 tablespoon canola oil

1 onion, halved, cut into wedges

1 zucchini, halved lengthwise,
    cut into chunks

3 cloves garlic, finely chopped

2 teaspoons herbes de Provence

1 cup no-salt-added diced tomatoes

1 cup canned small white beans, rinsed
    and drained

1 tablespoon ground flaxseed

¼ teaspoon salt

¾ pound large shrimp, peeled

¼ teaspoon red-pepper flakes

① Heat a large nonstick skillet over medium-high heat. Add the oil and heat for 1 minute. Add the onion and zucchini. Cover and cook, stirring occasionally, for about 10 minutes, or until the onion and zucchini are browned. Add the garlic and herbes de Provence. Cook for 1 minute, or until fragrant. Add the tomatoes (with juice), beans, flaxseed, and salt. Stir. Cover and simmer gently for 10 minutes to blend the flavors.

② Add the shrimp to the pan. Stir. Cover and simmer for 4 to 6 minutes, or until the shrimp are opaque. Sprinkle with the red-pepper flakes and serve.

Makes 4 servings (6 cups)

PER SERVING: 207 calories, 23 g protein, 18 g carbohydrates, 6 fat (1 g saturated fat), 129 mg cholesterol, 536 mg sodium

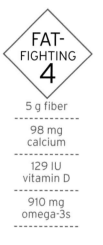

FAT-FIGHTING
4

5 g fiber

98 mg calcium

129 IU vitamin D

910 mg omega-3s

Shrimp Arrabiata

PREP TIME: 15 MINUTES ◆ COOK TIME: 4-7 HOURS

1 can (28 ounces) whole tomatoes
   in thick puree
1 large onion, chopped
1 red bell pepper, chopped
3 cloves garlic, minced
1 teaspoon dried oregano

1 teaspoon dried basil
¼ teaspoon crushed red pepper
1 pound medium shrimp, peeled and
   deveined
6 ounces whole grain spaghetti
   (such as Barilla Plus)

**FAT-
FIGHTING
4**

7 g fiber

136 mg
calcium

151 IU
vitamin D

3,520 mg
omega-3s

MAKE IT
FAST

1 Combine the tomatoes, onion, pepper, garlic, oregano, basil, and crushed red pepper in a 4- to 6-quart slow cooker. Cook on high for 4 to 6 hours or on low for 5 to 7 hours.

2 Add the shrimp and cook for 30 minutes, or until opaque (if cooking on low, increase the heat to high).

3 Meanwhile, prepare the pasta according to package directions. Drain. Divide among 4 plates and top with the sauce.

Makes 4 servings

PER SERVING: 320 calories, 30 g protein, 44 g carbohydrates, 3 g fat (0.5 g saturated fat), 151 mg cholesterol, 453 mg sodium

Shrimp Stir-Fry with Sugar Snap Peas in Peanut Sauce

PREP TIME: 20 MINUTES ◆ TOTAL TIME: 28 MINUTES

2 tablespoons omega-3-enriched peanut butter
1/4 cup warm water
2 teaspoons reduced-sodium soy sauce
1 teaspoon honey
1 teaspoon grated fresh ginger
1 clove garlic, finely chopped

2 teaspoons canola oil
1 1/2 cups sugar snap peas
1/2 cup shredded carrot
4 scallions, sliced
3/4 pound peeled shrimp
1 tablespoon flaxseed oil

FAT-FIGHTING 4

2 g fiber

82 mg calcium

129 IU vitamin D

2,480 mg omega-3s

MAKE IT FAST

① Place the peanut butter in a small bowl. Gradually add the water while whisking constantly until incorporated. Whisk in the soy sauce, honey, ginger, and garlic. Set aside.

② Heat a large nonstick skillet over medium-high heat. Add the canola oil and heat for 1 minute. Add the snap peas, carrot, and scallions. Toss. Cook, tossing occasionally, for 1 to 2 minutes, or until crisp-tender. Add the shrimp. Cook, tossing, for 2 minutes, or until they start to turn opaque. Add the reserved sauce. Reduce the heat to low. Cook for 1 minute, or until the mixture is hot. Remove from the heat and stir in the flaxseed oil.

Makes 4 servings

PER SERVING: 222 calories, 20 g protein, 9 g carbohydrates, 12 g fat (1.5 g saturated fat), 129 mg cholesterol, 270 mg sodium

MAKE IT AGAIN
Serve any leftovers as a lunch salad on a bed of baby spinach. Drizzle lightly with wine vinegar.

Lime-Ginger Scallops

PREP TIME: 15 MINUTES ◆ TOTAL TIME: 30 MINUTES

3 tablespoons lime juice
2 teaspoons honey
1 tablespoon grated fresh ginger
2 carrots, julienned

2 ribs celery, julienned
1 red onion, cut into thin wedges
1 pound bay scallops
¼ cup chopped cilantro (optional)

1 Whisk together the lime juice, honey, and ginger in a small bowl. Set aside. Coat a large, nonstick skillet with cooking spray and heat over medium-high heat. Add the carrots, celery, and onion and cook for 8 minutes, stirring frequently. Place on a serving plate and keep warm.

2 Recoat the pan with cooking spray and cook the scallops over medium-high heat for 5 minutes, stirring, or until browned and opaque. Stir in the reserved lime mixture, stirring to loosen the brown bits. Stir in the cilantro, if using. Serve over the vegetables.

Makes 4 servings

PER SERVING: 141 calories, 20 g protein, 13 g carbohydrates, 1 g fat (0.5 g saturated fat), 37 mg cholesterol, 221 mg sodium

FAT-FIGHTING 4

2 g fiber
---
54 mg calcium
---
0 IU vitamin D
---
230 mg omega-3s

MAKE IT FAST

Indian-Spiced Scallops

PREP TIME: 10 MINUTES ◆ TOTAL TIME: 35 MINUTES

1 pound fresh or frozen sea or bay scallops
2 teaspoons garam masala
2 teaspoons canola oil
1 large onion, halved lengthwise and sliced

1 red bell pepper, cut into thin strips
1/2 cup unsweetened apple juice
1/4 cup fat-free Greek-style yogurt
1/4 cup chopped cilantro

FAT-
FIGHTING
4

1 g fiber
- - - - - - - - - -
50 mg
calcium
- - - - - - - - - -
0 IU
vitamin D
- - - - - - - - - -
240 mg
omega-3s
- - - - - - - - - -

1 Toss together the scallops and garam masala in a medium bowl.

2 Heat the oil in a large nonstick skillet over medium-high heat. Cook the scallops for 4 to 10 minutes (depending on the size of the scallops), turning occasionally, or until browned and opaque. Remove to a plate.

3 Add the onion and pepper to the same skillet and cook, stirring, for 6 minutes, or until well browned. Stir in the apple juice and cook, stirring to loosen the brown bits, for 3 minutes. Return the scallops and any accumulated juices to the pan. Remove from the heat. Let stand for 2 minutes. Stir in the yogurt and cilantro. Serve immediately.

Makes 4 servings

PER SERVING: 167 calories, 21 g protein, 12 g carbohydrates, 3 g fat (0.5 g saturated fat), 37 mg cholesterol, 202 mg sodium

NOTE

Garam masala, a blend of ground spices, is a commonly used seasoning in Indian cuisine. You can find it in Indian groceries and in specialty stores.

Crab Gumbo

PREP TIME: 15 MINUTES ◆ TOTAL TIME: 2–5 HOURS

2 cups fat-free, reduced-sodium
　chicken broth
1 large onion, chopped
1 green bell pepper, chopped
2 ribs celery, chopped
2 carrots, chopped
3 plum tomatoes, seeded and chopped

1 tablespoon Worcestershire sauce
1 teaspoon dried thyme
1 teaspoon dried oregano
¼ teaspoon ground red pepper
1 (10-ounce) package frozen okra
2 cans (6 ounces each) crabmeat
2 cups cooked brown rice

Makes 4 servings

1 Combine the broth, onion, bell pepper, celery, carrots, tomatoes, Worcestershire sauce, thyme, oregano, and ground red pepper in a 3- to 6-quart slow cooker. Cover and cook on low for 5 to 6 hours or on high for 2 to 3 hours.

2 Add the okra and crab and cook for 1 hour on low or ½ hour on high heat. Divide into 4 bowls and top each with ½ cup rice.

PER SERVING: 267 calories, 23 g protein, 39 g carbohydrates, 2 g fat (0.5 g saturated fat), 76 mg cholesterol, 602 mg sodium*

＊ Limit sodium to less than 2,300 mg per day.

FAT-
FIGHTING
4

6 g fiber
- - - - - - - - - - - - -
201 mg
calcium
- - - - - - - - - - - - -
0 IU
vitamin D
- - - - - - - - - - - - -
0 mg
omega-3s
- - - - - - - - - - - - -

Portuguese Mussel Stew

PREP TIME: 15 MINUTES ◆ TOTAL TIME: 35 MINUTES

1 large onion, chopped
1 teaspoon canola oil
3 large cloves garlic, finely chopped
1 can (14.5 ounces) no-salt-added
   diced tomatoes
1 cup no-salt-added canned chickpeas,
   rinsed and drained
½ cup fat-free, reduced-sodium
   chicken broth

2 tablespoons light omega-3-enriched
   mayonnaise
⅛-¼ teaspoon prepared red-pepper
   paste
12 thin slices whole wheat baguette,
   toasted
3 cups coarsely chopped kale
2 pounds mussels in shells

FAT-
FIGHTING
4

7 g fiber
- - - - - - - - - -
139 mg
calcium
- - - - - - - - - -
0 IU
vitamin D
- - - - - - - - - -
1,050 mg
omega-3s
- - - - - - - - - -

1 Combine the onion and oil in a deep, wide skillet. Cover and set over medium heat. Cook, stirring occasionally, for 5 minutes, or until the onion starts to soften. Add the garlic and cook, stirring, for 1 minute, or until fragrant. Add the tomatoes, chickpeas, and broth. Simmer for about 5 minutes to allow the flavors to blend.

2 Meanwhile, combine the mayonnaise and red-pepper paste in a small bowl. Stir. Spread on the toasts. Set aside.

3 Add the kale to the skillet with the tomato mixture. Cover and cook for 2 minutes, or until the kale is wilted. Add the mussels and stir. Cover and cook at a brisk simmer for 5 minutes, or until the mussels open. Discard any unopened shells.

4 Spoon the mixture with broth into 4 large bowls. Top with the toasts.

Makes 4 servings

PER SERVING: 384 calories, 23 g protein, 51 g carbohydrates, 10 g fat (1 g saturated fat), 34 mg cholesterol, 690 mg sodium*

∗ Limit sodium to less than 2,300 mg per day.

NOTE
The mussels can be served in the shell or removed before serving. To remove, break off half a shell that has no mussel attached. Use it as a scoop/cutter to release the remaining mussels from the shells. Discard the shells.

Clam-and-Chickpea Paella

PREP TIME: 15 MINUTES ◆ TOTAL TIME: 35 MINUTES

1 small onion, chopped

½ red bell pepper, chopped

3 cloves garlic, finely chopped

1 teaspoon paprika

1 teaspoon canola oil

1 cup no-salt-added canned chickpeas, rinsed and drained

1 cup fat-free, reduced-sodium chicken broth

½ cup quick brown rice

3 cups baby spinach

2 cans (10 ounces each) baby clams, drained and rinsed

Ground black pepper

1 tablespoon flaxseed oil

FAT-FIGHTING 4

5 g fiber

- - - - - - - - - - - -

164 mg calcium

- - - - - - - - - - - -

0 IU vitamin D

- - - - - - - - - - - -

1,820 g omega-3s

- - - - - - - - - - - -

① Combine the onion, bell pepper, garlic, paprika, and oil in a deep, wide pot. Cover and set over medium heat. Cook, stirring occasionally, for 5 minutes, or until the pepper starts to soften, reducing the heat if the the pepper starts to brown. Add the chickpeas, broth, and rice. Stir. Cover and simmer for 10 minutes, or until most of the broth is absorbed.

② Stir in the spinach. Cook for 1 minute, or until the spinach is partially wilted. Stir in the clams. Cover and simmer for 2 minutes, or until the clams are heated through.

Remove from the heat. Season to taste with the black pepper. Stir in the flaxseed oil.

Makes 4 servings

PER SERVING: 260 calories, 20 g protein, 29 g carbohydrates, 8 g fat (1.5 g saturated fat), 74 mg cholesterol, 639 mg sodium*

- -

✳ Limit sodium to less than 2,300 mg per day.

MAKE IT AGAIN

Any leftover paella can be used as an omelet filling.

Seared Tuna with Tomatoes and Arugula

PREP TIME: 10 MINUTES ◆ TOTAL TIME: 25 MINUTES

2 tuna steaks (about 8 ounces each), each cut in half
¼ teaspoon salt
¼ teaspoon ground black pepper
1 large onion, cut into wedges
2 cloves garlic, chopped
1 cup cherry tomatoes, halved
2 tablespoons balsamic vinegar
1 bag (5 ounces) baby arugula

1 Sprinkle the tuna with the salt and pepper. Coat a large nonstick skillet with cooking spray and heat over medium-high heat. Add the tuna and cook for 6 minutes, turning once, or until just opaque. Remove to a plate and keep warm.

2 Recoat the skillet with cooking spray. Cook the onion and garlic over medium-high heat for 4 minutes, or until lightly browned. Add the tomatoes and vinegar and cook for 3 minutes.

3 Divide the arugula among 4 plates. Top each with a tuna steak and the tomato mixture.

Makes 4 servings

PER SERVING: 201 calories, 28 g protein, 7.7 g carbohydrates, 6 g fat (1.5 g saturated fat), 43 mg cholesterol, 204 mg sodium

FAT-FIGHTING 4

2 g fiber

81 mg calcium

0 IU vitamin D

1,390 mg omega-3s

MAKE IT FAST

Tabbouleh with Tuna and Red Pepper

PREP TIME: 25 MINUTES ◆ TOTAL TIME: 45 MINUTES + MARINATING AND STANDING TIME

1 tablespoon canola oil
Grated peel and juice of 1 navel orange
12 ounces tuna steak
1 red bell pepper, cut into strips
$\frac{1}{2}$ small onion, coarsely chopped
$1\frac{3}{4}$ cups peeled and cubed acorn squash
$\frac{3}{4}$ cup fat-free, reduced-sodium chicken or vegetable broth

$\frac{1}{2}$ cup fine tabbouleh
1 tablespoon ground flaxseed
$\frac{1}{4}$ teaspoon salt
$\frac{1}{4}$ cup chopped parsley
Ground black pepper

FAT-FIGHTING 4

6 g fiber

52 mg calcium

0 IU vitamin D

1,490 mg omega-3s

1 Preheat the grill.

2 Combine $\frac{1}{2}$ tablespoon of the oil, the grated orange peel, and juice in a zip-top bag. Place the tuna and bell pepper in the bag and massage to thoroughly coat with the marinade. Set aside for 15 minutes, flipping occasionally.

3 Remove the bell pepper from the marinade. Place on a perforated grill pan set over indirect heat on the grill. Stir occasionally.

4 Combine the onion and remaining $\frac{1}{2}$ tablespoon oil in a skillet. Cook over medium heat, stirring occasionally, for 5 minutes, or until softened. Add the squash and broth. Cover and simmer for 5 minutes, or until the squash is tender but still slightly firm. Carefully pour the marinade from the bag into the pan. Add the tabbouleh, flaxseed, and salt. Cover and reduce the heat so the mixture simmers for 5 minutes, or until the tabbouleh is cooked. Stir in the parsley. Remove from the heat and set aside. Season to taste with the black pepper.

5 Grill the tuna for 2 minutes per side on direct heat, or until seared. Move to indirect heat and cook for 6 to 8 minutes, or until the tuna yields only slightly when pressed. Remove and allow it to sit for 5 minutes. Remove the pepper strips from the grill.

6 Divide the tabbouleh among 4 plates. Cut the tuna into very thin diagonal slices. Fan out over the tabbouleh. Top with the pepper strips.

Makes 4 servings

PER SERVING: 273 calories, 24 g protein, 25 g carbohydrates, 8 g fat (1.5 g saturated fat), 32 mg cholesterol, 272 mg sodium

Tuna Cakes

PREP TIME: 15 MINUTES ◆ TOTAL TIME: 35 MINUTES

2 cans (12 ounces each) water-packed
tuna, drained
1 slice whole wheat bread, toasted and
finely chopped
2 tablespoons finely chopped, roasted red
bell pepper (from a jar)

2 scallions, finely chopped
1 omega-3-enriched egg, beaten
1 tablespoon omega-3-enriched
mayonnaise
1½ teaspoons lemon-pepper seasoning

1 Preheat the oven to 350°F. Coat a
baking sheet with cooking spray.

2 Combine the tuna, bread, pepper,
scallions, egg, mayonnaise, and seasoning
in a bowl. With 2 forks, toss the mixture,
breaking up the large chunks of tuna, to
blend well. With clean hands, shape into
8 cakes. Place on the baking sheet.

3 Bake for 18 to 20 minutes, or until the
cakes are golden and heated through.

Makes 8 servings (1 cake each)

PER SERVING: 113 calories, 17 g protein,
2 g carbohydrates, 3 g fat (1 g saturated fat),
52 mg cholesterol, 368 mg sodium

MAKE IT AHEAD

Cool the tuna cakes and place on
a tray. Place in the freezer for
24 hours, or until frozen solid. Pack
in zip-top freezer bags for longer
storage. Thaw and reheat in the
microwave for a quick lunch.

FAT-
FIGHTING
4

0 g fiber

19 mg
calcium

2 IU
vitamin D

710 mg
omega-3s

Sesame-Ginger Tuna Kebabs

PREP TIME: 30 MINUTES ◆ TOTAL TIME: 36 MINUTES + MARINATING TIME

1 pound tuna fillet, cut into 16 cubes
16 medium mushrooms
1/2 cup light Asian dressing

16 cherry tomatoes
8 scallions, trimmed and cut into
**   2" pieces**

1 Soak 4 wooden skewers in water for 30 minutes. Combine the tuna, mushrooms, and dressing in a bowl, tossing to coat. Set aside for 15 minutes. Coat a grill rack or broiler rack with cooking spray. Preheat the grill or broiler.

2 Alternately thread 4 tuna cubes, 4 mushrooms, 4 cherry tomatoes, and 2 scallion pieces onto each skewer. Grill or broil for 6 minutes, turning once, or until the fish flakes easily when tested with a fork. (Brush with the remaining dressing during the first 4 minutes of cooking.)

Makes 4 servings

PER SERVING: 220 calories, 30 g protein, 14 g carbohydrates, 5 g fat (0.5 g saturated fat), 51 mg cholesterol, 54 mg sodium

FAT-FIGHTING 4

2 g fiber
- - - - - - - - - - - - -
49 mg calcium
- - - - - - - - - - - - -
13 IU vitamin D
- - - - - - - - - - - - -
2,000 mg omega-3s
- - - - - - - - - - - - -

MAKE IT A MEAL
Serve with Asian Zucchini Slaw (page 143) and 1/2 cup brown rice.

Smoked Salmon Sushi

PREP TIME: 25 MINUTES ◆ TOTAL TIME: 1 HOUR 10 MINUTES

1⅓ cups water
⅓ cup short-grain brown rice
1 tablespoon rice wine vinegar
3 tablespoons reduced-sodium soy sauce
1 teaspoon wasabi paste
4 sheets roasted nori (seaweed for sushi)
2 carrots, cut into thin strips

1 small cucumber, peeled, halved
   lengthwise, seeded, and cut into
   very thin strips
4 ounces smoked salmon, cut into
   thin strips
3 tablespoons pickled ginger (*gari*),
   cut into thin strips

FAT-
FIGHTING
4

2 g fiber

66 mg
calcium

0 IU
vitamin D

730 mg
omega-3s

① Bring the water and rice to a boil over high heat. Reduce the heat to low, cover, and simmer for 45 minutes, or until tender and the water is absorbed. Remove to a colander or sieve and move the rice to the edges to cool quickly. Place in a medium bowl and toss with the vinegar. Set aside to cool. Combine the soy sauce and wasabi paste in a small bowl.

② Cut the nori sheets diagonally in half to form 2 triangles, using kitchen shears. Place the nori on a flat surface. Divide the rice onto the sheets, spreading to within 1" of the edges. Arrange the strips of carrot and cucumber down the center of the triangle. Top with the salmon and ginger. Brush some water on the 2 equal sides of the triangle and roll to form a cone (similar to an ice-cream cone). Repeat with the remaining cones. Drizzle with the remaining soy mixture.

Makes 4 servings (2 pieces each)

PER SERVING: 211 calories, 21 g protein, 22 g carbohydrates, 4 g fat (1 g saturated fat), 44 mg cholesterol, 643 mg sodium*

✳ Limit sodium to less than 2,300 mg per day.

Balsamic-Glazed Salmon

PREP TIME: 10 MINUTES ◆ TOTAL TIME: 20 MINUTES + MARINATING TIME

2 tablespoons honey
1 tablespoon balsamic vinegar
¼ teaspoon salt

¼ teaspoon ground black pepper
1 pound center-cut salmon fillet, skinned
and cut into 4 equal pieces

1 Combine the honey, vinegar, salt, and pepper in a zip-top bag. Add the salmon, seal, and refrigerate for 30 minutes to 8 hours.

2 Preheat the broiler. Coat the rack of a broiler pan with cooking spray. Place the salmon on the rack, skinned side down, and broil, 6" from the heat, for 6 to 10 minutes or until the fish is opaque.

Makes 4 servings

PER SERVING: 217 calories, 20 g protein, 19 g carbohydrates, 11 g fat (2 g saturated fat), 58 mg cholesterol, 205 mg sodium

FAT-
FIGHTING
4

0 g fiber
- - - - - - - - - - - -
14 mg
calcium
- - - - - - - - - - - -
0 IU
vitamin D
- - - - - - - - - - - -
1,980 mg
omega-3s
- - - - - - - - - - - -

Chinese Salmon

PREP TIME: 10 MINUTES ◆ TOTAL TIME: 20 MINUTES

2 tablespoons packed brown sugar
1 teaspoon Chinese five-spice powder
$\frac{1}{4}$ teaspoon salt

1 pound salmon fillet, skinned and cut into 4 equal pieces

❶ Preheat the broiler. Coat the rack of a broiler pan with cooking spray. Combine the sugar, five-spice powder, and salt in a small bowl.

❷ Place the salmon on the rack, skinned side down, and rub with the spice mixture. Broil, 6" from the heat, for 6 to 10 minutes, or until the fish is opaque.

Makes 4 servings

PER SERVING: 236 calories, 23 g protein, 7 g carbohydrates, 12 g fat (3 g saturated fat), 67 mg cholesterol, 214 mg sodium

FAT-
FIGHTING
4

0 g fiber
----
25 mg
calcium
----
0 IU
vitamin D

2,300 mg
omega-3s

MAKE IT
FAST

Curried Salmon with Cucumber-Radish Raita

PREP TIME: 10 MINUTES ◆ TOTAL TIME: 20 MINUTES

1 cup fat-free Greek-style yogurt
2 tablespoons chopped cilantro
¼ teaspoon ground cumin
1 cucumber, peeled, halved lengthwise, seeded, and thinly sliced crosswise
4 radishes, halved lengthwise and thinly sliced

1 clove garlic, minced
1 pound salmon fillet, skinned and cut into 4 equal pieces
1 teaspoon mild curry powder

1 Stir together the yogurt, cilantro, and cumin in a medium bowl. Stir in the cucumber, radishes, and garlic and set aside. Rub the salmon with the curry powder.

2 Coat a large nonstick skillet with cooking spray. Cook the salmon over medium-high heat, turning once, for 6 to 10 minutes, or until just opaque.

3 Place a salmon fillet on each of 4 plates. Serve with the *raita* (yogurt salad).

Makes 4 servings

PER SERVING: 248 calories, 28 g protein, 4 g carbohydrates, 13 g fat (3 g saturated fat), 67 mg cholesterol, 91 mg sodium

FAT-FIGHTING 4

1 g fiber
----
64 mg calcium
----
0 IU vitamin D

2,280 mg omega-3s

MAKE IT FAST

Pan-Seared Salmon with Fresh Apple-Basil Relish

PREP TIME: 12 MINUTES ◆ TOTAL TIME: 22 MINUTES

1 Gala apple, unpeeled
1/2 cup slivered fresh basil
1/2 rib celery, finely chopped
2 scallions, thinly sliced
1 tablespoon ground flaxseed

1 tablespoon canola oil
2 teaspoons cider or white wine vinegar
1/4 teaspoon salt
3/4 pound salmon fillet, cut into 4 equal
    pieces

FAT-
FIGHTING
4

2 g fiber

- - - - - - - - - - -

36 mg
calcium

- - - - - - - - - - -

0 IU
vitamin D

- - - - - - - - - - -

2,510 mg
omega-3s

- - - - - - - - - - -

MAKE IT
FAST

1 Coarsely shred the apple on a mandoline, in a food processor with a shredding disk, or on the largest holes of a box grater. Transfer to a mixing bowl. There should be 2 cups of shredded apple. Add the basil, celery, scallions, flaxseed, oil, vinegar, and 1/8 teaspoon of the salt. Toss and set aside.

2 Coat a large nonstick skillet with cooking spray and heat over medium-high heat for several minutes, or until hot. Place the salmon in the pan. Season the tops lightly with the remaining 1/8 teaspoon salt. Cook

for 4 minutes, or until browned on the bottom. Flip and cook for 4 to 6 minutes, or until the fish is opaque. Cooking time will vary with the thickness of the fillets. With a spatula, lift off the salmon skin and discard. Divide the relish among 4 plates. Top with the salmon.

Makes 4 servings

PER SERVING: 234 calories, 18 g protein, 9 g carbohydrates, 14 g fat (2 g saturated fat), 50 mg cholesterol, 202 mg sodium

Salmon and Spinach with Penne in Dill Sauce

PREP TIME: 15 MINUTES ◆ TOTAL TIME: 35 MINUTES

¼ cup fat-free ricotta cheese

3 tablespoons nonfat dry milk

3 tablespoons finely chopped fresh dill

1 tablespoon prepared horseradish

½ cup fat-free, reduced-sodium chicken or vegetable broth

1 tablespoon canola oil

½ pound salmon fillet, skinned and cut into 4 equal pieces

1 onion, finely chopped

1 bag (6 ounces) baby spinach, coarsely chopped

⅛ teaspoon salt

3 ounces whole grain penne (such as Barilla Plus)

1 tablespoon ground flaxseed

Ground black pepper

1 Set a medium covered pot of water over high heat. Combine the ricotta, dry milk, dill, and horseradish in a small bowl. Stir until smooth. Gradually stir in ¼ cup of the broth. Set aside.

2 Set a large nonstick skillet over medium-high heat for 1 minute. Add the oil and heat. Place the salmon in the pan. Cook for 4 minutes, or until browned on bottom. Flip. Add the onion to the pan. Stir to coat with oil. Cook for 4 minutes, stirring the onion frequently, or until it starts to color. Add the spinach, salt, and remaining ¼ cup broth. Stir. Cover the pan and reduce the heat so the mixture simmers.

3 When the water comes to a boil, add the pasta. Stir. Cook for 5 minutes, or until al dente. Drain.

4 When the salmon is opaque, remove it to a plate. Stir the reserved ricotta mixture into the spinach mixture. Add the pasta and flaxseed. Season generously with the pepper. Add the salmon and break into large chunks. Toss to mix.

Makes 4 servings

PER SERVING: 279 calories, 20 g protein, 25 g carbohydrates, 11 g fat (2 g saturated fat), 35 mg cholesterol, 291 mg sodium

FAT-FIGHTING
4

5 g fiber

144 mg calcium

0.17 IU vitamin D

2,000 mg omega-3s

Salmon Niçoise

PREP TIME: 15 MINUTES ◆ TOTAL TIME: 45 MINUTES

1½ cups fat-free, reduced-sodium chicken broth
3 large cloves garlic
½ cup green lentils
⅛ teaspoon salt + a pinch
Ground black pepper
¾ pound salmon fillet, skinned and cut into 4 equal pieces

1 cup tiny cauliflower florets
½ cup grape tomatoes, halved
½ cup fat-free plain yogurt
1 tablespoon ground flaxseed
2 teaspoons coarse mustard
1 tablespoon finely chopped parsley

FAT-FIGHTING **4**

5 g fiber

----

71 mg calcium

----

10 IU vitamin D

1,700 mg omega-3s

----

1 Bring the 1¼ cups of the broth and garlic to a boil in a deep skillet. Add the lentils and a pinch of salt. Cover and simmer for 10 minutes.

2 Season the salmon with the pepper and ⅛ teaspoon salt. Place the salmon fillets in the pan. Cover and simmer for 10 minutes, or until the salmon is opaque. Carefully remove the salmon to a plate, scraping any lentils back into the pan. Remove the garlic and place in a small bowl.

3 Stir the cauliflower into the lentils. Cover the pan and cook for 10 minutes, adding some of the reserved broth if needed, or until the lentils are cooked and the cauliflower is crisp-tender. Cook, uncovered, if needed to evaporate any remaining broth. Stir in the tomatoes.

4 Mash the garlic with the back of a spoon. Add the yogurt, flaxseed, and mustard. Stir to combine. Add about two-thirds of the sauce to the lentils. Toss. Spoon the lentil mixture onto 4 plates and top with the salmon and a dollop of the remaining sauce. Sprinkle with the parsley.

Makes 4 servings

PER SERVING: 270 calories, 25 g protein , 19 g carbohydrates, 11 g fat (2 g saturated fat), 51 mg cholesterol, 354 mg sodium

MAKE IT AGAIN
Any leftovers make a delightful chilled salad. Splash with a few drops of lemon juice or vinegar before serving.

Salmon-Broccoli Tetrazzini

PREP TIME: 15 MINUTES ◆ TOTAL TIME: 50 MINUTES + STANDING TIME

$\frac{1}{4}$ cup fat-free ricotta cheese

$\frac{1}{4}$ cup fat-free milk

3 tablespoons nonfat dry milk

$\frac{1}{4}$ cup grated Parmesan cheese

$\frac{1}{4}$ teaspoon salt

$\frac{1}{8}$ teaspoon ground red pepper

$\frac{1}{8}$ teaspoon grated nutmeg

3 ounces whole grain penne (such as Barilla Plus)

2 cups tiny broccoli florets

1 small leek, sliced, white and light-green parts

1 slice ($\frac{3}{4}$ ounce) reduced-fat Swiss cheese, finely chopped

2 cans (6 ounces each) boneless, skinless salmon, drained

1 tablespoon ground flaxseed

FAT-FIGHTING 4

3 g fiber

216 mg calcium

6.4 IU vitamin D

800 mg omega-3s

1 Preheat the oven to 350°F. Coat a 12" × 8" baking dish with cooking spray. Set a covered pot of water over high heat. Combine the ricotta, milk, dry milk, 2 tablespoons of the Parmesan, salt, red pepper, and nutmeg in a small bowl. Stir until smooth. Set aside.

2 Meanwhile, when the water boils, add the pasta. Stir and bring to a boil. Cook for 3 minutes. Add the broccoli and leek. Cook for 2 to 3 minutes, or until the pasta is al dente. Reserve $\frac{1}{2}$ cup of the cooking water before draining the pasta mixture. Drain and return the mixture to the pan. Add the reserved ricotta mixture and the Swiss cheese. Toss to combine the ingredients. Add the salmon, flaxseed, and a few tablespoons of the reserved cooking water to loosen the mixture. It should look fairly wet. Transfer to the baking dish. Sprinkle with the remaining 2 tablespoons Parmesan. Cover the top loosely with foil.

3 Bake for 25 minutes. Remove the foil and bake for about 5 more minutes, or until the tetrazzini is bubbling and golden. Remove and allow to sit for 10 minutes before serving.

Makes 4 servings

PER SERVING: 255 calories, 29 g protein, 24 g carbohydrates, 6 g fat (2 g saturated fat), 42 mg cholesterol, 513 mg sodium

Seared Snapper on Herbed, Mashed Edamame

PREP TIME: 10 MINUTES ◆ TOTAL TIME: 45 MINUTES

1½ cups water
2 cups frozen shelled edamame
4 shallots, minced
½ teaspoon dried tarragon
1 tablespoon fresh lemon juice

1½ pounds snapper, cod, or haddock
fillets, cut into 4 pieces
½ teaspoon salt
½ teaspoon ground black pepper

1 Bring the water, edamame, shallots, and tarragon to a boil in a small saucepan over high heat. Reduce the heat to low, cover, and simmer for 20 minutes, or until very tender. Combine in a blender or food processor and blend or process until smooth, adding the lemon juice and a little water if needed. Return to the saucepan, cover, and keep warm.

2 Sprinkle the fish with the salt and pepper. Coat a large nonstick skillet with cooking spray and heat over medium-high heat. Add the fish and cook, turning once, for 8 to 10 minutes, or until the fish flakes easily.

3 Divide the edamame mixture onto 4 plates. Top each with a piece of fish.

Makes 4 servings

PER SERVING: 279 calories, 43 g protein, 11 g carbohydrates, 5 g fat (0.5 g saturated fat), 63 mg cholesterol, 434 mg sodium

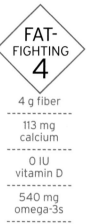

FAT-
FIGHTING
4

4 g fiber
----
113 mg
calcium
----
0 IU
vitamin D
----
540 mg
omega-3s

Chili-Rub Haddock Baked with Sweet Potatoes

PREP TIME: 15 MINUTES ◆ TOTAL TIME: 50 MINUTES

1/4 cup unsweetened applesauce
1 tablespoon ground flaxseed
1 teaspoon grated fresh ginger
1/8 teaspoon + 1/4 teaspoon salt
2 sweet potatoes, peeled and thinly sliced
2 teaspoons chili powder

1 clove garlic, finely chopped
4 (2"-thick) haddock fillets (4 ounces each)
1 tablespoon canola oil
1/4 cup fat-free sour cream
2 scallions, finely sliced

FAT-FIGHTING 4

3 g fiber

83 mg calcium

0 IU vitamin D

680 mg omega-3s

1 Preheat the oven to 375°F. Coat a 12" × 8" baking dish with cooking spray. Add the applesauce, flaxseed, ginger, and 1/8 teaspoon salt. Stir to mix. Add the sweet potatoes and toss thoroughly to coat with the applesauce mixture. Cover with aluminum foil.

2 Bake the potatoes for 20 minutes, or until tender but still slightly firm.

3 Meanwhile, combine the chili powder, garlic, and 1/4 teaspoon salt in a small dish. Toss to mix. Sprinkle over the haddock. Drizzle with the oil. Rub the haddock to coat evenly.

4 Remove the aluminum foil from the baking pan. Place the fillets atop the sweet potato nest. Return, uncovered, to the oven.

Bake for 15 minutes, or until the fish flakes easily.

5 Combine the sour cream and scallions in a small bowl. Plate the potatoes and haddock. Dollop the sour cream mixture on the side.

Makes 4 servings

PER SERVING: 215 calories, 24 g protein, 17 g carbohydrates, 5 g fat (1 g saturated fat), 66 mg cholesterol, 344 mg sodium

MAKE IT AHEAD
The haddock portion of this recipe can be doubled. Cool and store in the refrigerator in an airtight container to use as a filling for fish tacos.

Seared Trout Kalamata

PREP TIME: 10 MINUTES ◆ TOTAL TIME: 20 MINUTES

½ cup fresh whole grain bread crumbs
2 tablespoons ground flaxseed
6 kalamata olives, minced
4 trout fillets (5-6 ounces each)

6 plum tomatoes, quartered lengthwise
2 teaspoons grated lemon peel
¼ teaspoon salt
4 lemon wedges

1 Preheat the oven to 400°F. Coat a large baking sheet with sides with cooking spray.

2 Combine the crumbs, flaxseed, and olives in a small bowl. Place the fillets on one side of the baking sheet and press the crumb mixture on the fillets. Place the tomatoes on the other side of the baking sheet. Coat the tomatoes with cooking spray and sprinkle with the grated lemon peel and salt. Roast for 5 minutes, or until the fish flakes easily.

3 Remove the fish and place 1 fillet on each of 4 plates. Return the tomatoes to the oven and continue roasting for 3 minutes more, or until browned. Serve the tomatoes and a lemon wedge alongside the fish.

Makes 4 servings

PER SERVING: 281 calories, 32 g protein, 10 g carbohydrates, 13 g fat (2 g saturated fat), 82 mg cholesterol, 337 mg sodium

MAKE IT A MEAL
Serve with the Whole Grain Pilaf with Artichokes (page 154).

FAT-
FIGHTING
4

4 g fiber
- - - - - - - - - - - -
109 mg
calcium
- - - - - - - - - - - -
0 IU
vitamin D
- - - - - - - - - - - -
2,180 mg
omega-3s
- - - - - - - - - - - -

MAKE IT
FAST

Baked Stuffed Trout

PREP TIME: 20 MINUTES ◆ TOTAL TIME: 50 MINUTES

4 slices bacon
2 whole trout (1 pound), boned
1/2 small carrot, finely chopped
1/2 small onion, finely chopped
1 teaspoon canola oil
1 slice whole wheat bread, toasted,
    finely chopped

1/2 cup frozen baby peas
1 omega-3-enriched egg, beaten
2 tablespoons chopped parsley
1/4 teaspoon dried thyme
1/8 teaspoon salt
Ground black pepper

FAT-
FIGHTING
4

2 g fiber

43 mg
calcium

4.5 IU
vitamin D

450 mg
omega-3s

1 Preheat the oven to 375°F. Coat a 13" × 9" baking pan with cooking spray. Place 2 slices of the bacon in the pan. Place 1 trout over each slice of bacon. Set aside.

2 Combine the carrot, onion, and oil in a small skillet. Cover and cook over medium-high heat for 5 minutes, or until softened. Remove from the heat to cool slightly. Add the bread, peas, egg, parsley, thyme, and salt. Season to taste with the pepper. Toss to mix.

3 Spoon the stuffing into the trout cavities, packing to fit. Place the remaining bacon slices atop the trout. Cover the pan tightly with aluminum foil. Bake for 25 minutes, or until the fish flakes easily.

4 Remove the pan from the oven and allow the trout to sit for 5 minutes. Remove the foil. Carefully remove the bacon slices to a nonstick skillet and continue to cook over medium-high heat, or until well done. Carefully remove the top fillets from each trout and place on plates. Top each with one-quarter of the stuffing. Transfer the 2 remaining fillets and stuffing to the plates, using a spatula. Top each fillet with a slice of the cooked bacon.

Makes 4 servings

PER SERVING: 175 calories, 16 g protein, 7 g carbohydrates, 9 g fat (2 g saturated fat), 80 mg cholesterol, 366 mg sodium

VEGETARIAN

Personal White Pizza

PREP TIME 10 MINUTES ◆ TOTAL TIME 25 MINUTES

3 large cloves garlic, finely chopped
2 teaspoons canola oil
½ cup fat-free ricotta cheese
2 tablespoons ground flaxseed
2 tablespoons nonfat dry milk

4 (9"-10") 96% fat-free, whole wheat
flour tortillas (such as Mission Foods)
4 tablespoons grated Parmesan cheese
2 slices (¾ ounce each) reduced-fat
Swiss cheese, finely chopped

1 Preheat the oven to 375°F.

2 Combine the garlic and oil in a small microwaveable bowl. Cover with plastic wrap, leaving a vent. Microwave for 1 minute, or until sizzling. Remove and let stand for 5 minutes.

3 Add the ricotta, flaxseed, and dry milk to the garlic mixture. Stir until smooth. Place the tortillas on 1 large or 2 smaller baking sheets. Spread the tortillas evenly with the ricotta mixture. Sprinkle the cheeses evenly over the tortillas.

4 Bake for 15 minutes, or until bubbly and golden.

Makes 4 servings

PER SERVING: 221 calories, 15 g protein, 31 g carbohydrates, 8 g fat (2 g saturated fat), 12 mg cholesterol, 369 mg sodium

FAT-
FIGHTING
4

3 g fiber
- - - - - - - - - - -
301 mg
calcium
- - - - - - - - - - -
0.11 IU
vitamin D
- - - - - - - - - - -
20 mg
omega-3s
- - - - - - - - - - -

MAKE IT
FAST

Black-Bean Enchiladas

PREP TIME: 15 MINUTES ◆ TOTAL TIME: 1 HOUR + STANDING TIME

2 teaspoons canola oil
1 large yellow or red bell pepper, chopped
1 onion, chopped
2 cloves garlic, finely chopped
³⁄₄ teaspoon chili powder
¹⁄₈ teaspoon salt
1 can (15 ounces) black beans, rinsed and drained

2 tablespoons ground flaxseed
1 can (15 ounces) no-salt-added diced tomatoes, drained
¹⁄₂ cup loosely packed chopped cilantro
¹⁄₄ teaspoon red-pepper flakes
8 (6") corn tortillas
¹⁄₂ cup (2 ounces) shredded 75% reduced-fat Cheddar cheese

1 Preheat the oven to 350°F. Coat a 13" × 9" baking dish with cooking spray.

2 Heat a nonstick skillet over medium heat for 1 minute. Add the oil and swirl to coat the bottom of the pan. Add the bell pepper, onion, garlic, chili powder, and salt. Stir. Cover and cook, stirring occasionally, for 5 minutes, or until softened. Add the beans and flaxseed. Cook for 5 minutes, or until simmering. Smash some of the beans with the back of a spoon to thicken the mixture.

3 Combine the tomatoes, cilantro, and red-pepper flakes in a bowl. Stir and set aside.

4 Place the tortillas in a zip-top bag. Seal, leaving a vent. Microwave for 1 to 2 minutes on high power, or until the tortillas are softened. Wearing mitts, carefully remove the tortillas and lay them on a work surface. Dollop equal amounts of the bean mixture in the center of each tortilla. Roll each into a tube. Place seam side down in the baking dish. Spoon the tomato mixture over the enchiladas. Cover tightly with aluminum foil.

5 Bake for 20 minutes. Carefully remove the foil and scatter the cheese evenly over the enchiladas. Bake for another 10 minutes, or until the cheese melts. Remove from the oven and allow the enchiladas to sit for 5 minutes before serving.

Makes 4 servings (2 enchiladas each)

PER SERVING: 284 calories, 8 g protein, 47 g carbohydrates, 7 g fat (4 g saturated fat), 0 mg cholesterol, 409 mg sodium

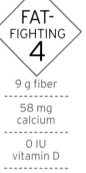

FAT-FIGHTING
4

9 g fiber

58 mg calcium

0 IU vitamin D

930 mg omega-3s

Southwestern Bean and Pumpkin Chili

PREP TIME: 10 MINUTES ◆ TOTAL TIME: 30 MINUTES

2 teaspoons canola oil
1 onion, chopped
1 small red bell pepper, chopped
1 teaspoon ground cumin
1/2 teaspoon dried oregano
1/8 teaspoon salt
1 clove garlic, finely chopped
1 cup canned, unseasoned pumpkin

1 cup no-salt-added canned white beans, rinsed and drained
1 1/2 cups water or fat-free, low-sodium vegetable broth
1 tablespoon flaxseed oil
1/4 cup chopped cilantro
Hot-pepper sauce

1 Heat a pot over medium-high heat. Add the canola oil and heat for 1 minute. Add the onion, bell pepper, cumin, oregano, and salt. Stir. Cover and cook, stirring occasionally, for 5 minutes, or until lightly browned. Add the garlic. Cook for 1 minute. Add the pumpkin, beans, and broth. Reduce the heat so the mixture simmers. Cook for 10 to 12 minutes to blend the flavors.

2 Remove from the heat. Stir in the flaxseed oil. Sprinkle with the cilantro and pass the hot-pepper sauce at the table.

Makes 4 servings

PER SERVING: 137 calories, 5 g protein, 20 g carbohydrates, 6 g fat (1 g saturated fat), 0 mg cholesterol, 356 mg sodium

MAKE IT AGAIN
Any leftover chili can be reheated as a side dish or as filling for tacos.

FAT-FIGHTING 4

6 g fiber

----

69 mg calcium

----

0 IU vitamin D

1,830 mg omega-3s

MAKE IT FAST

Greek Quinoa Toss

PREP TIME: 15 MINUTES ◆ TOTAL TIME: 40 MINUTES

1 cup frozen shelled edamame

1½ cups water

¾ cup quinoa, rinsed

¼ teaspoon salt

2 tablespoons fresh lemon juice

1 tablespoon canola oil

1 tablespoon fresh minced oregano
  or ½ teaspoon dried

1 clove garlic, minced

3 cups baby spinach

1 cup grape tomatoes, halved

¼ cup crumbled reduced-fat feta cheese

1 Prepare the edamame according to package directions. Rinse under cold water and drain.

2 Meanwhile, bring the water to a boil over high heat. Stir in the quinoa and salt and return to a boil. Reduce the heat to low, cover, and simmer for 20 minutes, or until all of the water is absorbed and the quinoa is tender.

3 Whisk together the lemon juice, oil, oregano, and garlic in a large bowl. Add the spinach, tomatoes, cheese, edamame, and quinoa. Toss to coat well.

Makes 4 servings

PER SERVING: 233 calories, 11 g protein, 30 g carbohydrates, 8 g fat (1 g saturated fat), 35 mg cholesterol, 313 mg sodium

FAT-FIGHTING
4

6 g fiber

91 mg calcium

0 IU vitamin D

10 mg omega-3s

MAKE IT A MEAL
Serve with Creamy Asparagus Soup (page 112).

Penne with Arugula and Pesto

PREP TIME: 10 MINUTES ◆ TOTAL TIME: 19-22 MINUTES

8 ounces whole grain penne
2 cups baby arugula leaves
1/2 cup walnuts, toasted
1/4 cup fresh basil leaves
3 cloves garlic, smashed

2 teaspoons olive oil
1/4 cup low-fat evaporated milk
1/3 cup grated Romano cheese
2 cups grape tomatoes, halved

1 Prepare the pasta according to package directions.

2 Meanwhile, combine the arugula, walnuts, basil, garlic, and olive oil in a blender or food processor. Process until the nuts are finely chopped. Add the milk and pulse until well blended. Add the cheese and pulse to blend.

3 Place the pasta and tomatoes in a serving bowl and toss with the sauce.

Makes 4 servings (about 6 cups)

PER SERVING: 329 calories, 14 g protein, 36 g carbohydrates, 15 g fat (3 g saturated fat), 8 mg cholesterol, 196 mg sodium

FAT-
FIGHTING
4

5 g fiber

208 mg
calcium

12 IU
vitamin D

1,190 mg
omega-3s

MAKE IT
FAST

Mock Italian Meatballs

PREP TIME: 25 MINUTES ◆ TOTAL TIME: 1 HOUR 10 MINUTES

1 can (14.5 ounces) diced tomatoes
2 teaspoons dried oregano
Ground black pepper
2½ pounds globe or Japanese eggplant, peeled and cut into ½"-thick slices
2 cloves garlic

½ cup grated pecorino cheese
¼ cup finely chopped parsley
¼ cup ground flaxseed
¼ cup nonfat dry milk
¼ teaspoon salt
1 tablespoon olive oil

FAT-FIGHTING 4

10.3 g fiber

273 mg calcium

0.22 IU vitamin D

80 mg omega-3s

1 Preheat oven to 375°F. Coat a 13" × 9" baking dish with cooking spray. Add the tomatoes. Sprinkle with the oregano and sprinkle generously with the pepper. Set aside.

2 Place the eggplant in a single layer on a large microwaveable plate or directly on a glass turntable. Microwave for 10 minutes, turning once, or until very soft. (This may have to be done in 2 batches.) Allow to cool to room temperature. Rinse with cold water. Drain and squeeze the eggplant dry.

3 In a blender or food processor, pulse the garlic until finely chopped. Add the eggplant, pecorino, parsley, flaxseed, dry milk, and salt. Pulse, scraping the sides of

the bowl as needed, until ground. Shape the mixture into 8 balls. Set in the prepared pan. Drizzle evenly with the oil.

4 Bake for about 25 minutes, or until the balls are heated through and the sauce is bubbling.

Makes 4 servings

PER SERVING: 242 calories, 12 g protein, 22 g carbohydrates, 12 g fat (4 g saturated fat), 16 mg cholesterol, 511 mg sodium

MAKE IT AHEAD
To save time, the eggplant slices can be microwaved several days in advance and refrigerated.

Asparagus, Red Onion, and Tofu Stir-Fry

PREP TIME: 15 MINUTES ◆ TOTAL TIME: 20 MINUTES + MARINATING TIME

½ cup vegetable broth
1 tablespoon molasses
1 tablespoon reduced-sodium soy sauce
2 teaspoons grated fresh ginger
2 cloves garlic, finely chopped
1 package (14 ounces) firm tofu, drained
    and cut into ½" cubes

2 teaspoons cornstarch
2 tablespoons canola oil
1 pound asparagus, diagonally cut into
    2" pieces
½ red onion, thinly sliced
1 tablespoon ground flaxseed
2 teaspoons toasted sesame seeds

1 Combine the broth, molasses, soy sauce, ginger, and garlic in a 13" × 9" ceramic baking dish. Whisk. Place the tofu in a single layer in the marinade. Toss gently. Set aside to marinate for 30 minutes, tossing occasionally.

2 Remove the tofu with a slotted spoon. Whisk the cornstarch into the marinade.

3 Heat a large nonstick skillet or wok over medium-high heat. Add 1 tablespoon of the oil and heat for 1 minute. Add the asparagus and onion. Cook, tossing, for 3 to 4 minutes, or until crisp-tender. Remove to a tray. Return the pan to the heat. Add the remaining 1 tablespoon oil and heat. Place the tofu in the pan. Cook, without tossing, for 1 minute, or until browned on bottom. Toss. Cook for 2 minutes more, or until all sides are browned. Return the asparagus, onion, and flaxseed to the pan along with the marinade. Toss for 1 minute, or until thickened. Serve sprinkled with the sesame seeds.

Makes 4 servings

PER SERVING: 222 calories, 13 g protein, 15 g carbohydrates, 13 g fat (1 g saturated fat), 0 mg cholesterol, 219 mg sodium

FAT-FIGHTING
4

4 g fiber

180 mg calcium

0 IU vitamin D

480 mg omega-3s

MAKE IT FAST

241

Vegetable Terrine

PREP TIME: 20 MINUTES ◆ TOTAL TIME: 25-27 MINUTES + CHILLING TIME

½ cup reduced-fat feta cheese
⅓ cup reduced-fat buttermilk
1 tablespoon flaxseed oil
¼ teaspoon ground black pepper
½ cucumber, thinly sliced
½ small red onion, very thinly sliced
1 cup canned sliced beets, drained
4 ounces baby bella mushrooms, sliced

3 cups baby spinach
½ cup fresh basil leaves, finely chopped
3 hard-cooked omega-3 enriched eggs, sliced
2 small whole wheat pitas (4" diameter), halved
Dried oregano

FAT-FIGHTING 4

5 g fiber

141 mg calcium

13.5 IU vitamin D

1,930 mg omega-3s

MAKE IT FAST

1 Combine the cheese, buttermilk, oil, and pepper in a glass trifle bowl or other high-sided 2½-quart glass serving dish. Stir. Place the cucumber in an even layer over the dressing. Continue creating layers with the onion, beets, mushrooms, spinach, basil, and egg. Cover tightly with plastic wrap. Refrigerate for up to 24 hours before serving.

2 Lightly coat 1 side of the pitas with olive oil spray. Sprinkle with oregano to taste.

Toast in a toaster oven or bake in the oven at 350°F for 5 to 7 minutes, or until toasted.

3 Toss the salad. Serve with the herbed pitas.

Makes 4 servings

PER SERVING: 237 calories, 14 g protein, 25 g carbohydrates, 10 g fat (3 g saturated fat), 141 mg cholesterol, 490 mg sodium

Everyday Soufflé

PREP TIME: 20 MINUTES ◆ TOTAL TIME: 1 HOUR 15 MINUTES

1 tablespoon dried bread crumbs
1 pound broccoli, cut into florets
3 large omega-3-enriched eggs, separated
1½ cups fat-free milk
⅓ cup all-purpose flour

¾ teaspoon dry mustard
1 clove garlic, minced
½ cup grated Romano cheese
3 large egg whites
⅛ teaspoon cream of tartar

1 Preheat oven to 375°F. Coat a 2-quart soufflé dish with cooking spray. Add the bread crumbs and shake to coat.

2 Place a steamer basket in a large pot with 2" of water. Bring to a boil over high heat. Place the broccoli in the basket and steam for 8 minutes, or until very tender. Drain and rinse under cold water. Place on a clean kitchen towel to dry. Finely chop and place in a large bowl.

3 Whisk together the 3 egg yolks in a small bowl and set aside. Whisk together the milk, flour, mustard, and garlic in a medium saucepan. Bring to a boil over medium heat. Reduce the heat and simmer, stirring constantly, for 3 minutes, or until slightly thickened. Remove from the heat. Whisk some of the milk mixture into the egg yolks. Whisk the egg yolk mixture into the saucepan. Cook for 2 minutes, or until thick. Pour into the bowl with the broccoli and stir in the cheese.

4 Beat all 6 egg whites and the cream of tartar in a large mixing bowl with an electric mixer on high speed until stiff, glossy peaks form, occasionally scraping down the sides of the bowl with a rubber spatula.

5 Stir about one-third of the whites into the broccoli mixture. Fold in the remaining whites. Pour into the prepared dish. Bake for 30 to 40 minutes, or until puffed and golden.

Makes 4 servings

PER SERVING: 251 calories, 22 g protein, 23 g carbohydrates, 7.3 g fat (3.7 g saturated fat), 146 mg cholesterol, 452 mg sodium

FAT-FIGHTING
4

5 g fiber
- - - - - - - - -
388 mg calcium
- - - - - - - - -
51 IU vitamin D
- - - - - - - - -
270 mg omega-3s
- - - - - - - - -

MAKE IT A MEAL
Serve with Spiced-Up Spinach Salad (page 138).

Roasted Ratatouille with Beans and Cheese

PREP TIME: 15 MINUTES ◆ TOTAL TIME: 50 MINUTES

1 onion, chopped
1 eggplant, peeled and cut into 1" pieces
1 zucchini, peeled and cut into 1" pieces
1 red bell pepper, cut into 1" pieces
2 tablespoons canola oil

1 can (15 ounces) no-salt-added
   chickpeas, rinsed and drained
1 cup marinara sauce
1 tablespoon balsamic vinegar
¾ cup part-skim ricotta cheese

① Preheat the oven to 400°F. Coat a baking sheet with cooking spray. Toss the onion, eggplant, zucchini, pepper, and oil in a large bowl. Place on the baking sheet and roast for 25 to 30 minutes, turning once, or until browned and tender.

② Heat the chickpeas and marinara sauce in a large microwaveable bowl, covered, on high for 1 to 2 minutes, or until hot. Stir in the vinegar and roasted vegetables.

③ Divide among 4 plates and top each with 3 tablespoons of the ricotta cheese.

Makes 4 servings (4 cups)

PER SERVING: 295 calories, 13 g protein, 33 g carbohydrates, 13 g fat (3 g saturated fat), 14 mg cholesterol, 344 mg sodium

FAT-FIGHTING
4

9 g fiber
----
197 mg
calcium
----
0 IU
vitamin D
----
740 mg
omega-3s

Spinach, Tomato, and Swiss Cheese Quiche

PREP TIME: 20 MINUTES ◆ TOTAL TIME: 50 MINUTES + STANDING TIME

1 tablespoon water
8 cups baby spinach
4 scallions, thinly sliced
2 egg whites
2 tablespoons ground flaxseed
2 slices (³⁄₄ ounce each) reduced-fat
   Swiss cheese, cut into slivers
2 tablespoons grated Parmesan cheese

¹⁄₂ cup canned diced tomatoes, drained
   and patted dry
2 omega-3-enriched eggs
1¹⁄₂ cups fat-free milk
2 tablespoons nonfat dry milk
Pinch of ground nutmeg
¹⁄₄ teaspoon salt
¹⁄₄ teaspoon ground black pepper

FAT-FIGHTING 4

4 g fiber

---

287 mg
calcium

---

47 IU
vitamin D

---

60 mg
omega-3s

---

1 Preheat the oven to 350°F. Coat a 9" quiche or pie dish with cooking spray.

2 Heat the water in a nonstick skillet. Add the spinach and scallions. Toss. Cover and cook for 2 minutes, or until wilted. Drain. Allow to cool. Squeeze very dry. Transfer to a work surface and chop the mixture very fine.

3 Beat 1 of the egg whites in a bowl. Add the flaxseed and spinach. Stir to combine. Transfer to the prepared dish. Press with the back of a fork to cover the bottom and sides of the pan. Top with the cheeses. Scatter on the tomatoes.

4 Beat the 2 eggs and the remaining egg white in the same bowl. Add the milk, dry milk, nutmeg, salt, and pepper. Beat to combine. Pour carefully into the pan.

5 Bake for 30 minutes, or until golden and set. Allow to sit for 10 minutes before serving.

Makes 4 servings

PER SERVING: 169 calories, 15 g protein, 16 g carbohydrates, 5 g fat (1 g saturated fat), 96 mg cholesterol, 560 mg sodium

Broccoli and Cheddar Bake

PREP TIME: 15 MINUTES ◆ TOTAL TIME: 1 HOUR 5 MINUTES + STANDING TIME

1 teaspoon canola oil
1 small onion, finely chopped
1 cup water
1 pound broccoli, stems and florets cut
    into bite-size pieces
2 tablespoons flour
2 cups fat-free milk
1 omega-3-enriched egg, beaten

2 egg whites, beaten
¾ cup (3 ounces) shredded
    75% reduced-fat Cheddar cheese
2 tablespoons grated Pecorino cheese
2 tablespoons ground flaxseed
¼ teaspoon ground red pepper
¼ teaspoon salt

FAT-
FIGHTING
4

3 g fiber

226 mg
calcium

55 IU
vitamin D

690 mg
omega-3s

1 Preheat the oven to 350°F. Coat a 13" × 9" baking dish with cooking spray.

2 Heat a medium saucepan over medium-low heat. Add the oil and onion. Cover and cook for 3 minutes, or until the onion starts to soften.

3 Meanwhile, heat the water in a skillet set over high heat. Bring to a boil. Add the broccoli. Reduce the heat so the mixture simmers briskly. Cover and cook for 4 minutes, or until the broccoli is bright green. Drain. Return to the skillet.

4 Add the flour to the saucepan. Gradually add the milk, whisking constantly, until smooth. Add the egg and egg whites. Cook, whisking constantly, for 5 minutes, or until thickened. Remove from the heat. Add the cheeses, flaxseed, red pepper, and salt. Stir until the Cheddar melts. Add to the broccoli mixture. Toss to coat. Pour into the prepared baking dish.

5 Bake for 30 minutes, or until bubbly and golden. Allow to sit for 10 minutes before serving.

Makes 4 servings

PER SERVING: 199 calories, 19 g protein, 16 g carbohydrates, 6 g fat (2 g saturated fat), 50 mg cholesterol, 336 mg sodium

Mushroom Ragout

PREP TIME: 10 MINUTES ◆ TOTAL TIME: 24 MINUTES

2 teaspoons canola oil
1 small onion, finely chopped
1¼ pounds baby bella mushrooms, sliced
½ teaspoon finely chopped fresh rosemary
⅛ teaspoon salt
2 tablespoons white whole wheat flour

2 tablespoons nonfat dry milk
1 tablespoon ground flaxseed
⅛ teaspoon grated nutmeg
1 cup reduced-fat buttermilk
¼ cup grated Parmesan cheese
1⅓ cup shredded reduced-fat Swiss cheese

FAT-
FIGHTING
4

3 g fiber

264 mg
calcium

4 IU
vitamin D

520 mg
omega-3s

MAKE IT
FAST

1 Heat a nonstick skillet over medium-high heat. Add the oil and heat for 1 minute. Add the onion. Cook, stirring, for 2 minutes, or until the onion starts to soften. Add the mushrooms, rosemary, and salt. Stir. Cover and cook for 4 minutes, or until the mushrooms give up liquid. Remove the cover and cook for 4 minutes, or until the liquid becomes syrupy.

2 Meanwhile, combine the flour, dry milk, flaxseed, and nutmeg in a bowl. Gradually add the buttermilk, whisking constantly, until smooth. Add to the skillet, stirring constantly, for 3 minutes, or until thickened. Remove from the heat. Stir in the cheeses until the Swiss melts.

Makes 4 servings

PER SERVING: 194 calories, 12 g protein, 17 g carbohydrates, 9 g fat (4 g saturated fat), 18 mg cholesterol, 242 mg sodium

African Groundnut Stew

PREP TIME: 15 MINUTES ◆ COOK TIME: 50 MINUTES

1 large onion, chopped
1 green bell pepper, chopped
1 clove garlic, minced
1 teaspoon ground ginger
1 teaspoon dried thyme
½ teaspoon ground allspice
4 cups fat-free, low-sodium vegetable or chicken broth

2 large sweet potatoes, peeled and cut into 1" pieces
2 large tomatoes, seeded and chopped
⅓ cup omega-3-enriched peanut butter
1 package (10 ounces) frozen sliced okra

1 Coat a large nonstick saucepan with cooking spray and heat over medium-high heat. Cook the onion, pepper, garlic, ginger, thyme, and allspice for 5 minutes, stirring, or until the vegetables are lightly browned.

2 Stir in the broth, sweet potatoes, and tomatoes and bring to a boil. Reduce the heat to low, cover, and simmer for 15 minutes, or until the potatoes are just tender.

3 Place the peanut butter in a small bowl. Remove about 1 cup of the simmering broth and whisk into the peanut butter. Return to the pot with the okra and cook for 10 minutes, or until the okra is cooked through.

Makes 4 servings

PER SERVING: 328 calories, 10 g protein, 48 g carbohydrates, 12 g fat (2 g saturated fat), 0 mg cholesterol, 298 mg sodium

FAT-FIGHTING
4

11 g fiber
---
147 mg calcium
---
0 IU vitamin D
---
680 mg omega-3s

Kansas City–Style Barbecued Tofu with Collard Greens

PREP TIME: 20 MINUTES ◆ TOTAL TIME: 44 MINUTES

1 teaspoon canola oil
1 small onion, finely chopped
1 block firm tofu (14 ounces), drained, cut
    into 8 cutlets, frozen, thawed, and
    squeezed dry (see box)
¾ cup no-salt-added tomato sauce

3 tablespoons molasses
½ teaspoon hot-pepper sauce
¼ teaspoon dry mustard
⅛ teaspoon ground cloves
6 cups coarsely chopped collard greens

FAT-FIGHTING 4

5 g fiber

812 mg calcium

0 IU vitamin D

750 mg omega-3s

1 Heat a large nonstick skillet over medium heat. Add the oil and onion. Cook, stirring, for 2 minutes, or until the onion starts to soften. Scrape the onion to the side. Add the tofu. Fry for 2 to 3 minutes, or until golden on the bottom. Flip and fry for 2 minutes more. Stir together the tomato sauce, molasses, hot-pepper sauce, dry mustard, and cloves in a small bowl. Stir into the pan. Scatter the collards on top. Cover and simmer for 5 minutes.

2 Stir the mixture gently. Cover and continue to simmer for 10 minutes, or until the collards are very tender. Pass additional hot-pepper sauce at the table.

Makes 4 servings

PER SERVING: 243 calories, 18 g protein, 24 g carbohydrates, 10 g fat (1 g saturated fat), 0 mg cholesterol, 54 mg sodium

MAKE IT AHEAD

Freezing and thawing tofu allows you to squeeze out the water, which gives the tofu more texture. To prepare the tofu for freezing, place it on a work surface with the long side of the block facing you. Cut into 8 equal cutlets. Line a tray or freezer-proof dish with plastic wrap. Place the cutlets in a single layer on the tray. Cover loosely with plastic wrap. Place in the freezer for at least 24 hours, or until frozen solid. When the cutlets are solid, they can be stacked in a zip-top freezer bag for longer keeping.

To use, remove the cutlets and allow to thaw for several days in the refrigerator or several hours at room temperature. Once thawed, you can squeeze out the water by placing a cutlet between a double thickness of paper towels and pressing gently.

SWEETS & TREATS

Rich Chocolate Torte

PREP TIME: 22 MINUTES ◆ TOTAL TIME: 1 HOUR 7 MINUTES + COOLING TIME

1 tablespoon + ¼ cup cocoa powder
1 cup walnuts
¾ cup sugar
5 omega-3-enriched eggs, separated
½ teaspoon cream of tartar

½ cup reduced-fat sour cream
5 ounces bittersweet chocolate (60% cocoa or higher), melted
1 teaspoon ground cinnamon

FAT-FIGHTING 4

2 g fiber

26 mg calcium

6 IU vitamin D

610 mg omega-3s

1 Preheat the oven to 350°F. Coat an 8" or 9" springform pan with cooking spray and dust with 1 tablespoon cocoa powder. Combine the walnuts and ¼ cup of the sugar in a blender or food processor. Pulse until finely ground. Set aside.

2 Beat the egg whites and cream of tartar in a large bowl with an electric mixer on high until foamy. Gradually add the remaining ½ cup sugar, beating, until stiff peaks form.

3 With the same beaters, beat the egg yolks in another bowl until thick. Add the sour cream, melted chocolate, cinnamon, and remaining ¼ cup cocoa and beat to blend well. Fold in the walnut mixture. Stir one-quarter of the egg whites into the chocolate mixture. Fold in the remaining whites in 2 batches.

4 Pour into the pan and bake for 45 minutes, or until a knife inserted in the center comes out clean. Cool the cake completely in the pan on a rack for at least 4 hours. (The cake is best made a day ahead and stored covered in the pan until serving.) Release the sides of the pan and cut the torte into 16 slices.

Makes 16 servings

PER SERVING: 159 calories, 4 g protein, 17 g carbohydrates, 10 g fat (3 g saturated fat), 59 mg cholesterol, 25 mg sodium

Warm Pear-and-Raspberry Strudel

PREP TIME: 20 MINUTES ◆ TOTAL TIME: 50 MINUTES + COOLING TIME

2 tablespoons honey

1 tablespoon cornstarch

$\frac{1}{2}$ teaspoon grated orange peel

$\frac{1}{16}$ teaspoon ground cinnamon

1 can (15 ounces) pear halves packed in juice, drained, patted dry, and thinly sliced

$\frac{1}{3}$ cup fresh or frozen raspberries

4 sheets frozen phyllo dough, thawed

1 tablespoon canola oil

1 tablespoon ground flaxseed

1 teaspoon confectioners' sugar

1 Preheat the oven to 375°F. Coat a medium baking sheet with cooking spray.

2 Combine the honey, cornstarch, orange peel, and cinnamon in a bowl. Add the pears and raspberries. Toss gently to coat with the cornstarch mixture.

3 Lay out 1 sheet of phyllo on a work surface. Lightly brush oil on the sheet with a pastry brush. Sprinkle with one-third of the flaxseed. Continue layering 2 sheets of phyllo, brushing lightly with oil and sprinkling with flaxseed. Cover with the last sheet of phyllo.

4 Gently spoon the pear mixture in a strip parallel to 1 end of the phyllo rectangle so that it's 1 $\frac{1}{2}$" away from the end and from either side. Fold the short (1 $\frac{1}{2}$") end of the phyllo over top of the filling, then fold in the 2 sides. Tightly holding each end, roll the

phyllo into a fat tube. Carefully transfer to the baking pan, seam side down. Brush lightly with oil.

5 Bake for 30 minutes, or until evenly browned and crisp. Shield any sections that are browning too fast with a piece of foil. Remove to cool slightly.

6 Cut the strudel into 6 pieces with a serrated knife. Dust lightly with the confectioners' sugar. Serve warm or at room temperature.

Makes 6 servings

PER SERVING: 118 calories, 1 g protein, 21 g carbohydrates, 4 g fat (0.5 g saturated fat), 0 mg cholesterol, 634 mg sodium*

∗ Limit sodium to less than 2,300 mg per day.

FAT-FIGHTING
4

2 g fiber

11 mg
calcium

0 IU
vitamin D

320 mg
omega-3s

Oats-Almond Mixed Berry Crisp

PREP TIME: 15 MINUTES ◆ TOTAL TIME: 1 HOUR + STANDING TIME

BERRIES
3 tablespoons confectioners' sugar
1 1/2 tablespoons cornstarch
2 cups sliced fresh strawberries
2 cups fresh blueberries
1 1/2 teaspoons almond extract

CRISP
3/4 cup old-fashioned oats
3 tablespoons sliced almonds
1 tablespoon light brown sugar
1 tablespoon canola oil

TOPPING
1/3 cup part-skim ricotta cheese
1 1/2 tablespoons confectioners' sugar
1/2 teaspoon pure vanilla extract

FAT-FIGHTING 4

4 g fiber
- - - - - - - - - - - - -
63 mg calcium
- - - - - - - - - - - - -
0 IU vitamin D
- - - - - - - - - - - - -
280 mg omega-3s
- - - - - - - - - - - - -

1 Preheat the oven to 350°F. Coat an 8" × 8" baking dish with cooking spray.

2 Prepare the berries: Combine the confectioners' sugar and cornstarch in a mixing bowl. Stir to mix. Add the strawberries, blueberries, and almond extract. Toss to coat the berries thoroughly. Transfer to the baking dish.

3 Prepare the crisp: Combine the oats, almonds, brown sugar, and oil in the same bowl that you used for the berries. Toss to coat thoroughly. Scatter evenly over the berry mixture.

4 Bake for 45 minutes, or until the berries' juices bubble and are no longer opaque. Remove and let stand at room temperature for 5 minutes.

5 Meanwhile, prepare the topping: Combine the ricotta, confectioners' sugar, and vanilla extract in a blender or mini food processor. Blend or process until smooth. Serve the crisp with a dollop of creamed ricotta on top.

Makes 6 servings

PER SERVING: 182 calories, 5 g protein, 29 g carbohydrates, 6 g fat (1 g saturated fat), 4 mg cholesterol, 19 mg sodium

NOTE
Any leftover crisp may be covered and refrigerated for up to 3 days.

Raspberry Soufflé

PREP TIME: 15 MINUTES ◆ TOTAL TIME: 40 MINUTES

6 tablespoons sugar
3 tablespoons all-purpose flour
½ cup fat-free milk
2 egg yolks from omega-3-enriched eggs, slightly beaten, at room temperature

3 tablespoons freshly squeezed lime juice
1 teaspoon lime zest
3 large egg whites, at room temperature
¼ teaspoon cream of tartar
1 cup raspberries

FAT-FIGHTING 4

1 g fiber

40 mg calcium

14 IU vitamin D

60 mg omega-3s

1 Preheat the oven to 375°F. Coat 6 ramekins (6 to 8 ounces each) with cooking spray. Sprinkle each with ½ teaspoon of the sugar, turning to coat. Place on a baking sheet with sides.

2 Whisk together the flour, milk, and 3 tablespoons of the remaining sugar in a small saucepan until blended. Bring to a boil over medium heat. Cook, stirring constantly, for 2 minutes, or until thickened. Pour about 2 tablespoons of the mixture into the egg yolks, beating well. Pour the yolks back into the milk mixture and return to the heat. Cook, stirring, for 1 minute. Pour into a large bowl and stir in the lime juice and zest. Set aside.

3 Beat the egg whites and cream of tartar in a large mixing bowl with an electric mixer on high speed until soft peaks form. Continue beating while gradually adding the remaining 2 tablespoons sugar, until very stiff and glossy peaks form. Gently stir one-quarter of the egg whites into the lime mixture. Fold in the raspberries. Fold in the remaining egg whites. Divide among the ramekins. Bake for 20 minutes, or until puffy and set. Serve immediately.

Makes 6 servings

PER SERVING: 108 calories, 4 g protein, 20 g carbohydrates, 2 g fat (0.5 g saturated fat), 60 mg cholesterol, 41 mg sodium

Blueberry Buckle

PREP TIME: 10 MINUTES ◆ TOTAL TIME: 1 HOUR 10 MINUTES + STANDING TIME

1 cup whole wheat pastry flour
¾ cup unbleached white flour
½ cup light brown sugar
2 teaspoons baking powder
¼ teaspoon ground cinnamon
¼ teaspoon salt
¾ cup fat-free milk

1 omega-3-enriched egg
1 teaspoon pure vanilla extract
2 tablespoons canola oil
2 ½ cups fresh blueberries
1 ¼ cups 7-grain crunch cereal
   (such as Kashi Crunch with
   Honey Almond Flax)

Makes 12 servings

PER SERVING: 163 calories, 4 g protein, 30 g carbohydrates, 3 g fat (0.5 g saturated fat), 15 mg cholesterol, 147 mg sodium

1 Preheat the oven to 350°F. Coat a 9" × 9" baking pan with cooking spray.

2 Whisk together the flours, sugar, baking powder, cinnamon, and salt in a large bowl. Whisk together the milk, egg, vanilla extract, and oil in a small bowl until well blended. Pour the wet ingredients into the dry ingredients and mix until just blended. Gently stir in the blueberries. Pour into the prepared pan. Sprinkle with the cereal.

3 Bake for 60 minutes, or until a wooden pick inserted in the center comes out clean. Let stand for 15 minutes before serving.

FAT-FIGHTING
4

3 g fiber

74 mg calcium

7.5 IU vitamin D

80 mg omega-3s

NOTE
This dish is fantastic with springtime-fresh blueberries, but frozen berries work just as well. Don't thaw before stirring into the batter. If desired, top with a dollop of frozen or refrigerated vanilla yogurt.

Orange Pudding Cake

PREP TIME: 15 MINUTES ◆ TOTAL TIME: 50 MINUTES + COOLING TIME

2 oranges
⅓ cup whole grain pastry flour
½ cup sugar
⅛ teaspoon salt
1 cup fat-free milk

2 tablespoons butter, melted
2 omega-3-enriched eggs, separated
1 egg white
2 ⅔ cups fresh raspberries

1 Preheat the oven to 350°F. Bring 6 cups of water to a boil. Coat an 8" glass baking dish with cooking spray.

2 From the oranges, grate 1 ½ teaspoons zest and squeeze ½ cup juice. Whisk together the flour, ¼ cup of the sugar, and the salt in a medium bowl. Add the milk, orange juice, butter, egg yolks, and orange zest and whisk until smooth.

3 Place all 3 egg whites in a large bowl and beat with an electric mixer on high until soft peaks form. Gradually add the remaining ¼ cup sugar while beating until stiff, glossy peaks form. Fold into the orange mixture. The batter will be lumpy and thin. Pour into the prepared baking dish.

4 Place the baking dish into a large roasting pan. Fill with boiling water until it reaches halfway up the baking dish. Bake for 35 minutes, or until puffed and browned and the center of the cake is set. Cool on a rack for 15 minutes. Place ⅓ cup of the raspberries into each of 8 bowls. Top with a slice of the pudding cake.

Makes 8 servings

PER SERVING: 147 calories, 4 g protein, 24 g carbohydrates, 5 g fat (2 g saturated fat), 61 mg cholesterol, 95 mg sodium

FAT-
FIGHTING
4

3 g fiber

61 mg
calcium

19 IU
vitamin D

700 mg
omega-3s

Blueberry-Lemon Streusel Snack Cake

PREP TIME: 25 MINUTES ◆ TOTAL TIME: 55 MINUTES + COOLING TIME

STREUSEL
3 tablespoons packed light brown sugar
1 tablespoon ground flaxseed

CAKE
3/4 cup white whole wheat flour
1/4 cup fat-free soy flour
3/4 teaspoon baking powder
1/2 teaspoon baking soda

2 omega-3-enriched eggs
1/3 cup granulated sugar
Dash of salt
1/2 cup fat-free buttermilk
1/4 cup canola oil
3 tablespoons fat-free dry milk
3/4 teaspoon lemon extract
3/4 cup fresh or frozen blueberries

1 Preheat the oven to 350°F. Coat an 8" × 8" glass baking dish with cooking spray.

2 Prepare the streusel: Combine the sugar and flaxseed in a small bowl. Stir with a fork, then set aside.

3 Prepare the cake: Combine the flours, baking powder, and baking soda on a large sheet of waxed paper. Blend with a fork.

4 Place the eggs, granulated sugar, and salt in the bowl of an electric mixer. Beat on low speed to incorporate. Increase the speed to high and beat for 2 to 3 minutes, or until the mixture is fluffy and lemon-colored. Add the buttermilk, oil, dry milk, and lemon extract. Mix on low speed just until combined. With the mixer running on low, gradually add the dry ingredients until the batter is smooth. Pour into the pan. Scatter the blueberries evenly on top.

5 Bake for 10 minutes. Sprinkle the reserved streusel evenly on the cake. Cover the cake loosely with a sheet of aluminum foil. Bake for an additional 20 minutes, or until a wooden pick inserted into the center comes out with moist crumbs clinging to it. (The center may feel slightly underdone but will firm up out of the oven.) Remove from the oven. Allow to cool for 15 minutes before cutting. Serve warm or at room temperature.

Makes 12 servings

PER SERVING: 141 calories, 4 g protein, 19 g carbohydrates, 6 g fat (1 g saturated fat), 30 mg cholesterol, 121 mg sodium

Walnut-Pumpkin Cheesecake

PREP TIME: 15 MINUTES ◆ TOTAL TIME: 1 HOUR 5 MINUTES + CHILLING TIME

1 cup 1% cottage cheese

8 ounces fat-free cream cheese

3 large omega-3-enriched eggs

½ cup pumpkin puree

⅓ cup + 2 tablespoons maple syrup

2 teaspoon pure vanilla extract

½ teaspoon ground cinnamon

¼ teaspoon ground cloves

¼ teaspoon ground ginger

½ cup walnuts

1 Preheat the oven to 350°F. Coat the bottom and sides of a 9" pie plate with cooking spray.

2 Place the cottage cheese in a blender or food processor. Blend or process for 3 minutes, or until very smooth, scraping down the sides. Add the cream cheese, eggs, pumpkin, ⅓ cup maple syrup, vanilla extract, cinnamon, cloves, and ginger. Process until very smooth. Pour into the prepared pie plate.

3 Bake for 40 minutes, or until the center is set and a knife inserted in the center comes out clean. Cool completely on a wire rack. Refrigerate for 3 hours or overnight.

4 Meanwhile, coat a small baking sheet with cooking spray. Combine the walnuts and remaining 2 tablespoons maple syrup in a small bowl. Place on the baking sheet. After removing the cake from the oven, bake the nuts for 10 minutes, or until lightly browned. Remove from the oven and let cool on a rack.

5 To serve, arrange the nuts around the edges of the cheesecake.

Makes 8 servings

PER SERVING: 180 calories, 11 g protein, 18 g carbohydrates, 7 g fat (1 g saturated fat), 71 mg cholesterol, 298 mg sodium

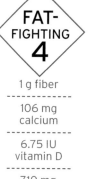

FAT-FIGHTING **4**

1 g fiber

106 mg calcium

6.75 IU vitamin D

710 mg omega-3s

Chocolate-Pecan Cheesecake

PREP TIME: 15 MINUTES ◆ TOTAL TIME: 50 MINUTES + CHILLING TIME

3 tablespoons bran cereal crumbs

1/4 teaspoon ground cinnamon

1/4 cup + 2 tablespoons unsweetened cocoa powder

1/2 teaspoon instant coffee

1/3 cup boiling water

8 ounces fat-free cream cheese, softened

4 ounces reduced-fat cream cheese, softened

1/2 cup fat-free ricotta

2/3 cup confectioners' sugar

2 omega-3-enriched eggs

1 egg white

2 teaspoons pure vanilla extract

1/2 ounce bittersweet chocolate, shaved

2 tablespoons finely chopped pecans

FAT-FIGHTING 4

1 g fiber

162 mg calcium

7 IU vitamin D

50 mg omega-3s

1 Position an oven rack in the bottom third of the oven. Preheat the oven to 325°F. Coat the bottom and sides of an 8" springform pan with cooking spray. Combine the cereal crumbs and cinnamon in a bowl. Sprinkle evenly over the pan bottom. Set aside.

2 Combine the cocoa powder, coffee, and water in a bowl. Stir until smooth. Set aside.

3 Combine the cream cheeses and ricotta in an electric mixer bowl. Beat at medium speed until smooth. Add the sugar. Reduce the speed to low and beat to incorporate. Add the eggs and egg white one at a time, beating until blended. Add the vanilla extract. Blend until smooth. Add the cocoa mixture and stir until completely incorporated. Pour into the prepared pan.

4 Bake for 30 to 35 minutes, or until the outer edges are set but the center still jiggles. Sprinkle the chocolate shavings and pecans evenly over the cheesecake. Return the cheesecake to the oven and bake for 2 to 3 minutes, or until the chocolate melts.

5 Remove to a rack to cool to room temperature. Cover and refrigerate overnight.

6 Remove the sides of the pan and cut into 8 wedges.

Makes 8 servings

PER SERVING: 168 calories, 11 g protein, 19 g carbohydrates, 6 g fat (2 g saturated fat), 55 mg cholesterol, 27 mg sodium

Chocolate Napoleons

PREP TIME: 12 MINUTES TOTAL TIME: 9 MINUTES

1 ½ cups fresh strawberries, sliced
12 refrigerated wonton wrappers
1 teaspoon ground cinnamon
6 ounces fat-free cream cheese

3 tablespoons cocoa powder
2 tablespoons honey
1 teaspoon pure vanilla extract

1 Preheat the oven to 325°F. Place the strawberries in a small bowl.

2 Place the wonton wrappers on a baking sheet and coat with cooking spray. Sprinkle with the cinnamon. Bake for 8 to 10 minutes, or until golden brown. Remove to a rack to cool completely.

3 Meanwhile, combine the cream cheese, cocoa powder, honey, and vanilla extract in a large bowl. Beat with an electric mixer on low speed until blended and smooth. If desired, place in a pastry bag with a star tip.

4 Place 1 wonton wrapper on each of 4 plates. Pipe or spoon about 1 ½ tablespoons of the chocolate mixture onto each wrapper. Top with another wrapper and more chocolate mixture, making 3 layers. Surround each serving with the berries.

Makes 4 servings

PER SERVING: 178 calories, 10 g protein, 31 g carbohydrates, 2 g fat (0.5 g saturated fat), 9 mg cholesterol, 397 mg sodium

FAT-FIGHTING 4

3 g fiber
----
226 mg calcium
----
0 IU vitamin D
----
40 mg omega-3s

MAKE IT FAST

Chocolate Crème Cups

PREP TIME: 15 MINUTES ◆ TOTAL TIME: 20 MINUTES + CHILLING TIME

2 cups fat-free evaporated milk
1 tablespoon unflavored gelatin
¼ cup finely chopped semisweet chocolate
1 tablespoon unsweetened cocoa powder

1 tablespoon honey
2 teaspoons pure vanilla extract
Pinch of salt
6 tablespoons fat-free whipped topping

1 Pour the milk into a saucepan. Sprinkle with the gelatin and set aside for 10 minutes to soften.

2 Cook the milk over medium-high heat, whisking constantly, for 5 minutes, or until the mixture is steaming hot but not boiling. Remove from the heat and whisk until no beads of gelatin remain.

3 Combine the chocolate and cocoa in a mixing bowl. Pour in the hot milk, whisking constantly until the chocolate melts. Add

the honey, vanilla extract, and salt. Whisk to dissolve. Ladle into six ½-cup custard cups or dessert bowls. Set on a tray. Cover and refrigerate overnight, or until set. Top each serving with 1 tablespoon of the whipped topping.

Makes 6 servings

PER SERVING: 131 calories, 8 g protein, 19 g carbohydrates, 3 g fat (2 g saturated fat), 3 mg cholesterol, 128 mg sodium

FAT-FIGHTING **4**

1 g fiber

251 mg calcium

68 IU vitamin D

10 mg omega-3s

MAKE IT FAST

Toasted Coconut Cream Tart

PREP TIME: 20 MINUTES ◆ TOTAL TIME: 45 MINUTES + CHILLING TIME

FAT-FIGHTING 4

0 g fiber

171 mg calcium

51 IU vitamin D

300 mg omega-3s

CRUST
1/3 cup old-fahioned oats
1 1/2 teaspoons brown sugar

FILLING
2 omega-3-enriched eggs,
    at room temperature
1 egg white, at room temperature

3 tablespoons cornstarch
3 tablespoons + 1/4 cup
    confectioners' sugar
1 (12 ounce) can fat-free evaporated milk
1 cup fat-free milk
1 tablespoon coconut extract
1/4 teaspoon cream of tartar
2 tablespoons flaked coconut

1 Preheat the oven to 350°F. Coat a 9" quiche or pie dish with cooking spray. Place the oats in a blender or food processor. Pulse to a coarse powder. Add the brown sugar and pulse to combine. Scatter the oat mixture into the prepared dish. Bake for 5 minutes, or until toasted. Remove and set aside.

2 Separate the eggs, putting the whites into the bowl of an electric mixer and the yolks in a small bowl. Set aside.

3 Combine the cornstarch and 3 tablespoons of the sugar in a saucepan. Whisk to blend. Gradually add the milks, whisking constantly until smooth. Add the reserved egg yolks and whisk until smooth. Place over medium-high heat and cook, stirring constantly, for 5 minutes, or until the mixture bubbles and thickens. Remove from the heat and stir in the coconut extract. Set aside.

4 Add the cream of tartar to the reserved egg whites. Beat on low speed for 1 minute to loosen the whites. Increase the speed to high and beat for 3 to 4 minutes, reducing the speed occasionally to gradually add the remaining 1/4 cup sugar. Beat until the whites hold peaks.

5 Carefully pour the custard into the reserved pie dish. Dollop on the meringue and spread lightly to reach the sides of the dish and cover the custard completely. Sprinkle with the coconut.

6 Bake for 15 minutes, or until the meringue is evenly browned. Remove to cool completely. Refrigerate for at least 8 hours before cutting.

Makes 8 servings

PER SERVING: 124 calories, 7 g protein, 20 g carbohydrates, 1.7 g fat (0.7 g saturated fat), 47 mg cholesterol, 90 mg sodium

Milk Chocolate Panna Cotta

PREP TIME: 5 MINUTES ◆ TOTAL TIME: 7 MINUTES + CHILLING TIME

½ cup fat-free milk
1 ½ teaspoons unflavored gelatin
3 tablespoons cocoa powder

2 tablespoons honey
1 ½ cups low-fat vanilla yogurt

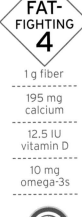

FAT-FIGHTING 4

1 g fiber

195 mg calcium

12.5 IU vitamin D

10 mg omega-3s

MAKE IT FAST

1 Place the milk in a small saucepan. Sprinkle the gelatin over the milk and let stand for 5 minutes to soften the gelatin. In a small cup, mix the cocoa powder and honey. Set aside.

2 Cook the milk mixture over medium heat, stirring for 2 minutes, or until the gelatin dissolves but the milk does not boil. Stir in the reserved chocolate mixture and remove from the heat. Place in a bowl and gradually stir in the yogurt. Pour into

4 (6-ounce) ramekins. Cover and refrigerate for 2 hours, or until set.

3 When ready to serve, dip the ramekins into hot water for 1 minute, then invert onto a dessert plate. Shake to loosen and lift off the ramekin.

Makes 4 servings

PER SERVING: 133 calories, 7 g protein, 25 g carbohydrates, 2 g fat (1 g saturated fat), 5 mg cholesterol, 80 mg sodium

Mini Chocolate Tarts

PREP TIME: 15 MINUTES ◆ TOTAL TIME: 25 MINUTES + CHILLING TIME

**4 sheets frozen phyllo dough
(14" x 18"), thawed**
8 ounces light silken tofu, drained
1 cup fat-free Greek yogurt

⅓ cup cocoa powder
⅓ cup honey
1 tablespoon pure vanilla extract

1 Preheat the oven to 350°F. Coat 12 muffin cups with cooking spray.

2 Place 1 sheet of phyllo dough on a work surface (cover remaining dough to prevent drying) and coat with buttered-flavored cooking spray. Top with another sheet of phyllo and recoat. Repeat layering, using all sheets. Cut in half lengthwise, then cut each half into 4 squares. Press into the muffin cups, folding the phyllo if necessary to fit and form a cup. Bake for 8 to 10 minutes, or until golden brown. Remove to a rack to cool completely.

3 Meanwhile, combine the tofu, yogurt, cocoa, honey, and vanilla extract in a blender or food processor. Blend or process until smooth, scraping down the sides with a rubber spatula. Refrigerate for 1 hour. Just before serving, fill the phyllo cups with ¼ cup of the chocolate mixture.

Makes 8 servings

PER SERVING: 111 calories, 5 g protein, 20 g carbohydrates, 2 g fat (1 g saturated fat), 1 g cholesterol, 76 mg sodium

FAT-
FIGHTING
4

1 g fiber

119 mg
calcium

37 IU
vitamin D

0 mg
omega-3s

MAKE IT
FAST

Chocolate–Peanut Butter Cupcakes

PREP TIME: 25 MINUTES ◆ TOTAL TIME: 60 MINUTES

¾ cup all-purpose flour
½ cup whole wheat pastry flour
½ cup unsweetened cocoa powder
1 teaspoon baking soda
1 teaspoon baking powder
½ teaspoon salt
¾ cup granulated sugar
4 egg whites
1 egg

3 tablespoons canola oil
1 teaspoon pure vanilla extract
1 ½ cups plain low-fat yogurt
¾ cup omega-3-enriched peanut butter
   (such as Smart Balance)
¾ cup confectioners' sugar
3 ounces fat-free cream cheese
¼ cup fat-free evaporated milk

FAT-FIGHTING 4

1 g fiber

----

41 g
calcium

----

3 IU
vitamin D

----

400 mg
omega-3s

----

1 Coat 24 muffin cups with cooking spray or line with cupcake papers.

2 Whisk together flours, cocoa, baking soda, baking powder, and salt in a medium bowl. Set aside.

3 Beat together the granulated sugar, egg whites, and egg in a large bowl with an electric mixer on medium speed for 5 minutes, or until thick and pale. Beat in the oil and vanilla extract. Alternately add the reserved flour mixture and yogurt and beat on low just until incorporated. Divide into the muffin cups, filling just over half full. Bake for 15 minutes, or until a wooden pick inserted in the center comes out clean. Remove to a rack to cool.

4 Meanwhile, to make the frosting, whisk together the peanut butter, confectioners' sugar, cream cheese, and milk until well blended. Spread 1 tablespoon over each cupcake.

Makes 24

PER CUPCAKE: 150 calories, 5 g protein, 19 g carbohydrates, 7 g fat (1 g saturated fat), 10 mg cholesterol, 193 mg sodium

Glazed Pineapple Cupcakes

PREP TIME 25 MINUTES ◆ TOTAL TIME: 40 MINUTES

¼ cup packed brown sugar
1 cup canned pineapple chunks packed in
    juice, drained (reserve 3 tablespoons
    juice)
½ cup white whole wheat flour
⅓ cup fat-free soy flour
¾ teaspoon baking powder
½ teaspoon baking soda

2 omega-3-enriched eggs
Dash of salt
5 tablespoons granulated sugar
½ cup fat-free plain yogurt
¼ cup canola oil
3 tablespoons nonfat dry milk
2 teaspoons pure vanilla extract

FAT-FIGHTING 4

1 g fiber

59 mg
calcium

6 IU
vitamin D

450 mg
omega-3s

1 Preheat the oven to 350°F. Coat a nonstick 12-cup muffin pan with cooking spray. Scatter 1 packed teaspoon of the brown sugar into the bottom of each cup. Cut each pineapple chunk in half. Place 4 pieces in a single layer in each cup.

2 Combine the flours, baking powder, and baking soda on a sheet of waxed paper. Blend with a fork.

3 Separate the eggs, putting the whites in the bowl of an electric mixer and the yolks into another mixing bowl. Add the salt to the whites and beat on low speed for 1 minute to loosen. Increase the speed to high. Beat for 2 to 3 minutes, gradually adding 1 tablespoon of the granulated sugar until the whites hold soft peaks. Set aside.

4 To the yolks, add the yogurt, oil, dry milk, reserved pineapple juice, vanilla extract, and remaining 4 tablespoons granulated sugar. With a fork, beat until smooth. Stir in the dry ingredients. Carefully fold the reserved whites into the batter. Dollop the batter into the muffin cups. Smooth the tops.

5 Bake for 15 minutes, or until browned and the cakes spring back when pressed with a fingertip. Remove from the oven. Let stand for 5 minutes. Place a heatproof tray over the pan. Using oven mitts, flip the pan over on the tray. Tap the cup bottoms to aid release. Serve warm.

Makes 12 servings

PER SERVING: 141 calories, 4 g protein, 19 g carbohydrates, 6 g fat (0.5 g saturated fat), 30 mg cholesterol, 114 mg sodium

MAKE IT AHEAD

The cupcakes may be cooled to room temperature. Place in a tightly covered plastic storage container and refrigerate for up to 1 day or freeze for up to 3 months. To reheat, place a refrigerated or thawed frozen cupcake in a 350°F toaster oven for 5 minutes, or until heated through.

Gooey Date Bars

PREP TIME: 15 MINUTES ◆ TOTAL TIME: 40 MINUTES

½ cup honey

⅓ cup fat-free plain yogurt

3 tablespoons canola oil

1 omega-3-enriched egg

1½ teaspoons pure vanilla extract

1 cup chopped pitted dates

¾ cup old-fashioned oats

½ cup white whole wheat flour

¼ cup ground flaxseed

¼ cup chopped walnuts

½ teaspoon baking soda

½ teaspoon ground cinnamon

⅛ teaspoon salt

Confectioners' sugar

1 Preheat the oven to 350°F. Coat an 8″ × 8″ baking pan with cooking spray.

2 Beat the honey, yogurt, oil, egg, and vanilla extract with a fork or whisk until smooth in a mixing bowl. Toss the dates, oats, flour, flaxseed, walnuts, baking soda, cinnamon, and salt in another bowl. Add to the batter. Stir to combine. Dollop into the prepared pan. Spread evenly.

3 Bake for 25 minutes, or until the top is browned and a wooden pick inserted into the center has moist crumbs clinging to it. Do not overbake. Remove to a rack to cool.

Cut into 16 squares. Dust lightly with the confectioners' sugar.

Makes 16 servings

PER SERVING: 145 calories, 3 g protein, 24 g carbohydrates, 5 g total fat (0.5 g saturated fat), 11 mg cholesterol, 66 mg sodium

FAT-FIGHTING **4**

2 g fiber

- - - - - - - - - - - -

23 mg cholesterol

- - - - - - - - - - - -

3 IU vitamin D

- - - - - - - - - - - -

640 mg omega-3s

- - - - - - - - - - - -

MAKE IT AHEAD

Store the bars in a tightly covered container at room temperature for up to 2 days, or freeze for up to 2 months.

Double-Chocolate Walnut Brownies

PREP TIME: 15 MINUTES ◆ TOTAL TIME: 40 MINUTES + COOLING TIME

FAT-FIGHTING 4

2 g fiber

33 mg calcium

1 IU vitamin D

420 mg omega-3s

3 ounces unsweetened chocolate, chopped
3 tablespoons canola oil
$\frac{1}{2}$ cup white whole wheat flour
$\frac{1}{4}$ cup unsweetened cocoa powder
1 tablespoon ground flaxseed
$\frac{3}{4}$ teaspoon baking powder
Pinch of salt

1 omega-3-enriched egg
1 omega-3-enriched egg white
1 cup packed brown sugar
$\frac{1}{3}$ cup reduced-sodium canned tomato puree or tomato sauce
2 teaspoons pure vanilla extract
$\frac{1}{4}$ cup chopped walnuts
Confectioners' sugar (optional)

1. Preheat the oven to 350°F. Coat an 8" × 8" baking pan with cooking spray.

2. Combine the chocolate and oil in a microwaveable bowl. Microwave on high power for 1 minute, or until the chocolate pieces are glossy and lose their shape. Stir until smooth.

3. Combine the flour, cocoa, flaxseed, baking powder, and salt on a large sheet of waxed paper. Stir to blend.

4. Beat the egg and egg white with a fork until smooth in a mixing bowl. Add the sugar and mix, breaking up any lumps. Add the tomato puree, vanilla extract, and chocolate mixture. Stir until smooth. Add the dry ingredients, mixing until thoroughly blended. Dollop the batter into the prepared pan. Scatter the walnuts evenly over the top, pressing lightly with a spatula to embed them partially in the batter.

5. Bake for 20 to 25 minutes, or until a wooden pick inserted into the center has moist crumbs clinging to it. Do not overbake. Cool for 10 minutes before cutting into 16 pieces. Dust lightly with confectioners' sugar, if desired.

Makes 16 servings

PER SERVING: 143 calories, 3 g protein, 20 g carbohydrates, 7 g fat (2 g saturated fat), 11 mg cholesterol, 62 mg sodium

MAKE IT AHEAD

Brownies taste best served warm. To keep them longer, cut and place them on a tray. Freeze for several hours, then wrap them individually in plastic wrap. Freeze for up to 3 months.

Mini Turnovers with Raspberries

PREP TIME: 20 MINUTES ◆ TOTAL TIME: 32 MINUTES + COOLING TIME

1 1/2 cups raspberries
2 tablespoons honey
1/2 cup part-skim ricotta cheese

1 teaspoon all-purpose flour
1/4 teaspoon ground cardamom
12 wonton wrappers

FAT-FIGHTING 4

4 g fiber

149 mg calcium

0 IU vitamin D

70 mg omega-3s

1 Preheat the oven to 350°F. Coat a baking sheet with cooking spray. Combine the raspberries and 1 tablespoon of the honey in a bowl, tossing to coat. Set aside. Stir together the ricotta, flour, cardamom, and remaining 1 tablespoon honey.

2 Place the wrappers on a flat surface and place a scant tablespoon of the ricotta mixture in the center of each. Moisten the edges of the wrapper with water and fold 1 corner over to form a triangle. Press the sides together to seal. Place the turnovers on the prepared baking sheet. Lightly coat the tops with cooking spray. Bake for 12 minutes, or until browned. Cool on a rack for at least 10 minutes.

3 Place 3 turnovers each on 4 plates. Top with the reserved raspberries.

Makes 4 servings

PER SERVING: 174 calories, 7 g protein, 29 g carbohydrates, 4 g fat (2 g saturated fat), 12 mg cholesterol, 171 mg sodium

Dark-Chocolate Crackle Cookies

PREP TIME: 15 MINUTES ◆ TOTAL TIME: 23 MINUTES + CHILLING TIME

¼ cup + 2 tablespoons omega-3-enriched tub margarine (such as Smart Balance)
¼ cup + 2 tablespoons unsweetened cocoa
2 teaspoons almond extract
¾ cup light-brown sugar

¼ cup + 2 tablespoons unsweetened applesauce
2 tablespoons honey
1 ¼ cups white whole wheat flour
Pinch of salt
4 teaspoons granulated sugar

1 Place the margarine in a microwaveable mixing bowl. Microwave on high power for 1 minute, or until the margarine melts. Remove. Add the cocoa and almond extract. Stir until smooth. Add the brown sugar, applesauce, and honey. Stir until smooth. Add the flour and salt. Stir until no white is visible. Cover the bowl with plastic wrap and refrigerate for several hours or overnight, or until the dough is very stiff.

2 Preheat the oven to 350°F. Coat several baking sheets with cooking spray. Place the granulated sugar in a small dish or plate. Scoop out a scant tablespoonful of the

dough. Roll between palms into a ball, flattening slightly. Dip 1 side into the sugar and place, sugar side up, on the baking sheet. Continue until all the cookies are shaped.

3 Bake for 7 to 8 minutes, or until the surface is set but still soft to the touch. Do not overbake. Allow the cookies to cool on the pan. Store in a tightly covered tin.

Makes 32 (2 per serving)

PER SERVING: 121 calories, 2 g protein, 23 g carbohydrates, 4 g fat (1 g saturated fat), 0 mg cholesterol, 13 mg sodium

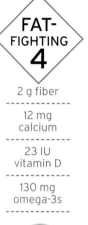

FAT-FIGHTING **4**

2 g fiber

12 mg calcium

23 IU vitamin D

130 mg omega-3s

MAKE IT FAST

Fruit 'n' Nut Bark

PREP TIME: 5 MINUTES ◆ TOTAL TIME: 8 MINUTES + CHILLING TIME

½ cup 60% chocolate baking chips
½ cup chopped walnuts

¼ cup dried cranberries

1 Line a baking sheet with parchment or waxed paper.

2 Place the baking chips in a medium bowl and microwave on medium for 2 minutes, stirring twice, or until just melted. Stir in the walnuts and cranberries.

3 Spread the mixture on the baking sheet to a 10" × 8" rectangle. Refrigerate for

1 hour, or until set. Cut or break the bark into 8 pieces.

Makes 8 servings

PER SERVING: 109 calories, 2 g protein, 11 g carbohydrates, 8 g fat (2 g saturated fat), 0 mg cholesterol, 1 mg sodium

FAT-
FIGHTING
4

1 g fiber

- - - - - - - - - - - -

11 mg
calcium

- - - - - - - - - - - -

0 IU
vitamin D

- - - - - - - - - - - -

670 mg
omega-3s

- - - - - - - - - - - -

MAKE IT
FAST

Maple-Walnut Bites

PREP TIME: 15 MINUTES ◆ TOTAL TIME: 1 HOUR 15 MINUTES + STANDING TIME

2 egg whites, at room temperature
¼ teaspoon cream of tartar

¼ cup maple sugar
½ cup walnuts, toasted and chopped

1 Preheat the oven to 250°F. Line 2 large baking sheets with parchment paper.

2 Beat the egg whites and cream of tartar in a large mixing bowl with an electric mixer on high speed until soft peaks form. Continue beating while gradually adding the maple sugar, until very stiff and glossy peaks form. Gently fold in the walnuts.

3 Drop by tablespoons onto the parchment paper. Bake for 1 hour. Turn off the oven and leave in the oven for 1 hour without opening the oven door.

Makes about 36 cookies (9 per serving)

PER SERVING: 122 calories, 4 g protein, 10 g carbohydrates, 8 g fat (0.8 g saturated fat), 0 mg cholesterol, 29 mg sodium

FAT-FIGHTING 4

1 g fiber

22 mg calcium

0 IU vitamin D

1,130 mg omega-3s

NOTE
You can purchase maple sugar in health food stores as well as in many supermarkets.

Grilled Mango Kebabs with Chocolate and Macadamia Nuts

PREP TIME: 15 MINUTES ◆ TOTAL TIME: 18 MINUTES

2 ripe mangoes
1 teaspoon canola oil
1 ounce bittersweet chocolate,
   finely chopped

1 to 2 tablespoons fat-free milk
1 tablespoon macadamia nuts,
   finely chopped

1 Preheat the grill.

2 With a sharp knife, cut both sides of each mango lengthwise along the pit, as close to the pit as possible. Lay each half skin side down on a cutting board. Score the flesh into 1" squares, without cutting through the skin. Invert the skin side so the fruit pops out. Cut the fruit cubes off close to the skin. (Reserve the fruit around the pits for another use.) Drizzle the cubes with oil and toss to coat. Thread the cubes onto 4 (12") skewers. Place on a tray.

3 Place the mangoes on the grill for about 30 seconds, or until browned on the bottom. With mitts, turn the skewers and grill for 30-second intervals, or until browned on all sides. Remove the cubes to 4 dessert dishes.

4 Combine the chocolate and milk in a microwaveable bowl. Microwave for 45 seconds, or until the chocolate loses its shape. Stir until smooth. Microwave for 10 seconds more if chunks remain. Drizzle the chocolate on the mango. Sprinkle with the nuts.

Makes 4 servings

PER SERVING: 129 calories, 1 g protein, 22 g carbohydrates, 6 g fat (2 g saturated fat), 0 mg cholesterol, 4 mg sodium

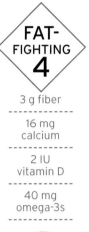

FAT-FIGHTING
4

3 g fiber

16 mg calcium

2 IU vitamin D

40 mg omega-3s

MAKE IT FAST

Mocha Pudding

PREP TIME: 5 MINUTES + CHILLING TIME

1 container (15 ounces) fat-free
  ricotta cheese
½ cup cocoa powder
⅓ cup confectioners' sugar

1 teaspoon pure vanilla extract
¼ teaspoon espresso powder
1 cup low-fat vanilla yogurt
12 chocolate-coated coffee beans

1 Combine the ricotta, cocoa powder, sugar, vanilla, espresso powder, and ¾ cup of the yogurt in a blender or food processor. Blend or process just until smooth.

2 Divide among 4 dessert dishes and refrigerate for 2 hours, or until set.

3 Top each pudding with 1 tablespoon of the remaining yogurt and 3 coffee beans.

Makes 4 servings

PER SERVING: 211 calories, 13 g protein, 31 g carbohydrates, 4 g fat (2 g saturated fat), 21 mg cholesterol, 154 mg sodium

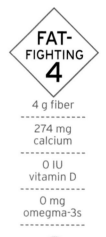

FAT-
FIGHTING
4

4 g fiber

274 mg
calcium

0 IU
vitamin D

0 mg
omegma-3s

MAKE IT
FAST

Tropical Yogurt Parfait

PREP TIME: 15 MINUTES

1 ½ cups cubed pineapple

1 mango, peeled, pitted, and chopped

1 cup raspberries

½ teaspoon chopped crystallized ginger

1 ½ cups fat-free vanilla Greek-style yogurt

¼ teaspoon ground cloves

¼ cup walnuts, toasted and coarsely chopped

FAT-FIGHTING 4

4 g fiber

143 mg calcium

0 IU vitamin D

740 mg omega-3s

MAKE IT FAST

1 Combine the pineapple, mango, raspberries, and ginger in a medium bowl. Combine the yogurt and cloves in a small bowl.

2 Layer half the fruit into 4 large parfait glasses or dessert dishes. Top with half the yogurt, then half the nuts. Repeat the layers, finishing with the walnuts.

Makes 4 servings

PER SERVING: 193 calories, 11 g protein, 29 g carbohydrates, 5 g fat (0.5 g saturated fat), 0 mg cholesterol, 37 mg sodium

SIPPABLES

Peach Lassi

PREP TIME: 5 MINUTES

½ cup low-fat Greek-style yogurt
½ cup frozen loose-pack peaches,
    cut into small chunks
2 tablespoons nonfat dry milk
½–¾ cup plain sparkling water

1 teaspoon pure vanilla extract
Pinch of ground cinnamon
Pinch of ground cardamom
½–¾ cup sparkling water

FAT-
FIGHTING
4

1 g fiber
----
320 mg
calcium

0.44 IU
vitamin D
----
0 mg
omega-3s

MAKE IT
FAST

Combine the yogurt, peaches, and dry milk in a blender or a food processor. Pulse for 1 minute, or until the peaches are finely chopped. With the machine running, add the vanilla extract, cinnamon, and cardamom. Gradually add the sparkling water until the desired consistency is reached. The mixture should be thick and frothy. Serve immediately.

Makes 1 serving (1¾ cup)

PER SERVING: 199 calories, 11 g protein, 37 g carbohydrates, 1 g fat (1 g saturated fat), 9 mg cholesterol, 146 mg sodium

Raspberry Lime Spritzer

PREP TIME: 10 MINUTES (INCLUDES MAKING THE SYRUP) ◆ TOTAL TIME: 13 MINUTES

6 ounces sparkling water

2 tablespoons raspberry syrup (recipe follows)

1 lime wedge

Combine the water and syrup in a tall glass. Squeeze in the lime juice. Stir. Add ice, if desired.

Makes 1 serving

PER SERVING: 67 calories, 0 g protein, 17 g carbohydrates, 0.5 g fat (0 g saturated fat), 0 mg cholesterol, 40 mg sodium

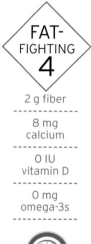

FAT-FIGHTING **4**

2 g fiber

8 mg calcium

0 IU vitamin D

0 mg omega-3s

MAKE IT FAST

Raspberry Syrup

1 cup frozen raspberries

2 tablespoons honey

1 Combine the raspberries and honey in a microwaveable bowl. Cover with plastic wrap, leaving a vent. Microwave on high for 2 to 3 minutes, or until steaming. Remove and allow to cool.

2 Set a fine mesh sieve over a bowl or other container. Pass the raspberry mixture through the sieve, pressing with the back of a spoon. There should be 6 tablespoons of syrup.

3 Place in a small covered jar and refrigerate for 2 weeks or freeze for 2 months.

MAKE IT AHEAD

The syrup recipe can be doubled or tripled. Pour 2-tablespoon portions into an ice cube tray and freeze for up to 2 months.

Kiwi Crème

PREP TIME: 5 MINUTES

1 kiwifruit, very ripe, peeled
⅓ cup fat-free evaporated milk
¼ cup crushed ice cubes

2 teaspoons confectioners' sugar
¼ teaspoon pure vanilla extract

Combine the kiwifruit, milk, ice, sugar, and vanilla extract in a blender or a food processor. Blend or process for 1 to 2 minutes, or until the mixture is thick. Pour into a tall glass.

Makes 1 serving

PER SERVING: 135 calories, 7 g protein, 26 g carbohydrates, 1 g fat (0.5 g saturated fat), 3 mg cholesterol, 100 mg sodium

FAT-FIGHTING
4

2 g fiber

273 mg
calcium

68 IU
vitamin D

300 mg
omega-3s

MAKE IT
FAST

Cherry-Almond Smoothie

PREP TIME: 5 MINUTES

6 ounces light silken tofu, drained
¼ cup slivered almonds
1½ cups frozen tart cherries

½ cup pomegranate-cherry 100% juice
1 teaspoon pure vanilla extract

Combine the tofu and almonds in a blender or food processor and pulse to blend. Add the cherries, juice, and vanilla extract. Process or blend to combine. Serve immediately.

Makes 2 servings (2 cups)

PER SERVING: 197 calories, 10 g protein, 23 g carbohydrates, 8 g fat (1 g saturated fat), 30 mg cholesterol, 30 mg sodium

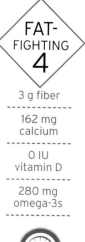

FAT-FIGHTING
4

3 g fiber
- - - - - - - - - - - - -
162 mg calcium
- - - - - - - - - - - - -
0 IU vitamin D
- - - - - - - - - - - - -
280 mg omega-3s
- - - - - - - - - - - - -

MAKE IT FAST

Gazpacho in a Glass

PREP TIME: 10 MINUTES

1 cup grape tomatoes, halved, or canned reduced-sodium diced tomatoes
1 tablespoon chopped celery
1 tablespoon chopped red bell pepper
1 tablespoon chopped onion
1 tablespoon chopped cucumber with skin
1 tablespoon chopped cilantro
1 tablespoon ground flaxseed
Wedge of lime
Pinch of salt
½ cup ice water
Hot-pepper sauce

FAT-FIGHTING 4

5 g fiber

47 mg calcium

0 IU vitamin D

1,860 mg omega-3s

MAKE IT FAST

Combine the tomatoes, celery, bell pepper, onion, cucumber, cilantro, flaxseed, squeeze of lime juice, salt, and ¼ cup of the water in a blender or a food processor. Pulse for 1 to 2 minutes, or until the mixture is finely chopped. Add up to ¼ cup more water and pulse to combine. Season to taste with the hot-pepper sauce.

Makes 1 serving

PER SERVING: 81 calories, 3 g protein, 11 g carbohydrates, 4 g fat (0.5 g saturated fat), 0 mg cholesterol, 181 mg sodium

MAKE IT AHEAD
To make more servings at once, simply quadruple the recipe. You can keep it in a tightly covered container in the refrigerator for up to 3 days. Shake well before serving.

Orange-Vanilla Shake

PREP TIME: 5 MINUTES

½ cup fat-free vanilla frozen yogurt
2 tablespoons frozen orange juice
  concentrate

1 tablespoon ground flaxseed
½ teaspoon pure vanilla extract

Combine the yogurt, orange juice concentrate, flaxseed, and vanilla extract in a blender or food processor. Pulse until blended. Serve immediately.

Makes 1 serving

PER SERVING: 201 calories, 7 g protein, 35 g carbohydrates, 4 g fat (0.5 g saturated fat), 2 mg cholesterol, 68 mg sodium

FAT-FIGHTING **4**

3 g fiber

200 mg calcium

0 IU vitamin D

1,860 mg omega-3s

MAKE IT FAST

Frosty Chocolate Milkshake

PREP TIME: 5 MINUTES

2 tablespoons unsweetened dark cocoa
powder
2 tablespoons confectioners' sugar
2 tablespoons boiling water

¾ cup 1% milk
⅓ cup crushed ice cubes
2 teaspoons pure vanilla extract

FAT-
FIGHTING
4

4 g fiber

235 mg
calcium

95 IU
vitamin D

0 mg
omega-3s

MAKE IT
FAST

In a glass measuring cup, whisk the cocoa, sugar, and water until a syrup forms. Add the milk and stir to completely dissolve the syrup. Pour into a blender or a food processor, along with the ice and vanilla. Blend or process for 1 to 2 minutes, or until the mixture is thick, creamy, and slightly lighter in color. A few tiny specks of ice may remain. Pour into a frosted 20-ounce glass and serve immediately.

Makes 1 serving

PER SERVING: 172 calories, 8 g protein, 30 g carbohydrates, 3 g fat (2 g saturated fat), 9 mg cholesterol, 86 mg sodium

Horchata

PREP TIME: 5 MINUTES

1 tablespoon blanched almonds
$\frac{1}{3}$ cup fat-free evaporated milk
$\frac{1}{4}$ cup crushed ice

$\frac{1}{8}$ teaspoon almond extract
Pinch of ground cinnamon
1 teaspoon honey

1 Grind the almonds into a powder in a blender or small food processor. Add the milk, ice, almond extract, and cinnamon. Blend or process for 1 minute, or until frothy.

2 Pour into a glass. Stir in the honey. Serve with a spoon to scoop up all the almond bits.

Makes 1 serving

PER SERVING: 143 calories, 8 g protein, 17 g carbohydrates, 5 g fat (0.5 g saturated fat), 3 mg cholesterol, 101 mg sodium

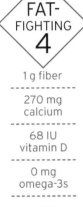

FAT-FIGHTING
4

1 g fiber

270 mg
calcium

68 IU
vitamin D

0 mg
omega-3s

MAKE IT
FAST

Chai Latte Frappé

PREP TIME: 16 MINUTES

1 chai-flavored tea bag
½ cup fat-free vanilla Greek-style yogurt

1 tablespoon ground flaxseed

1 Prepare the tea using just ¼ cup boiling water. Let steep for 5 minutes. Discard the tea bag and place the tea in the freezer to chill for 10 minutes.

2 Combine the tea, yogurt, and flaxseed in a blender and pulse until blended. Serve immediately.

Makes 1 serving (½ cup)

PER SERVING: 128 calories, 13 g protein, 13 g carbohydrates, 3 g fat (0.5 g saturated fat), 0 mg cholesterol, 48 mg sodium

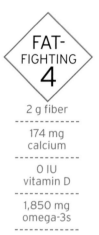

FAT-
FIGHTING
4

2 g fiber

174 mg
calcium

0 IU
vitamin D

1,850 mg
omega-3s

MAKE IT
FAST

Coffeehouse Latte

PREP TIME: 5 MINUTES

¼ cup fat-free evaporated milk
½ cup brewed regular or
    decaffeinated coffee

1 teaspoon honey
Ground cinnamon
Cocoa powder

1 Place the milk in a 1-pint microwaveable glass jar. Microwave on high power for 1 minute, or until hot. Screw on the jar lid. Holding the jar with an oven mitt, shake the milk vigorously for about 30 seconds, or until frothy.

2 Pour the coffee into a large cup. Add the honey and stir. Pour in the frothed milk. Dust with cinnamon and/or cocoa.

Makes 1 serving

PER SERVING: 73 calories, 4 g protein, 14 g carbohydrates, 0 g fat (0 g saturated fat), 0 mg cholesterol, 83 mg sodium

NOTE
The hot milk can also be frothed with a battery-operated cappuccino whip or a stove-top plunger cappuccino frother.

FAT-FIGHTING 4

0 g fiber

66 mg calcium

48 IU vitamin D

0 mg omega-3s

MAKE IT FAST

PART
3
DTOUR RESOURCES

Menus and More to Help
You Stay on Track

14 DAYS OF DTOUR MENUS

We know that changing your diet can be hard, which is why we've designed the DTOUR recipes to be as easy—and delicious!—as possible. Many are ready to eat in 30 minutes or less. And because each category of recipes follows specific nutritional guidelines, you can mix and match them to create daily menus to your liking.

But you may be of the same mind as some of our DTOUR test panelists, who preferred a more structured dietary approach. "Just tell me what to eat!" they told us. With them—and you—in mind, we've asked our dietitian, Barbara Quinn, MS, RD, CDE, to develop 2 weeks' worth of sample menus using a selection of our DTOUR recipes. You can follow the menus as presented here, or use them as a jumping-off point to building your own meals and snacks.

First, you'll need to choose your calorie level, if you haven't already done so. (Page 28 explains how.) Each of our daily menus comes in a 1,400- and a 1,600-calorie version. As you'll see, most of the menus are a bit over or under their calorie mark, and that's okay. Trying to get a precise number of calories every day would be maddening. As long as you aren't straying too far from your calorie budget, you'll lose weight.

That said, it's important to pay attention to your serving sizes. If you don't, the calories can quickly add up. Keep in mind that many of the DTOUR recipes make 4 to 6 servings. You can store any leftovers for another meal.

Each day's menu features 3 meals and 2 snacks, with 1 snack between lunch and dinner and the other after dinner. As a rule of thumb, you should time your snacks with your meals so that you're eating every 3 to 4 hours. This helps keep your blood sugar on an even keel. So if you eat breakfast around 6 o'clock in the morning but don't get your lunch break until noon, then you should plan your snack for around 9 o'clock.

If you follow these menus to the letter, you will meet or exceed DTOUR's recommended daily intakes for the Fat-Fighting 4: 25 to 30 grams of fiber; 1,200 milligrams of calcium; 155 IU of vitamin D; and 2,500 to 2,700 milligrams of omega-3s. Remember that for vitamin D, the the daily intake is from foods. Your body also manufactures the vitamin with adequate sun exposure. (If you don't spend much time in the sun, you might want to consider taking a vitamin D supplement, as discussed on page 31.)

We have suggested beverages to accompany many of the meals and snacks. Where we haven't, you're welcome to add sparkling water, coffee, tea, or a reduced-calorie beverage containing no more than 20 calories per serving.

By the way, if a menu features a meal or snack that doesn't appeal to you, you can substitute any other recipe, as long as the calories per serving are nearly the same. Feel free to experiment! We do recommend eating a variety of foods so you're getting a good mix of a range of nutrients. With 200 recipes to choose from, you just might find some new favorites here!

DAY 1

1,400 CALORIES

BREAKFAST

☐ 1 Peanutty Pocket (p. 89)

☐ ½ cup fat-free milk

LUNCH

☐ 1 Tuscan Tuna Salad Wrap (p. 126)

☐ 1 ounce mozzarella string cheese

☐ 1 fresh orange

SNACK

☐ 1 serving Cherry Almond Smoothie (p. 293)

DINNER

☐ 1 serving Spaghetti Carbonara (p. 66)

☐ 2 servings Roasted Asparagus with Toasted Walnuts (p. 151)

SNACK

☐ ½ cup fresh or frozen blueberries

☐ 1 cup low-fat or light yogurt

DAY 1 TOTALS: 1,419 calories, 72 g protein, 139 g carbohydrate, 49 g fat (11 g saturated fat), 1,765 mg sodium

- -

FAT-FIGHTING 4: 26 g fiber, 1,146 mg calcium, 184 IU vitamin D, 3,068 mg omega-3s

1,600 CALORIES

BREAKFAST

☐ 1 Peanutty Pocket (p. 89)

☐ 1 cup fat-free milk

LUNCH

☐ 1 Tuscan Tuna Salad Wrap (p. 126)

☐ 1 ounce mozzarella string cheese

☐ 1 fresh orange

SNACK

☐ 1 serving Cherry Almond Smoothie (p. 293)

DINNER

☐ 1 serving Spaghetti Carbonara (p. 66)

☐ 2 servings Roasted Asparagus with Toasted Walnuts (p. 151)

☐ Garlic Toast: Toast 1 slice sourdough bread and spread with mixture of 1 teaspoon olive oil and 1 clove garlic, finely chopped. Place in hot oven or broiler until browned.

SNACK

☐ ½ cup fresh or frozen blueberries

☐ 1 cup low-fat or light yogurt

DAY 1 TOTALS: 1,596 calories, 85 g protein, 177 g carbohydrate, 63 g fat (13 g saturated fat), 1,985 mg sodium

- -

FAT-FIGHTING 4: 30 g fiber, 1,319 mg calcium, 184 IU vitamin D, 3,398 mg omega-3s

DAY 2

1,400 CALORIES

BREAKFAST

- ☐ ½ Breakfast Burrito (p. 79)
- ☐ 1 Coffeehouse Latte (p. 300)
- ☐ 1 fresh orange, sliced

LUNCH

- ☐ 1 Endive Cheese Pita (p. 56)
- ☐ 2 tablespoons chopped walnuts

SNACK

- ☐ 2 servings (2 pieces) Fruit 'n' Nut Bark (p. 280)
- ☐ 1 cup fat-free milk

DINNER

- ☐ Grilled Salmon with Wasabi Aioli Sandwich (p. 125)

SNACK

- ☐ 1 Gooey Date Bar (p. 275)
- ☐ ½ cup fat-free milk

DAY 2 TOTALS: 1,381 calories, 80 g protein, 162 g carbohydrate, 50 g fat (11 g saturated fat), 2,234 mg sodium

----

FAT-FIGHTING 4: 20 g fiber, 1,493 mg calcium, 301 IU vitamin D, 5,524 mg omega-3s

1,600 CALORIES

BREAKFAST

- ☐ ½ Breakfast Burrito (p. 79)
- ☐ 1 scrambled egg
- ☐ 1 Coffeehouse Latte (p. 300)
- ☐ 1 fresh orange, sliced

LUNCH

- ☐ 1 Endive Cheese Pita (p. 56)
- ☐ 3 tablespoons chopped walnuts

SNACK

- ☐ 2 servings (2 pieces) Fruit 'n' Nut Bark (p. 280)
- ☐ 1 cup fat-free milk

DINNER

- ☐ Grilled Salmon with Wasabi Aioli Sandwich (p. 125)

SNACK

- ☐ 1 Gooey Date Bar (p. 275)
- ☐ 1 cup fat-free milk

DAY 2 TOTALS: 1,554 calories, 92 g protein, 169 g carbohydrate, 60 g fat (13 g saturated fat), 2,369 mg sodium

----

FAT-FIGHTING 4: 21 g fiber, 1,684 mg calcium, 368 IU vitamin D, 6,245 mg omega-3s

DAY 3

1,400 CALORIES

BREAKFAST

- ☐ 1 serving Breakfast Oats with Pears (p. 83)
- ☐ 1 cup fat-free milk

LUNCH

- ☐ 1 Cubano Panini (p. 123)
- ☐ 1 serving Spiced-Up Spinach Salad (p. 138)

SNACK

- ☐ 2 tablespoons hummus
- ☐ 1 rye crispbread cracker

DINNER

- ☐ 1 serving Ranch Chicken Fingers (p. 183)
- ☐ 1 serving Spiced-Up Spinach Salad, left over from lunch (p. 138)

SNACK

- ☐ 1 serving Cheese-and-Nut Stacks (p. 44)

DAY 3 TOTALS: 1,418 calories, 84 g protein, 156 g carbohydrate, 57 g fat (8 g saturated fat), 2,200 mg sodium

- -

FAT-FIGHTING 4: 26 g fiber, 784 mg calcium, 100 IU vitamin D, 7,100 mg omega-3s

1,600 CALORIES

BREAKFAST

- ☐ 1 serving Breakfast Oats with Pears (p. 83)
- ☐ 1 cup fat-free milk

LUNCH

- ☐ 1 Cubano Panini (p. 123)
- ☐ 1 serving Spiced-Up Spinach Salad (p. 138)

SNACK

- ☐ 4 tablespoons hummus
- ☐ 2 rye crispbread crackers

DINNER

- ☐ 1 serving Ranch Chicken Fingers (p. 183)
- ☐ 1 serving Spiced-Up Spinach Salad, left over from lunch (p. 138)

SNACK

- ☐ 1 serving + 2 Cheese-and-Nut Stacks (p. 44)

DAY 3 TOTALS: 1,581 calories, 89 g protein, 201 g carbohydrate, 63 g fat (11 g saturated fat), 2,458 sodium

- -

FAT-FIGHTING 4: 34 g fiber, 1,166 mg calcium, 175 IU vitamin D, 7,470 mg omega-3s

DAY 4

1,400 CALORIES

BREAKFAST

- ❑ 1 serving Seattle Salmon Hash (p. 82)
- ❑ 1 slice reduced-calorie high-fiber bread
- ❑ 1 cup fat-free milk

LUNCH

- ❑ 1 Chipotle Grilled Cheese Sandwich (p. 116)
- ❑ 1 cup raw carrot slices
- ❑ 1 cup fresh tomato slices

SNACK

- ❑ 1 medium banana
- ❑ 1 tablespoon omega-3-enriched peanut butter

DINNER

- ❑ 1 serving Balsamic-Glazed Flank Steak with Broccoli Raab and Chickpea Puree (p. 162)
- ❑ 1 serving Spicy Sweet Potato "Fries" with Creole Mustard Dipping Sauce (p. 45)

SNACK

- ❑ 1 serving Mini Turnovers with Raspberries (p. 278)

DAY 4 TOTALS: 1,390 calories, 78 g protein, 168 g carbohydrate, 49 g fat (14 g saturated fat), 2,233 mg sodium

- -

FAT-FIGHTING 4: 30 g fiber, 1,098 mg calcium, 100 IU vitamin D, 6,590 mg omega-3s

1,600 CALORIES

BREAKFAST

- ❑ 1 serving Seattle Salmon Hash (p. 82)
- ❑ 1 slice reduced-calorie high-fiber bread
- ❑ 1 tablespoon canola oil margarine
- ❑ 1 cup fat-free milk

LUNCH

- ❑ 1 Chipotle Grilled Cheese Sandwich (p. 116)
- ❑ 1 cup raw carrot slices
- ❑ 1 cup fresh tomato slices
- ❑ ½ cup fat-free milk

SNACK

- ❑ 1 medium banana
- ❑ 1 tablespoon omega-3-enriched peanut butter

DINNER

- ❑ 1 serving Balsamic-Glazed Flank Steak with Broccoli Raab and Chickpea Puree (p. 162)
- ❑ 1 serving Spicy Sweet Potato "Fries" with Creole Mustard Dipping Sauce (p. 45)

SNACK

- ❑ 1 serving Mini Turnovers with Raspberries (p. 278)
- ❑ ½ cup fat-free milk

DAY 4 TOTALS: 1,582 calories, 86 g protein, 60 g carbohydrate, 60 g fat (16 g saturated fat), 2,463 mg sodium

- -

FAT-FIGHTING 4: 30 g fat, 1,414 mg calcium, 200 IU vitamin D, 6,594 mg omega-3s

DAY 5

1,400 CALORIES

BREAKFAST

- ❏ 1 Breakfast "Banana Split" (p. 95)
- ❏ 1 ounce almonds (23 whole kernels)

LUNCH

- ❏ 2 servings (2 halves) Mexicana Deviled Eggs (p. 42)
- ❏ 1 serving Field Greens with Pear and Walnuts (p. 136)
- ❏ 4 reduced-fat whole grain crackers (such as Triscuits)

SNACK

- ❏ 1 Orange-Vanilla Shake (p. 295)

DINNER

- ❏ 1 Open-Faced Sweet-and-Spicy Chicken Sandwich (p. 119)
- ❏ 1 Gazpacho in a Glass (p. 294)

SNACK

- ❏ 9 (1 serving) Maple-Walnut Bites (p. 282)

DAY 5 TOTALS: 1,406 calories, 80 g protein, 156 g carbohydrate, 55 g fat (6 g saturated fat), 1,273 mg sodium

- -

FAT-FIGHTING 4: 24 g fiber, 1,051 mg calcium, 115 IU vitamin D, 5,760 mg omega-3s

1,600 CALORIES

BREAKFAST

- ❏ 1 Breakfast "Banana Split" (p. 95)
- ❏ 1 slice reduced-calorie high-fiber bread
- ❏ 1 ounce almonds (23 whole kernels)

LUNCH

- ❏ 2 servings (2 halves) Mexicana Deviled Eggs (p. 42)
- ❏ 1 serving Field Greens with Pear and Walnuts (p. 136)
- ❏ 8 reduced-fat whole grain crackers (such as Triscuits)

SNACK

- ❏ 1 Orange-Vanilla Shake (p. 295)

DINNER

- ❏ 1 Open-Faced Sweet-and-Spicy Chicken Sandwich (p. 119)
- ❏ 1 ounce reduced-fat provolone cheese
- ❏ 1 Gazpacho in a Glass (p. 294)

SNACK

- ❏ 9 (1 serving) Maple-Walnut Bites (p. 282)
- ❏ 1 cup fat-free milk

DAY 5 TOTALS: 1,601 calories, 91 g protein, 180 g carbohydrate, 63 g fat (10 g saturated fat), 1,718 mg sodium

- -

FAT-FIGHTING 4: 29 g fiber, 1,285 mg calcium, 114 IU vitamin D, 5,810 omega-3s

DAY 6

1,400 CALORIES

BREAKFAST

❏ 1 slice (2 servings) Baked French Toast (p. 88)

LUNCH

❏ 1 serving Citrus Arugula Salad with Grilled Chicken (p. 130)

❏ 1 cup fat-free milk

SNACK

❏ 1 cup fresh apple slices

❏ 1 tablespoon omega-3-enriched peanut butter

DINNER

❏ 1 Grilled Vegetable Stack (p. 114)

❏ 2 servings Hot-and-Sour Soup (p. 103)

SNACK

❏ 1 Kiwi Crème (p. 292)

❏ 2 tablespoons unsalted almonds

DAY 6 TOTALS: 1,401 calories, 96 g protein, 148 g carbohydrate, 49 g fat (11 g saturated fat), 1,641 mg sodium

----

FAT-FIGHTING 4: 22 g fiber, 1,610 g calcium, 328 IU vitamin D, 2,050 mg omega-3s

1,600 CALORIES

BREAKFAST

❏ 1 slice (2 servings) Baked French Toast (p. 88)

❏ 1 tablespoon trans-fat-free, low-saturated-fat margarine

LUNCH

❏ 1 serving Citrus Arugula Salad with Grilled Chicken (p. 130)

❏ 1 cup fat-free milk

❏ 1 slice reduced-calorie, high-fiber bread and 1 teaspoon trans-fat-free, low-saturated-fat margarine

SNACK

❏ 1 cup fresh apple slices

❏ 1 tablespoon omega-3-enriched peanut butter

DINNER

❏ 1 Grilled Vegetable Stack (p. 114)

❏ 2 servings Hot-and-Sour Soup (p. 103)

SNACK

❏ 1 Kiwi Crème (p. 292)

❏ 2 tablespoons unsalted almonds

DAY 6 TOTALS: 1,603 calories, 99 g protein, 160 g carbohydrate, 66 g fat (13 g saturated fat), 1,891 mg sodium

----

FAT-FIGHTING 4: 26 g fiber, 1,632 mg calcium, 328 IU vitamin D, 2,050 mg omega-3s

DAY 7

1,400 CALORIES

BREAKFAST

❏ 1 Italian Egg Sandwich (p. 75) with 1 teaspoon olive oil added to the skillet

LUNCH

❏ 1 serving Chinese Chopped Salad with Shrimp (p. 142)

❏ ½ medium avocado, sliced

❏ ½ cup fat-free milk

SNACK

❏ 1 medium fresh pear

❏ 2 tablespoons light cream cheese

DINNER

❏ 1 serving Santa Fe Chicken (p. 193)

❏ 1 serving Spinach and Fennel Salad (p. 139)

SNACK

❏ 2 servings Clam Dip with Crudités (p. 62)

DAY 7 TOTALS: 1,413 calories, 106 g protein, 140 g fat, 50 g fat (15 g saturated fat), 2,231 mg sodium

----

FAT-FIGHTING 4: 31 g fiber, 1,327 mg calcium, 220 IU vitamin D, 854 mg omega-3s

1,600 CALORIES

BREAKFAST

❏ 1 Italian Egg Sandwich (p. 75) with 1 teaspoon olive oil added to the skillet

LUNCH

❏ 1 serving Chinese Chopped Salad with Shrimp (p. 142)

❏ ½ medium avocado, sliced

❏ ½ cup fat-free milk

SNACK

❏ 1 medium fresh pear

❏ 2 tablespoons light cream cheese

DINNER

❏ 1 serving Santa Fe Chicken (p. 193)

❏ 2 servings Spinach and Fennel Salad (p. 139)

SNACK

❏ 2 servings Clam Dip with Crudités (p. 62)

DAY 7 TOTALS: 1,601 calories, 120 g protein, 160 g carbohydrate, 56 g fat (15 g saturated fat), 2,456 mg sodium

----

FAT-FIGHTING 4: 34 g fiber, 1,436 mg calcium, 295 IU vitamin D, 1,104 mg omega-3s

DAY 8

1,400 CALORIES

BREAKFAST

- ❑ 1 Carrot-Walnut Muffin (p. 90)
- ❑ 1 teaspoon canola oil margarine
- ❑ 1 cup fat-free milk

LUNCH

- ❑ 1 serving Creamy Italian Pasta Salad (p. 132)
- ❑ 10 large black olives

SNACK

- ❑ 1 serving Cheese-and-Nut Stacks (p. 44)

DINNER

- ❑ 1 serving Smoky Black Bean Soup (p. 105)
- ❑ 1 serving Savory Artichoke Tomato Tart (p. 52)

SNACK

- ❑ 1 serving Raspberry Soufflé (p. 258)
- ❑ 2 tablespoons unsalted almonds

DAY 8 TOTALS: 1,426 calories, 70 g protein, 146 g carbohydrate, 42 g fat (8 g saturated fat), 1,538 mg sodium

----

FAT-FIGHTING 4: 26 g fiber, 985 mg calcium, 124 IU vitamin D, 1,460 mg omega-3s

1,600 CALORIES

BREAKFAST

- ❑ 1 Carrot-Walnut Muffin (p. 90)
- ❑ 1 teaspoon canola oil margarine
- ❑ 1 cup fat-free milk

LUNCH

- ❑ 1 serving Creamy Italian Pasta Salad (p. 132)
- ❑ 10 large black olives
- ❑ 1 ounce low-fat mozzarella cheese

SNACK

- ❑ 1 serving Cheese-and-Nut Stacks (p. 44)

DINNER

- ❑ 1 serving Smoky Black Bean Soup (p. 105)
- ❑ 1 serving Savory Artichoke Tomato Tart (p. 52)

SNACK

- ❑ 1 serving Raspberry Soufflé (p. 258)
- ❑ 4 tablespoons unsalted almonds

DAY 8 TOTALS: 1,609 calories, 81 g protein, 150 g carbohydrate, 57 g fat (12 g saturated fat), 1,713 mg sodium

----

FAT-FIGHTING 4: 28 g fiber, 1,253 mg calcium, 124 IU vitamin D, 1,500 mg omega-3s

DAY 9

1,400 CALORIES

BREAKFAST

❏ 1 serving Farmers' Market Scrambled Eggs (p. 72) includes 1 slice toasted light whole grain bread and 1 cup fat-free milk

❏ 1 teaspoon trans-fat-free, low-saturated-fat margarine

LUNCH

❏ 2 servings Spiced-Up Spinach Salad (p. 138)

SNACK

❏ 1 Carrot-Walnut Muffin (p. 90)

❏ ½ cup fat-free milk

DINNER

❏ 1 serving Southern "Fried" Chicken Fingers with Mashed Sweet Potatoes (p. 181)

❏ 1 medium tomato, sliced

SNACK

❏ 1 Frosty Chocolate Milkshake (p. 296)

DAY 9 TOTALS: 1,397 calories, 78 g protein, 171 g carbohydrate, 50 g fat (9 g saturated fat), 1,949 mg sodium

- -

FAT-FIGHTING 4: 29 g fiber, 1,163 mg calcium, 266 IU vitamin D, 5,774 mg omega-3s

1,600 CALORIES

BREAKFAST

❏ 1 serving Farmers' Market Scrambled Eggs (p. 72) includes 1 slice toasted light whole grain bread and 1 cup fat-free milk

❏ 1 teaspoon trans-fat-free, low-saturated fat margarine

LUNCH

❏ 2 servings Spiced-Up Spinach Salad (p. 138)

❏ 1 ounce low-fat mozzarella cheese

SNACK

❏ 1 Carrot-Walnut Muffin (p. 90)

❏ ½ cup fat-free milk

❏ 1 tablespoon trans-fat-free, low-saturated-fat margarine

DINNER

❏ 1 serving Southern "Fried" Chicken Fingers with Mashed Sweet Potatoes (p. 181)

❏ 1 medium tomato, sliced

SNACK

❏ 1 Frosty Chocolate Milkshake (p. 296)

DAY 9 TOTALS: 1,579 calories, 85 g protein, 171 g carbohydrate, 67 g fat (13 g saturated fat), 2,224 mg sodium

- -

FAT-FIGHTING 4: 29 g fiber, 1,385 mg calcium, 266 IU vitamin D, 5,814 mg omega-3s

DAY 10

1,400 CALORIES

BREAKFAST

- ❐ 1 slice reduced-calorie, high-fiber bread
- ❐ 2 tablespoons omega-3-enriched peanut butter
- ❐ 1 cup fat-free milk

LUNCH

- ❐ 1 Buffalo Chicken Salad Sandwich (p. 118)
- ❐ 1 fresh orange

SNACK

- ❐ 1 small fresh apple
- ❐ 1 ounce low-fat mozzarella cheese

DINNER

- ❐ 1 serving Moroccan Lentil Soup (p. 108)

SNACK

- ❐ 1 serving Blueberry Buckle (p. 259)
- ❐ ½ ounce walnuts (about 7 walnut halves)

DAY 10 TOTALS: 1,420 calories, 84 g protein, 159 g carbohydrate, 53 g fat (12 g saturated fat), 1,729 mg sodium

- -

FAT-FIGHTING 4: 32 g fiber, 999 mg calcium, 108 IU vitamin D, 2,530 omega-3s

1,600 CALORIES

BREAKFAST

- ❐ 1 slice reduced-calorie, high-fiber bread
- ❐ 2 tablespoons omega-3-enriched peanut butter
- ❐ 2 tablespoons raisins
- ❐ 1 cup fat-free milk

LUNCH

- ❐ 1 Buffalo Chicken Salad Sandwich (p. 118)
- ❐ 1 fresh orange

SNACK

- ❐ 1 small fresh apple
- ❐ 1 ounce low-fat mozzarella cheese

DINNER

- ❐ 1 serving Moroccan Lentil Soup (p. 108)

SNACK

- ❐ 1 serving Blueberry Buckle (p. 259)
- ❐ 1 ounce walnuts (about 14 halves)

DAY 10 TOTALS: 1,577 calories, 87 g protein, 177 g carbohydrate, 63 g fat (13 g saturated fat), 1,731 mg sodium

- -

FAT-FIGHTING 4: 34 g fiber, 1,024 mg calcium, 108 IU vitamin D, 3,830 mg omega-3s

DAY 11

1,400 CALORIES

BREAKFAST

- ❐ 1 Egg and Tomato Sandwich (p. 73)
- ❐ ½ cup fat-free milk

LUNCH

- ❐ 1 serving Moroccan Lentil Soup, left over from Day 10 dinner (p. 108)

SNACK

- ❐ 1 cup low-fat or light yogurt
- ❐ 2 tablespoons flaxseed meal
- ❐ 4 dried apricots

DINNER

- ❐ 1 Pork and Vegetable Tostada (p. 171)
- ❐ 1 serving Cilantro Jicama Salad (p. 137)

SNACK

- ❐ 1 medium banana

DAY 11 TOTALS: 1,406 calories, 85 g protein, 184 g carbohydrate, 38 g fat (12 g saturated fat), 1,774 mg sodium

----

FAT-FIGHTING 4: 34 g fiber, 1,203 mg calcium, 153 IU vitamin D, 234 mg omega-3s

1,600 CALORIES

BREAKFAST

- ❐ 1 Egg and Tomato Sandwich (p. 73)
- ❐ ½ cup fat-free milk

LUNCH

- ❐ 1 serving Moroccan Lentil Soup, left over from Day 10 dinner (p. 108)

SNACK

- ❐ 1 cup low-fat or light yogurt
- ❐ 2 tablespoons flaxseed meal
- ❐ 4 dried apricots

DINNER

- ❐ 1 Pork and Vegetable Tostada (p. 171)
- ❐ 1 serving Cilantro Jicama Salad (p. 137)

SNACK

- ❐ 1 medium banana
- ❐ 2 tablespoons omega-3-enriched peanut butter

DAY 11 TOTALS: 1,600 calories, 93 g protein, 189 g carbohydrate, 56 g fat (15 g saturated fat), 1,888 mg sodium

----

FAT-FIGHTING 4: 34 g fiber, 1,203 mg calcium, 153 IU vitamin D, 1,234 mg omega-3s

DAY 12

1,400 CALORIES

BREAKFAST

❏ 1 serving Coconut Cream of Wheat with Strawberries and Pistachios (p. 84)

❏ 1 medium boiled egg

LUNCH

❏ 1 Curry Fish Sandwich (p. 124)

❏ 1 medium fresh orange

SNACK

❏ 1 Horchata (p. 298)

DINNER

❏ 1 serving Slow Cooker Beef Pot Roast with Root Vegetables (p. 164)

❏ 1 serving Sweet-and-Sour Cabbage (p. 144)

SNACK

❏ 8 reduced-fat whole-grain crackers (such as Triscuits)

❏ 1 ounce low-fat mozzarella cheese

DAY 12 TOTALS: 1,400 calories, 84 g protein, 167 g carbohydrate, 53 g fat (10 g saturated fat), 2,047 mg sodium

- -

FAT-FIGHTING 4: 31 g fiber, 1,186 mg calcium, 170 IU vitamin D, 3,648 mg omega-3s

1,600 CALORIES

BREAKFAST

❏ 1 serving Coconut Cream of Wheat with Strawberries and Pistachios (p. 84)

❏ 1 medium boiled egg

LUNCH

❏ 1 Curry Fish Sandwich (p. 124)

❏ 1 medium avocado, sliced

❏ 1 medium fresh orange

SNACK

❏ 1 Horchata (p. 298)

❏ 2 tablespoons walnuts (about 7 halves)

DINNER

❏ 1 serving Slow Cooker Beef Pot Roast with Root Vegetables (p. 164)

❏ 1 serving Sweet-and-Sour Cabbage (p. 144)

SNACK

❏ 8 reduced-fat whole-grain crackers (such as Triscuits)

❏ 1 ounce low-fat mozzarella cheese

DAY 12 TOTALS: 1,575 calories, 93 g protein, 169 g carbohydrate 68 g fat (12 g saturated fat), 2,109 mg sodium

- -

FAT-FIGHTING 4: 32 g fiber, 1,225 mg calcium, 170 IU vitamin D, 4,966 mg omega-3s

DAY 13

1,400 CALORIES

BREAKFAST

❏ 1 serving Spinach Frittata (p. 74): includes 1 slice whole-grain toast and 1 cup fat-free milk

❏ 1 tablespoon fat-free, low-saturated-fat margarine

LUNCH

❏ 1 Knife-and-Fork Turkey Reuben (p. 120)

❏ 1 cup fat-free milk

SNACK

❏ 1 Orange-Vanilla Shake (p. 295)

DINNER

❏ 1 serving Chinese Salmon (p. 220)

❏ 1 serving Ginger Roasted Squash (p. 150)

SNACK

❏ 3 dates stuffed with 1 tablespoon pecans

DAY 13 TOTALS: 1,428 calories, 89 g protein, 151 g carbohydrate, 56 g fat (11 g saturated fat), 2,188 mg sodium

----

FAT-FIGHTING 4: 22 g fiber, 1,372 mg calcium, 218 IU vitamin D, 4,420 mg omega-3s

1,600 CALORIES

BREAKFAST

❏ 1 serving Spinach Frittata (p. 74): includes 1 slice whole-grain toast and 1 cup fat-free milk

❏ 1 tablespoon fat-free, low-saturated-fat margarine

LUNCH

❏ 1 Knife-and-Fork Turkey Reuben (p. 120)

❏ 1 cup fat-free milk

❏ 1 cup cantaloupe or watermelon cubes

SNACK

❏ 1 Orange-Vanilla Shake (p. 295)

DINNER

❏ 1 serving Chinese Salmon (p. 220)

❏ 1 serving Ginger Roasted Squash (p. 150)

SNACK

❏ 6 dates stuffed with 2 tablespoons pecans

DAY 13 TOTALS: 1,598 calories, 90 g protein, 182 g carbohydrate, 65 g fat (11 g saturated fat), 2,215 mg sodium

----

FAT-FIGHTING 4: 27 g fiber, 1,404 mg calcium, 218 IU vitamin D, 4,420 mg omega-3s

DAY 14

1,400 CALORIES

BREAKFAST

❐ 1 slice (1 serving) Banana-Peanut Bread (p. 92)

❐ ½ cup fat-free milk

LUNCH

❐ 2 Tuna Cakes (p. 215)

❐ 1 serving Garbanzo and Roasted Tomato Salad (p. 133)

SNACK

❐ 1 cup low-fat plain yogurt

❐ 1 cup sliced strawberries

DINNER

❐ 1 serving Southern-Style Pork, Black-Eyed Peas, and Collard Greens (p. 169)

❐ 1 slice low-calorie, high-fiber bread

❐ 1 tablespoon trans-fat-free, low-saturated-fat margarine

SNACK

❐ 1 Tropical Yogurt Parfait (p. 286)

DAY 14 TOTALS: 1,405 calories, 98 g protein, 150 g carbohydrate, 49 g fat (8 g saturated fat), 1,683 mg sodium

- -

FAT-FIGHTING 4: 27 g fiber, 1,046 mg calcium, 57 IU vitamin D, 3,844 mg omega-3s

1,600 CALORIES

BREAKFAST

❐ 1 slice (1 serving) Banana-Peanut Bread (p. 92)

❐ 1 tablespoon trans-fat-free, low-saturated-fat margarine

❐ ½ cup fat-free milk

LUNCH

❐ 2 Tuna Cakes (p. 215)

❐ 1 serving Garbanzo and Roasted Tomato Salad (p. 133)

❐ 6 reduced-fat whole-grain crackers (such as Triscuits)

SNACK

❐ 1 cup low-fat plain yogurt

❐ 1 cup sliced strawberries

DINNER

❐ 1 serving Southern-Style Pork, Black-Eyed Peas, and Collard Greens (p. 169)

❐ 1 slice low-calorie, high-fiber bread

❐ 1 tablespoon trans-fat-free, low-saturated-fat margarine

SNACK

❐ 1 Tropical Yogurt Parfait (p. 286)

DAY 14 TOTALS: 1,597 calories, 100 g protein, 167 g carbohydrate, 62 g fat (10 g saturated fat), 1,903 mg sodium

- -

FAT-FIGHTING 4: 29 g fiber, 1,046 mg calcium, 57 IU vitamin D, 3,844 mg omega-3s

DTOUR ON THE GO

While we've tried to make the DTOUR recipes as fast and easy to prepare as possible, we realize that you may not always have the time—or the inclination—to cook a meal from scratch. With that in mind, we've assembled a short list of prepared and fast-food options that will fit into the DTOUR plan. Swap them into your daily menus as you need to, though we do recommend enjoying them in moderation.

FROZEN DINNERS

Look for dinners containing 300 to 400 calories, with 25 to 35 grams of carbohydrates (or up to 45 grams if the meal is closer to 400 calories), 5 or more grams of fiber, and not more than 3 grams of saturated fat. Ideally, a frozen meal will also deliver a generous amount of omega-3s and at least 10 percent of the Daily Values for calcium (1,000 milligrams) and vitamin D (400 IU).

Amy's Bowls Brown Rice and Vegetables

Amy's Bowls Light in Sodium Brown Rice & Vegetables

Amy's Indian Mattar Tofu

Amy's Indian Palak Paneer

Amy's Organic Bowls Brown Rice, Black-Eyed Peas & Veggies Bowl

Healthy Choice Beef Tips Portobello

Healthy Choice Classic Meat Loaf

Healthy Choice Country Herb Chicken

Healthy Choice Creamy Garlic Shrimp

Healthy Choice Oven Roasted Chicken

Healthy Choice Cafe Steamers Chicken Red Pepper Alfredo

Healthy Choice Cafe Steamers Grilled Basil Chicken

Healthy Choice Cafe Steamers Grilled Chicken Marinara

Healthy Choice Cafe Steamers Grilled Whiskey Steak

Healthy Choice Cafe Steamers Roasted Beef Merlot

Healthy Choice Cafe Steamers Roasted Chicken Fresca

Healthy Choice Cafe Steamers Roasted Chicken Marsala

Healthy Choice Select Entrées Salisbury Steak

Healthy Choice Select Entrées Slow Roasted Turkey Medallions

Lean Cuisine Café Classics Chicken Carbonara

Lean Cuisine Café Classics Parmesan Crusted Fish

Lean Cuisine Café Classics Sun-Dried Tomato Pesto Chicken

Lean Cuisine Chicken Florentine Lasagna

Lean Cuisine Comfort Classics Cheese Lasagna & Chicken

Lean Cuisine Comfort Classics Chicken Parmesan

Lean Cuisine Dinnertime Selects Chicken Tuscan

Lean Cuisine Dinnertime Selects Roasted Turkey Breast

Lean Cuisine Dinnertime Selects Steak Tips Dijon

Lean Cuisine Spa Cuisine Classics Chicken in Peanut Sauce

Lean Cuisine Spa Cuisine Classics Chicken Mediterranean

Lean Cuisine Spa Cuisine Classics Chicken Pecan

Lean Cuisine Spa Cuisine Classics Grilled Chicken Primavera

Lean Cuisine Spa Cuisine Classics Salmon with Basil

Lean Cuisine Spa Cuisine Classics Szechuan Style Stir Fry with Shrimp

Lean Cuisine Spaghetti with Meatballs

Smart Ones Chicken Enchiladas Monterey

Smart Ones Chicken Mirabella

Smart Ones Chicken Parmesan

Smart Ones Chicken Santa Fe

Smart Ones Meat Loaf

Smart Ones Picante Chicken and Pasta

Smart Ones Shrimp Marinara

Smart Ones Spicy Szechuan Style Vegetable & Chicken

Smart Ones Turkey Medallions with Mushroom Gravy

South Beach Living Chicken Fettuccine Alfredo

South Beach Living Kung Pao Chicken

South Beach Living Meatloaf with Gravy

South Beach Living Garlic Parmesan Chicken

South Beach Living Roasted Turkey

South Beach Living Savory Pork

SOUPS

In general, canned soups need to be reduced- or low-sodium, with no more than 2 grams of saturated fat and zero trans fat per serving. They should provide at least 3 grams of dietary fiber, and total carbohydrates minus dietary fiber should not exceed 30 grams.

Campbell's Chunky Healthy Request Grilled Chicken and Sausage Gumbo

Campbell's Chunky Healthy Request Chicken Corn Chowder

Campbell's Chunky Healthy Request Old Fashioned Vegetable Beef

Campbell's Chunky Healthy Request Sirloin Burger

Campbell's Chunky Healthy Request Vegetable

Campbell's Healthy Request Vegetable Beef

Campbell's Low Sodium Chunky Vegetable Beef

Campbell's Low Sodium Split Pea

Campbell's Select Harvest Light Italian-Style Vegetable

Campbell's Select Harvest Light Savory Chicken with Vegetables

Campbell's Select Harvest Light Southwestern-Style Vegetable

Campbell's Select Harvest Light Vegetable Beef and Barley

Campbell's Select Harvest Light Vegetable and Pasta

Healthy Choice Beef Pot Roast

Healthy Choice Chicken Tortilla

Healthy Choice Country Vegetable

Healthy Choice Minestrone

Progresso Reduced Sodium Garden Vegetable

Progresso Reduced Sodium Minestrone

Progresso Reduced Sodium Light Vegetable

FAST FOODS

Most fast-food restaurants post the nutritional values of their menu options either on site or online. Entrées should contain no more than 300 to 450 calories, with 30 to 40 grams of carbohydrates, 10 to 15 grams of total fat but less than 3 grams of saturated fat, and at least 5 grams of fiber. If they provide 300 milligrams of calcium, 100 IU of vitamin D, and at least 200 milligrams (0.2 gram) of omega-3s, that's even better.

Burger King Cheeseburger

Burger King Chicken Tenders 4-piece

Burger King Garden Salad (no dressing)

Burger King Ham Omelet Sandwich

Burger King Hamburger

Burger King Spicy Chick'n Crisp Sandwich (without mayo)

Burger King Tendergrill Chicken Garden Salad (without dressing)

Burger King Whopper Jr. Sandwich (without mayo)

Burger King Whopper Jr. Sandwich with cheese (without mayo)

Hardee's BBQ Chicken Sandwich

Hardee's Cinnamon 'n Raisin Biscuit

Hardee's Small Cheeseburger

Hardee's Small Hamburger

McDonald's Chicken McNuggets 4-piece

McDonald's Chipotle BBQ Snack Wrap Grilled

McDonald's English Muffin

McDonald's Hamburger

McDonald's Honey Mustard Snack Wrap Grilled

McDonald's Premium Southwest Salad with Grilled Chicken (without dressing)

McDonald's Premium Southwest Salad without chicken (without dressing)

McDonald's Premium Bacon Ranch Salad with Grilled Chicken (without dressing)

McDonald's Premium Bacon Ranch Salad without chicken (without dressing)

McDonald's Premium Caesar Salad with Grilled Chicken (without dressing)

McDonald's Premium Caesar Salad without chicken (without dressing)

McDonald's Ranch Snack Wrap Grilled

Subway 6" Ham without cheese

Subway 6" Oven-Roasted Chicken Breast

Subway 6" Roast Beef

Subway 6" Subway Club

Subway 6" Turkey Breast

Subway 6" Turkey Breast and Ham

Subway 6" Veggie Delight

Subway Ham Mini-Sub

Subway Roast Beef Mini-Sub

Subway Turkey Breast Mini-Sub

Wendy's Caesar Side Salad

Wendy's Chicken Caesar Salad (without toppings or dressing)

Wendy's Chili (small or large)

Wendy's Grilled Chicken Go Wrap

Wendy's Homestyle Chicken Go Wrap

Wendy's Spicy Chicken Go Wrap

Wendy's Jr. Hamburger

Wendy's Jr. Cheeseburger

Wendy's Mandarin Chicken Salad (without toppings or dressing)

Wendy's Ultimate Chicken Grill Sandwich

DTOUR PRODUCT RECOMMENDATIONS

Take this list to the supermarket with you! It's meant to help guide your choices as you stock your refrigerator and pantry for DTOUR. For each food group, we've established basic nutritional criteria and identified the brands that either meet these criteria or come very close. It's by no means an exhaustive list, but you'll have an idea of what to look for. You may want to try several different brands of a particular food until you find one you like.

BREAD

What to look for: whole grains; at least 3 grams of dietary fiber, no trans fat, less than 1 gram of saturated fat, and no more than 18 grams of carbohydrate per slice. Reduced-calorie, high-fiber breads are the best choice. *Tip:* When reading labels, be sure to note whether a serving is one slice or two.

Aunt Millie's Cracked Wheat with Whole Grain

Aunt Millie's Healthy Goodness Fiber for Life Light 100% Whole Wheat

Aunt Millie's Hearth Organic 100% Whole Wheat

Aunt Millie's Organic 100% Whole Wheat

Brownberry 100% Whole Wheat

Brownberry 12 Grain

Brownberry Grains and More

Brownberry Health Nut

Brownberry Natural Wheat

Brownberry Oat Nut

Gold Medal 100% Whole Wheat

Healthy Life 100% Whole Wheat

Healthy Life 100% Whole Grain Flaxseed

Healthy Life 100% Whole Grain Sugar Free Wheat

Healthy Life 100% Whole Grain Sugar Free Rye

Healthy Life Double Fiber 100% Whole Wheat

Healthy Life Double Fiber Flaxseed with Omega-3 ALA

Healthy Life Double Fiber Wheatberry with Bulgur Crunch

Nature's Pride 100% Whole Wheat

Nature's Pride 12 Grain

Nature's Pride Double Fiber 100% Whole Wheat

Nature's Pride Healthy Multi-Grain

Nature's Pride Stone Ground Whole Wheat with Honey

Pepperidge Farm Classic Soft 100% Whole Wheat

Sara Lee Classic 100% Whole Wheat

Wonder Soft 100% Whole Wheat

CEREALS

What to look for: whole grain hot or cold cereal with at least 2 grams of fiber per serving. Sugar should not appear in the #1 or #2 position on the ingredients list.

COLD CEREALS

General Mills Basic 4

General Mills Fiber One Honey Clusters

General Mills Fiber One Raisin Bran Clusters

General Mills Cheerios

General Mills Multi-Grain Cheerios

General Mills Kix

General Mills Oatmeal Crisp Hearty Raisin

General Mills Oatmeal Crisp Crunchy Almond

General Mills Total Raisin Bran

Kashi 7 Whole Grain Flakes

Kashi GoLean

Kashi GoLean Crunch

Kashi GoLean Crunch Honey Almond Flax

Kashi Good Friends Original

Kashi Good Friends Cinna-Raisin Crunch

Kashi Granola Apple Orchard

Kashi Granola Cocoa Beach

Kashi Granola Mountain Medley

Kashi Granola Summer Berry

Kashi Heart to Heart Honey Toasted Oat

Kashi Heart to Heart Oat Flakes & Wild Blueberry Clusters

Kashi Honey Puffs

Kashi Nuggets

Kashi U

Kashi Vive Probiotic Digestive Wellness

Kellogg's All-Bran Complete Wheat Flakes

Kellogg's All-Bran Strawberry Medley

Kellogg's All-Bran Yogurt Bites

Kellogg's All-Bran Complete Wheat Flakes

Kellogg's Cracklin' Oat Bran

Kellogg's Frosted Mini-Wheats Unfrosted Bite Size

Kellogg's Mueslix

Kellogg's Raisin Bran

Kellogg's Raisin Bran Extra

Kellogg's Smart Start Strong Heart Antioxidants

Kellogg's Smart Start Strong Heart Strawberry Oat Bites

Kellogg's Smart Start Strong Heart Toasted Oat

Post Grape-Nuts

Post Grape-Nuts Flakes

Post Selects Great Grains Banana Nut Crunch

Post Selects Great Grains Crunchy Pecans

Post Selects Great Grains Raisins, Dates and Pecans

Post Shredded Wheat Original

Post Shredded Wheat Wheat 'n Bran

Quaker Life

Quaker Life Cinnamon

Quaker Life Maple & Grown Sugar

Quaker Natural Granola Lowfat

Quaker Natural Granola Oats & Honey

Quaker Natural Granola Oats & Honey & Raisins

Uncle Sam Toasted Whole-Wheat Flakes and Flaxseed

HOT CEREALS

Kashi GoLean Creamy Truly Vanilla

Kashi GoLean Hearty Honey Cinnamon

McCann's Steel Cut Irish Oatmeal

McCann's Quick & Easy Steel Cut Irish Oatmeal

McCann's Quick-Cooking Irish Oatmeal

Quaker Instant Oatmeal Original

Quaker Instant Oatmeal High Fiber Cinnamon Swirl

Quaker Instant Oatmeal High Fiber Maple & Brown Sugar

Quaker Lower Sugar Instant Oatmeal–Apples and Cinnamon

Quaker Lower Sugar Instant Oatmeal–Peaches & Cream

Quaker Oats Old-Fashioned

Quaker Simple Harvest All-Natural Multigrain Instant Hot Cereal

Quaker Weight Control Instant Oatmeal–Banana Bread

Quaker Weight Control Instant Oatmeal–Cinnamon

Quaker Weight Control Instant Oatmeal–Maple & Brown Sugar

Quick Quaker Oats

CHEESES

What to look for: reduced-fat or low-fat varieties that contain no more than 3 to 6 grams of fat per ounce, and no more than 2 to 4 grams of saturated fat per ounce

Frigo CheeseHeads Mozzarella and Cheddar Swirls

Frigo CheeseHeads Mozzarella String

Frigo CheeseHeads Light String

Kraft Italian Five Cheese (shredded)

Kraft Cracker Barrel Extra Sharp Cheddar with 2% Milk

Kraft Deli Deluxe 2% Milk American Slices

Kraft Fat-Free Shredded Cheddar

Kraft Low-Moisture, Part-Skim Mozzarella (finely shredded)

Kraft Mild Cheddar with 2% Milk (shredded)

Kraft Mozzarella with 2% Milk (shredded)

Kraft Natural Cheese Mexican Style Four Cheese (shredded)

Kraft Sharp Cheddar with 2% Milk (shredded)

Kraft Singles 2% Milk Sharp Cheddar

Kraft Singles 2% Milk Slices

Kraft Singles Fat Free American

Kraft Singles American

Kraft Mild Cheddar with 2% Milk (block)

Kraft Colby with 2% Milk (block)

Kraft Low-Moisture, Part-Skim Mozzarella (block)

Kraft Sharp Cheddar with 2% Milk (block)

Kraft Snackables String

Kraft Snackables String with 2% Milk

Kraft Snackables Twists

Kraft Velveeta Slices

Sargento Light String Cheese with 2% Milk

Sargento Classic Mozzarella, shredded

Sargento Natural Baby Swiss Slices

Sargento Natural Swiss Slices

Sargento Natural Muenster Slices

Sargento Natural Pepper Jack Slices

Sargento Natural Provolone Slices

Sargento Natural Reduced Fat Provolone Slices

Weight Watchers Shredded Cheddar individual portions

Weight Watchers Shredded Mexican individual portions

Weight Watchers Shredded Natural Light String Cheese

CRACKERS

What to look for: whole grain crackers containing no more than 3 grams of total fat and 1 gram of saturated fat, plus at least 2 grams of fiber

Old London Whole Grain Melba Toast

Triscuit Baked Whole Grain Wheat Reduced Fat

Wasa Crispbread

ICE CREAM

What to look for: varieties that contain no more than 2 grams of saturated fat and no more than 18 grams of total carbohydrate per ½-cup serving. *Tip:* Brands that are low-carb may be higher in saturated fat, while brands that are low-fat may be higher in carbs.

Blue Bunny Hi Lite Chocolate

Blue Bunny Hi Lite Homemade Vanilla

Blue Bunny Hi Lite Vanilla

Blue Bunny Premium Light Butter Pecan

Blue Bunny Premium Light Chocolate Raspberry Cheesecake

Blue Bunny Premium Light Vanilla

Breyers Smooth & Dreamy Creamy Chocolate

Breyers Smooth & Dreamy Creamy Vanilla

Breyers Smooth & Dreamy Vanilla Bean

Breyers Smooth & Dreamy Vanilla Chocolate Strawberry

Edy's Fun Flavors Butter Pecan

Edy's Loaded Cookies 'n Cream

Edy's Loaded Chocolate Chip Mint Brownie

Edy's Slow Churned Butter Pecan

Edy's Slow Churned Chocolate

Edy's Slow Churned Coffee

Edy's Slow Churned French Vanilla

Edy's Slow Churned Neapolitan

Edy's Slow Churned Vanilla

Edy's Slow Churned Vanilla Bean

Edy's Slow Churned No Sugar Added Butter Pecan

Edy's Slow Churned No Sugar Added Coffee

Edy's Slow Churned No Sugar Added Cookies 'n Cream

Edy's Slow Churned No Sugar Added French Vanilla

Edy's Slow Churned No Sugar Added Neapolitan

Edy's Slow Churned No Sugar Added Triple Chocolate

Edy's Slow Churned No Sugar Added Vanilla

Edy's Slow Churned No Sugar Added Vanilla Bean

Edy's Slow Churned Yogurt Blends Black Cherry Vanilla Swirl

Edy's Slow Churned Yogurt Blends Chocolate Vanilla Swirl

Edy's Slow Churned Yogurt Blends Peach

Edy's Slow Churned Yogurt Blends Strawberry

Edy's Slow Churned Yogurt Blends Vanilla

Note: Edy's and Dreyer's ice creams are the same products, but Edy's is available in the eastern United States, and Dreyer's is found in the western states.

MARGARINE

What to look for: soft tub, canola or omega-3 enriched, trans fat free, with no more than 2 grams of saturated fat per serving (1 tablespoon)

Brummel and Brown with natural yogurt

I Can't Believe it's Not Butter Light

I Can't Believe It's Not Butter Mediterranean Blend

I Can't Believe It's Not Butter Original

Olivio

Promise

Smart Balance Light

Smart Balance with Flax Oil

Smart Balance Omega

MILK OR MILK SUBSTITUTES

What to look for: low-fat (1%) or fat-free (skim), providing at least 30 percent of the Daily Value for calcium (1,000 milligrams) and at least 30 percent of the DV for vitamin D (400 IU)

8th Continent Fat Free Original Soymilk

8th Continent Fat Free Vanilla Soymilk

8th Continent Light Original Soymilk

8th Continent Light Vanilla Soymilk

8th Continent Light Chocolate Soymilk

Light Silk Soymilk Chocolate

Light Silk Soymilk Plain

Light Silk Soymilk Vanilla

Rice Dream Original

POPCORN

What to look for: no more than 3 grams of total fat and 1 gram of saturated fat per serving; trans fat free. *Tip:* Don't be fooled by "mini bags" of popcorn. Some may hold far more fat and saturated fat than you want.

Jolly Time Healthy Pop Butter

Jolly Time Healthy Pop Caramel Apple

Jolly Time Healthy Pop Kettle Corn

Orville Redenbacher Smart Pop Butter

Orville Redenbacher Smart Pop Butter Mini Bags

Orville Redenbacher Smart Pop Kettle Korn

Orville Redenbacher Smart Pop Kettle Korn Mini Bags

Orville Redenbacher Smart Pop Movie Theater Butter

Orville Redenbacher Smart Pop Popcorn

Orville Redenbacher Smart Pop Popcorn Mini Bags

Pop Secret 94% Fat Free Butter

Pop Secret 100 Calorie Popcorn Homestyle

Unpopped kernels for hot air poppers (various brands)

YOGURTS

What to look for: light, low-fat, or fat-free, containing no more than 1 gram of saturated fat and no more than 15 grams of total carbohydrates per serving. *Tip:* Some types of fat-free and light yogurts provide way more than 15 grams of total carbohydrates per serving.

Activia Light Blueberry

Activia Light Cherry

Activia Light Peach

Activia Light Strawberry

Activia Light Raspberry

Activia Light Strawberry-Banana

Activia Light Vanilla

Dannon Light & Fit Blueberry

Dannon Light & Fit Peach

Dannon Light & Fit Strawberry

Dannon Light & Fit Strawberry Banana

INDEX

Underscored page references indicate boxed text. **Boldfaced** page references indicate photographs.

CUSTOMIZE IT!
DIABETES DTOUR ONLINE
POWERED BY Prevention | The perfect companion to the book!

AS A MEMBER YOU'LL GET:

MEALS
- Customized meal plans filled with fat-fighting nutrients
- Delicious sugar-busting recipes
- Weekly shopping lists

MANAGEMENT
- Weight, calorie, blood sugar, and medication trackers
- Progress reports
- Fat-blasting fitness program
- Personal, private journal

MOTIVATION
- Direct access to certified nutrition and fitness experts
- Members-only message boards for advice and support
- Tips to control your sugar from the editors of *Prevention*

Join today at dtour.com/cookbook

Jean's
BIG
NUMBER:
2
dress sizes lost!

Tom's
BIG
NUMBER:
58
percent drop
in blood sugar!

Jean Nick & Tom Colbaugh,
ages 48 & 54

BECOME A MEMBER TODAY!
Special offer available only at dtour.com/cookbook

201272501